MOROCCO

Contents

the magazine 5
- ✦ A Cold Country with a Hot Sun
- ✦ Best of Morocco ✦ Matters of Belief
- ✦ A Moroccan Feast ✦ A Very Important Date
- ✦ From Sultans… to Steeplechasers
- ✦ An Architectural Mosaic
- ✦ Berber First, Moroccan Second
- ✦ Pirates and Corsairs ✦ Paul Bowles's Morocco

Finding Your Feet 33
- ✦ First Two Hours
- ✦ Getting Around
- ✦ Accommodation
- ✦ Food and Drink
- ✦ Shopping
- ✦ Entertainment

Marrakech 45
Getting Your Bearings ✦ **In Three Days**
Don't Miss
- ✦ Djemaa el-Fna ✦ Souks ✦ Ben Youssef Medersa
- ✦ The Ramparts and Gates ✦ Gardens of Marrakech

At Your Leisure ✦ 9 more places to explore
Where to… ✦ Stay ✦ Eat and Drink ✦ Shop
- ✦ Be Entertained

The Atlantic Coast 71
Getting Your Bearings ✦ **In Five Days**
Don't Miss
- ✦ Rabat and Salé
- ✦ Casablanca
- ✦ Essaouira

At Your Leisure ✦ 8 more places to explore
Where to… ✦ Stay ✦ Eat and Drink ✦ Shop
- ✦ Be Entertained

The North 95

Getting Your Bearings ✦ In Five Days
Don't Miss
✦ Tangier
✦ Tetouan
✦ Chefchaouen
At Your Leisure ✦ 7 more places to explore
Where to... ✦ Stay ✦ Eat and Drink ✦ Shop
✦ Be Entertained

Imperial Cities and Middle Atlas 117

Getting Your Bearings ✦ In Five Days
Don't Miss
✦ Fes
✦ Volubilis
✦ Meknes
At Your Leisure ✦ 9 more places to explore
Where to... ✦ Stay ✦ Eat and Drink ✦ Shop
✦ Be Entertained

Atlas Mountains and the South 139

Getting Your Bearings ✦ In Six Days
Don't Miss
✦ Tizi n'Test
✦ Toubkal National Park ✦ The Dadès Valley: La Route des Kasbahs ✦ Aït Benhaddou
At Your Leisure ✦ 12 more places to explore
Where to... ✦ Stay ✦ Eat and Drink ✦ Shop
✦ Be Entertained

Walks & Tours 163

✦ 1 Caleche Ride in Marrakech
✦ 2 The Toubkal Region
✦ 3 Along the Tizi n'Tichka

Practicalities 173

✦ Before You Go ✦ When to Go
✦ When You Are There
✦ Survival Phrases
✦ Glossary

Atlas 181

Index 187

Written by Sylvie Franquet

Copy edited by Maria Morgan
Verified by Josephine Quintero
Indexed by Marie Lorimer

© Automobile Association Developments Limited 2003
Maps produced under licence from map data © New Holland
Publishers (UK) Limited 2002
Maps © Automobile Association Developments Limited 2003

Automobile Association Developments Limited retains the copyright
in the original edition © 2003 and in all subsequent editions,
reprints and amendments.

All rights reserved. No part of this publication may be reproduced,
stored in a retrieval system, or transmitted in any form or by any
means – electronic, photocopying, recording or otherwise – unless
the permission of the publishers has been obtained beforehand.

The contents of this publication are believed correct at the time of
printing. Nevertheless, the publishers cannot be held responsible
for any errors or omissions or for changes in the details given in this
guide or for the consequences of any reliance on the information
provided by the same.

Published in the United States by AAA Publishing,
1000 AAA Drive,
Heathrow, Florida 32746
Published in the United Kingdom by AA Publishing

ISBN 1-56251-833-X

Color separation by Leo Reprographics
Printed and bound in China by Leo Paper Products

10 9 8 7 6 5 4 3 2 1

A01027	

the magazine

A Cold Country with a Hot Sun

Morocco's Diverse Geography

Arab geographers called the highlands of North Africa "Jzirat el Maghreb" – the Island of the West or Sunset. This "island" was surrounded by the Atlantic Ocean, the Mediterranean Sea and, in the south, by the vast sand sea of the Sahara Desert. Morocco, on the westernmost tip of this "island", had everything from lush valleys to arid sand dunes and barren mountains, from cool rivers and lakes in the Middle Atlas to sunny beaches on its Atlantic coast.

Even in the middle of the countryside there is some stunning architecture

The landscape ranges from lush fields in the Middle Atlas to desert in the south

Many visitors are lured by the beauty and infinity of the desert, which is vast

Marshal Lyautey, the French colonial administrator who laid the groundwork for modern Morocco, described it as "a cold country with a hot sun". It's an appropriate description, as it's a common misconception that temperatures are always soaring in Morocco. In fact, in the mountains, which form a considerable part of the country, the temperature swings between dazzling summer and icy winter when most of the peaks are under snow. In the summer months, the desert is blazing during the day but cools down considerably when the sun drops. The Atlantic coast, particularly near Agadir, enjoys pleasant temperatures all year round: in summer it's a lot cooler than Marrakech and the desert towns, while in winter it's still hot enough for sunbathing.

the magazine

Swim in the Mediterranean Sea, in the wild Atlantic Ocean, in Middle Atlas lakes or in High Atlas rivers

Beach Delights

Morocco has 2,800km of coastline facing the Atlantic and 530km on the Mediterranean. The coast, backed by the fertile Sous and Sebou plains, is the most densely inhabited region and by far the richest. Much of the Atlantic coast is considerably rougher and windier than the Mediterranean, and it has some splendid surfing beaches, among them Sidi Kaouiki (► 83, 94), Sidi Ifni and Dar-Bouazza (► 94) near Casablanca. Tangier (► 100–103) is the country's largest passenger harbour, while Casablanca (► 79–80) is the largest industrial harbour in Morocco.

Waiting for the Rain

Water is a problem in Morocco. It is essential not only for agriculture, the staple of the economy, but also for fountains, gardens and all the daily needs of the cities and villages. Sometimes there is too much, for instance in 1996 when flash floods in the Ourika Valley and elsewhere in the Atlas Mountains killed thousands of Moroccan holidaymakers, and caused huge amounts of damage. But, more often, there is not enough water: a drought that began in 1999 shows little sign of abating and has affected agricultural output, forcing farming families to join the exodus of around 450,000 people who leave for the cities each year. Economic hardship is one reason, but it's also the lure of a better life.

the magazine **7**

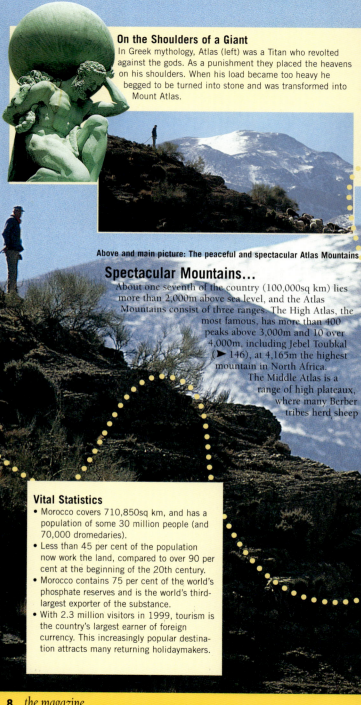

On the Shoulders of a Giant
In Greek mythology, Atlas (left) was a Titan who revolted against the gods. As a punishment they placed the heavens on his shoulders. When his load became too heavy he begged to be turned into stone and was transformed into Mount Atlas.

Above and main picture: The peaceful and spectacular Atlas Mountains

Spectacular Mountains...

About one seventh of the country (100,000sq km) lies more than 2,000m above sea level, and the Atlas Mountains consist of three ranges. The High Atlas, the most famous, has more than 400 peaks above 3,000m and 10 over 4,000m, including Jebel Toubkal (▶146), at 4,165m the highest mountain in North Africa.

The Middle Atlas is a range of high plateaux, where many Berber tribes herd sheep

Vital Statistics
- Morocco covers 710,850sq km, and has a population of some 30 million people (and 70,000 dromedaries).
- Less than 45 per cent of the population now work the land, compared to over 90 per cent at the beginning of the 20th century.
- Morocco contains 75 per cent of the world's phosphate reserves and is the world's third-largest exporter of the substance.
- With 2.3 million visitors in 1999, tourism is the country's largest earner of foreign currency. This increasingly popular destination attracts many returning holidaymakers.

8 *the magazine*

and goats. The highest point here is Jebel Bounaceur at 3,340m.

The Anti Atlas, featuring Jebel Sarhro at 2,712m, is a barren range skirting the desert alongside the Draa Valley. The mountains of the Atlas are made of sedimentary rocks with intrusions of granite and quartzite. The northern coast is separated from the rest of the country by the Rif Mountains (► 109), an extension of the *cordillera* of southern Spain.

Below: Be prepared when exploring the desert, as sand storms can be disorientating

…Just Right for Skiing

The French introduced skiing to Morocco in the 1930s and now resorts cater to all abilities. The best time to go is from December to March and you need to climb to around 2,000m to find suitable snow. Morocco's foremost ski resort is Oukaïmeden (► 162), from where Africa's highest cable lift glides to the top of Jebel Oukaïmeden (3,273m). Tours for more experienced skiers are possible in the area around Tazaghart, accompanied by highly trained Berber guides with extensive knowledge of the mountains and deserts. The modest ski pistes of Mischliffen, Azrou and Ifrane (► 138) are popular weekend spots where the inhabitants of Fes like to relax.

Not Forgetting the Desert

Beyond the Draa Valley and the Anti Atlas lies the vast Sahara Desert. Most of the desert in Morocco consists of *hamadas* – barren, wind-swept rocky plateaux – and, less commonly, of *ergs* – picturesque sand dunes that here seldom rise to spectacular heights. Many *oueds* (rivers) cross the sands, brought to life by rainstorms but quickly drying up again. Oases are rare, except near the Draa and Ziz valleys (► 154, 155), which are fed by water from the Anti Atlas. The Western Sahara near the Atlantic does see a little more rain and some mist coming off the ocean, making the area greener and less barren. The only other riches of the desert are the phosphates hidden beneath its surface. .

the magazine 9

Best of Morocco

Best experiences

- Wander around the **souks**, especially in Marrakech (➤ 52–53), Fes (➤ 122–125) and Essaouira (➤ 81–83).
- Walk in the **Atlas Mountains** (➤ 167–169).
- Try syrupy **mint tea**, poured from a height to make it bubbly.
- **Boogie-board** in at Sidi Kaouki beach (➤ 83, 94) and elsewhere along the Atlantic coast.
- Play **golf** on superb courses in extraordinary settings, particularly the Red Course at the Dar es Salaam Golf Club in Rabat (➤ 94).
- Have dinner (or at least a fresh orange juice) in **Djemaa el-Fna** in Marrakech (➤ 50–51).
- Look at the shrine of **Sidi Chamarouche** (from a distance) if you have the blues (➤ 169).
- Linger over a **massage** in Essaouira's Hammam Mounia (➤ 23).
- **Sleep** like Moroccan royalty in a luxurious *riad* hotel (➤ 39).
- Hold your nose at the **tanneries** in Fes (➤ 124).

Riad hotels combine modern luxuries with traditional Moroccan hospitality

Best for peace and quiet

- **Gorges du Zegzel** in the Beni Snassen Mountains (➤ 110).
- **Jardin Majorelle**, Marrakech (➤ 60).
- The hills and lakes of the **Middle Atlas** (➤ 131–133).
- **Beaches** south of Essaouira (➤ 83).
- The **sand dunes** of Mhamid (➤ 154).

Best oases

- **Tinerhir** (➤ 154): one of the largest and most beautiful oases, noted for its dense vegetation and numerous *ksour* and kasbahs.
- **Zagora** (➤ 153–154): departure point of caravans on the 52-day desert journey to Timbuctoo in Mali.
- **Erfoud** (➤ 155): between the rivers Rheris and Ziz, this small oasis near the impressive

Erg Chebbi sand dunes has arguably the best dates in Morocco.
- **Figuig**: an amazing oasis with seven *ksour*, completely isolated near the Algerian border.
- **Akka:** this small, traditional oasis in the very south, off the tourist map, is an old centre of the slave trade (buses from Ouazarzate and Agadir).

Best cafés with a view

- **Café Maure** in Rabat's kasbah overlooks the Andalucian Garden and the Atlantic (➤ 78).
- **Café Hafa** in Tangier (➤ 113), for superb views over the bay.
- Café of **La Kasbah** hotel in Aït Benhaddou (➤ 156) has marvellous views of the amphitheatre of kasbahs across the river.
- The **Hotel Mirage** café at Cap Spartel (➤ 111) has great sea views, especially at sunset.
- **Café de Paris**, Djemaa el-Fna, Marrakech (➤ 51) from the roof terrace you can see the snow-capped Atlas range on a clear day.

Best moussems and festivals

- The **marriage festival** of the Berber Aït Haddidou tribe in Imilchil, when men and women try to find suitable partners. Dates vary (➤ 133).
- The **Gnaoua** festivals in Essaouira (➤ 82), usually each June.
- **Erfoud Date Festival**, end of October (➤ 155).
- **Festival of Sacred Music** in Fes, end of May or beginning of June (➤ 138).
- **Moussem of Moulay Idriss**, September: the largest religious *moussem* (➤ 131).

Best kasbah

If you only go to one... kasbah, let it be the spectacular **Aït Benhaddou** (➤ 150), the setting for films such as *Lawrence of Arabia* (1962) and *Gladiator* (2000).

The palm groves of Tinerhir oasis near Todra Gorge

Watch the crowds on Djemaa el-Fna from a distance

Above: Berber girl looking for a husband at the Imilchil marriage festival. Left: The lively date festival at Erfoud

the magazine

Matters of Belief

Religion is no simple matter in Morocco. Although the majority of Moroccans are Muslims, the Berbers have maintained some of their older pagan customs, particularly a large number of saints. So, while orthodox Islam insists there should be no intermediary between man and Allah, saints play a large part in Moroccan life. In addition, the *chorfa* (plural of *cherif* or *sherif*) – descendants of the Prophet Mohammed – are venerated as wise men. Morocco's Alaouite dynasty of kings are *chorfa*.

The Basics of Islam

Muslims believe in the "Five Pillars" of Islam: the *Shahaada* (the confirmation that there is no God but Allah and Mohammed is His messenger); *Salaat* (prayers five times daily); *Soum* (fasting during Ramadan); *Zakaat* (giving alms for the poor) and *Haj* (making a pilgrimage to Mecca). Muslims live by their holy book, the **Koran** (or Qu'ran), which is believed to be the direct word of God given to the Prophet Mohammed.

The *Hadith*, the sayings of the Prophet on how to conduct daily life, is also part of the Koran.

Muslims should pray five times a day, facing Mecca in Saudi Arabia. Some go to the mosque, while others pray in shops, at the roadside, in the desert – wherever they happen to be. Most men go to a mosque for **Friday noon prayers** and to hear the weekly sermon, so businesses and museums are usually closed at that time.

During the **Holy month of Ramadan**, which commemorates the revealing of the Koran to Mohammed, fasting from sunrise to sunset should be observed by everyone except children, travellers, the sick, the elderly and pregnant women.

12 *the magazine*

Believers perform their ritual ablutions before they pray in the mosque

Inshallah, bismillah and el hamdu lillah

The name of Allah is constantly invoked. The most common phrase is probably ***inshallah***, literally meaning "if God wills", although it can also mean "maybe", "yes", "no", "could be", "for sure" or variations on that theme. Muslims believe that all things happen because Allah (God) wants them to happen; no human should presume to know God's will. Before a meal or a departing on a journey they say ***bismillah***, short for *bismillah er rahman er rahim* – "in the name of God the compassionate and merciful". To express surprise or in times of trouble Muslims whisper ***Allahu Akbar*** ("God is great"), and to express pleasure or relief they may say ***el hamdu lillah*** ("Praise be to God").

Moroccans use the Hand of Fatma to protect them from the evil eye

The "**evil eye**" is the name given to a variety of spells, usually cast by a jealous person. As part of popular Islam, many Moroccans (particularly the more traditional Berbers) make great efforts to avoid these spells. For instance, as too much beauty or good fortune attracts the evil eye, you should never tell a mother that she has a beautiful baby. Mothers protect their babies by putting a "**hand of Fatma**" (Fatima was Mohammed's daughter) charm around the child's neck. This might be a leather pouch containing Koranic verses or a blue bead. Popular belief is that even the most beautiful carpet should have some imperfection, and the Berbers traditionally weave one in accordingly.

White Koubbas and Moussems

Pilgrims consider saints to be wise men (though there are a few women) or doctors, so they visit their ***koubbas*** or ***marabouts*** (tombs) to seek advice or a cure. Some people tie strips of fabric to the grilles of tombs to bind their contracts with the saints. Others put oil inside the tomb, where it becomes infused with the saint's *baraka* (blessing) and is then

the magazine 13

used to heal a sick person. Women in particular seek help and advice from *marabouts*, particularly about infertility, psychological problems and childbirth.

Where Sufi brotherhoods have formed around particular saints, the tomb is called a *zaouia*. The most important *zaouias* in Morocco are the Aïssaoua in Meknes, the Gnaoua (➤ 82) and the Regraga in Essaouira and the Taïbia in Ouezzane.

The birthday of the saint is usually celebrated with a festival known as a **moussem**, which involves several days of feasting and prayers.

Muslims can pray wherever they are, but many Moroccans head for the local mosque at some point in the day

The Magic of Pickled Reptiles
Traditional life in Morocco is still ruled by *jinns* (genies) – good or evil spirits who control people and their actions – and both white and black magic are frequently used to counter them. Apothecary stalls in the souks sell dried chameleons, porcupines, animal skins and other exotic produce that are used to make magic potions as prescribed by a *shouaf* (witch doctor), who gives advice on casting or dealing with spells.

14 *the magazine*

Bismillah!

A real Moroccan feast is not for the faint of heart or weak of stomach. The many courses of rich food may be unfamiliar to Western palates, but it's a feast in every sense, with bright colours, a variety of smells and a multitude of tastes from ultra-sweet to hot and sour. The Moroccan duty of hospitality ensures a warm welcome, a relaxed atmosphere and a generously filled table.

A Moroccan Feast

Hospitality Reigns

The sharing of food – a big bowl of couscous or a steaming tagine, for example – is a social affair; but in Morocco it is also an expression of solidarity, of family or tribal bonding. Hospitality is an honour for the wealthy but also a way of survival for the poor. To evoke this spirit of hospitality, Moroccans like to tell a pre-Islamic story that celebrates a prince who spent his fortune on entertaining passing guests honourably. Even simple travellers who had lost their way were given hospitality, until in the end he had nothing left. One day the king visited him, having heard that the prince owned a fantastic horse. At the end of the meal when the king finally mentioned the delicate subject of buying the animal, the prince admitted that in order to fulfil his duty of hospitality he had had to kill the animal. The irony is that the tradition of hospitality led to both host and guest losing out.

Moroccan food is as varied as it is delicious

A Veritable Feast

Moroccans eat at low, round tables, while sitting on cushions or a sofa. Before a meal, a bowl is usually brought to the table and hands are washed. Traditionally, only the right hand is used for eating, and food is scooped up with a chunk of bread. The invitation to eat is "*bismillah*" (► 13), after which the host will take the first bite.

As a guest you should try to taste each of the dishes, though you don't have to eat everything as it's considered polite to leave some food, as well as to belch to show you've had plenty. Guests talk very little as they eat, and especially avoid touchy or exciting subjects that might distract people from the numerous pleasures of the table.

The meal starts with a soup such as *harira*, a rich meat soup eaten with dates. This might be followed by several types of salad, then by several tagines (stews) or grilled meat or fish. Then couscous and finally fruit and sweets might be served.

The meal ends with a much-needed digestive mint tea. Take your time to enjoy it: as the people from the High Atlas say: "Listen to our stories like you drink tea, with little sips, so you get its full flavour."

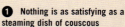

❶ Nothing is as satisfying as a steaming dish of couscous
❷ The best and sweetest dates are found in Zagora
❸ Dining Moroccan-style: low tables and comfortable sofas
❹ A delicious chicken *mqualli* with olives and almonds
❺ It's the spices that make Moroccan cuisine so delicious

Tagine of chicken *mqualli*

This popular tagine delightfully blends the bitterness of the olives with the sweet-sour taste of preserved lemons.

1 large chicken, cut into eight
40g butter
2 tablespoons olive oil
1 onion, grated or very finely chopped
½ teaspoon ginger
½ teaspoon saffron
½ teaspoon cinnamon
salt & pepper
a bunch of flat parsley, chopped
a bunch coriander, chopped
15 juicy green olives
1–2 preserved lemons chopped

Put the chicken in a large saucepan with the oil, butter, onions, spices and one large glass of water and simmer gently for 1½ hours, or until the meat falls off the bone. Stir from time to time, turn the chicken over and add more water as required, to obtain a good gravy. When the meat is ready, add the lemon and olives and cook for a few more minutes. Serve hot with flat bread and a salad.

Bright colours, a multitude of tastes and good company makes for a veritable Moroccan feast

Ras el-Hanout

Ras el-Hanout ("Head of the Shop"), the most exotic Moroccan flavouring, is used on special occasions, and in certain winter stews. It's a pungent mixture of 27 spices: cardamon, mace, galangal, guinea pepper, two kinds of nutmeg, four spices pimiento, cantharide, Indian and Chinese cinnamon, cyparacée, long pepper, cloves, curcuma, grey and white ginger, oris root, black pepper, lavender, rose-buds, Chinese cinnamon, ash berries, belladonna, fennel flowers, gouza el-asnab, asclepiadic fruit, cubeb and monk's pepper.

A VERY IMPORTANT DATE

No picturebook of Morocco is complete without the slender and elegant silhouette of the palm tree. It's not only beautiful but it's also an essential element in both Arab and Berber culture. As the Berber proverb says: "It is good to know the truth and speak the truth, but it is even better to know the truth and speak about palm trees."

The country has a wide variety of palm trees, but the date palm (*phoenix dactylifera*) is the most important. It's said that the date palm needs to have its feet in the water and its head in the fire, so it's perfectly adapted to the Moroccan south and is the only crop grown in the region. It's vital to the people there for several reasons:

• The trees can bear fruit for over 150 years.

• They protect the soil from erosion by the desert wind and provide protection from the blistering sun, both for humans and for the crops grown in their shade.

• Every part of the palm tree is used: dates are a key ingredient in the Moroccan diet, the flowers provide a popular aphrodisiac, the trunk and leaves are used as building materials, the sap makes an inebriating liqueur and the fibres are woven into ropes.

Over one million people still live off palm groves, but in recent years the extent of the groves has nearly halved, to about 44,000ha. One reason is that young people are shunning the hard labour of the soil. In addition, a large number of trees in North Africa have been blighted by an (as yet) incurable fungal disease called *bayoud*.

18 *the magazine*

Religious Dates

The trees also have a religious importance in Islamic, Christian and Jewish traditions. The Prophet Mohammed was born in a palm grove at a time when dates were often the only solid food. To remember this, Muslims traditionally break the Ramadan fast each night with a date and a spoonful of water.

A North African tradition has it that the date palm originated in the Garden of Eden when a full-grown tree bearing ripe fruit sprang from the spot where Adam had just cut his nails and hair. The angel Gabriel appeared behind the tree and told Adam that it was to be his food. When Adam had to leave the garden he took the palm with him as the main fruit of the world.

When the ancient Jewish leader Moses led his people out of Egypt, they were hungry and thirsty until they came to the palm grove of Elim. The Bible also mentions the beauty, mythology and usefulness of palm trees.

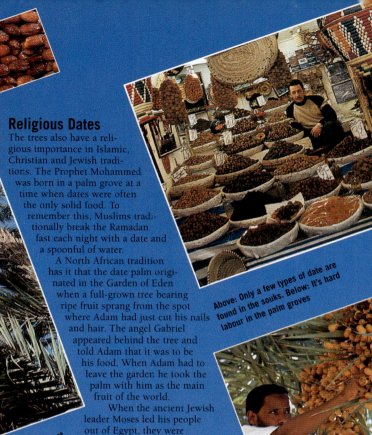

Above: Only a few types of date are found in the souks. Below: It's hard labour in the palm groves

The date harvest, the culmination of the year's work, is celebrated with a huge party

---

Notable Dates

- The sweetest dates are found in Zagora (▶ 153–154).
- The *boussekri* has firm flesh and, eaten with mint tea or milk, is the usual snack of shepherds.
- The *majhoul* date, less sweet but naturally preserved, is usually left on the branch to ripen.
- The oblong *boutoub* also keeps well, while the soft *boufggous* date is dipped in cumin-flavoured water.
- In villages, dates are kept in earthenware jars and buried in the ground – *akbourn* or buried dates have a strong smell and bitter taste because of their fermentation.
- Less tasty dates are fed to goats and sheep.

the magazine 19

From Sultans..

Morocco's Major Dynasties

788–974
Moulay Idriss I (▶ 131), the political refugee and founder of Fes, heads Morocco's first Muslim dynasty – the **Idrissids**.

c1060–1147
The **Almoravid** Islamic reform movement – the first Berber dynasty – is founded in the Sahara by Ibn Yaasin. His successors Abu Bekr and Youssef ben Tachfine, founder of Marrakech, expand the empire to include Muslim kingdoms in Spain.

1147–1268
Ibn Toumert preaches war against the Almoravids and the resulting Berber **Almohad** dynasty, founded in the High Atlas, marks the high point of Moroccan history. It dominates Northern Africa and Muslim Spain, with Yacoub el-Mansour later declaring himself sultan of Seville.

13th–15th centuries
Merenids from the eastern plains rule the country, establishing its borders.

16th–17th centuries
Morocco flourishes under the **Saadians**. Abu el-Abbas Ahmed el-Mansour, the most famous Saadian king (reigned 1578–1603), was named "el-Mansour" – the Victorious – after he defeated the Portuguese in the battle of the Three Kings in 1578.

Travellers and Tales

Ibn Battutah
The explorer and geographer Abu Abdallah Mohammed (1304–77), was known as Ibn Battutah (or Battuta), and called the "Traveller of Islam". He was born in Tangier but in 1325 his intended pilgrimage to Mecca resulted in a journey of almost 30 years across the Middle East, North Africa, Asia Minor, Africa and China. His book *Rihla* (Travels) contains detailed and entertaining descriptions of the different cities, landscapes and people he encountered.

His adventures were recently and brilliantly captured by Tim Mackintosh-Smith in his book *Travels with a Tangerine: A Journey in the Footnotes of Ibn Battutah* (published by John Murray in 2001). Battutah's modest *marabout* lies in the medina of Tangier, and is located in the street named after him.

Tahar Ben Jelloun
The country's most famous author was born in Tangier but now lives in Paris. He writes very Moroccan stories in French, in which dreamlike

the magazine

to Steeplechasers

17th century onwards
The present **Alaouite** dynasty has reigned since 1666, beginning with Moulay Rachid and his notorious successor Moulay Ismail (▶ 128–130). King Hassan II (1929–99), the eldest son of Mohammed V, reigned for 38 years (from 1961) and his image is still seen everywhere in Morocco. In 1975, he organised the Green March, during which some 350,000 Moroccans walked south to "recapture" the Western Sahara from the Spanish. He modernised the country's economy, held the country's first free elections in 1997, and appointed the first socialist prime minister, Abderrahmane Youssoufi, in 1998. The current king, Hassan II's son, Mohammed VI, is also playing an active political role.

Dominating the kingdom for nearly four decades, King Hassan II exerted a powerful influence over Morocco

narratives tell of the harsh reality of daily life. His most acclaimed book, *The Sand Child* (1985), tells of a girl from the south who is brought up as a boy in order to circumvent Islamic inheritance laws regarding females.

Mohammed Mrabet

This writer (born *c*1940) is influenced by Morocco's oral tradition of storytelling and has written over a dozen novels and collections of short stories, most of which have been translated by Paul Bowles (▶ 32). His works include *M'Hashish* (1969) and *Chocolate Creams and Dollars* (1993).

Author of *The Sand Child*, Tahar Ben Jelloun, who now lives in Paris

the magazine 21

Front-runners

Said Aouita dominated the athletics world

The athlete **Said Aouita** (born in Rabat in 1960) became a national hero by winning the 1984 Olympic 5,000m gold medal in Los Angeles. The following year he became the first person for 30 years to hold world records at both 1,500m and 5,000m. After setting a new record for 5,000m at the 1987 World Championships in Rome, Aouita also claimed world records for 2,000m and 3,000m.

Said Aouita's success has since led to Moroccan athletes leading the middle- and long-distance events, even breaking the Kenyan and Ethiopian dominance on the 3,000m steeplechase.

In this Muslim country, even Morocco's female athletes are getting in on the action, among them the 5,000m runners **Zahra Ouaziz** and **Asmae Leghzaoui**.

Other notable achievements include:

• **1,500m: Hicham El-Guerrouj** (born 1974) leads the way: he has established around 15 world best times, and set the current record in Rome in 1998.

• **3,000m steeplechase: Brahim Boulami** (born 1972) set a new world record in Brussels, Belgium, on 24 August, 2001. Other exponents on the all-time list include Ali Ezzine, Abdelaziz Sahere, Elarbi Khattabi and Hicham Bouaouiche.

• **5,000m:** Said Aouita's 1987 world record has since been bettered by his countrymen Salah Hissou, Khalid Boulami and Brahim Lahlafi. Other Moroccans joining them on the all-time list include Khalid Skah, Brahim Jabbour and, most recently, Abderrahim Goumri in 2001.

• **10,000m:** Leading Moroccans in the longest track event include Salah Hissou, Ismail Sghyr, Khalid Skah and **Brahim Boutayeb** (born 1967) – Olympic champion in Seoul in 1988.

• **Marathon: Khalid Khannouchi** (born 1971) set a new world record in Chicago, on 24 October, 1999, while **Abdelkader El-Mouaziz** (born 1969) was the winner of the 2001 London Marathon.

Athletes often train in the Atlas Mountains and excel in middle- and long-distance races

the magazine

An Architectural Mosaic

Most Moroccan minarets are modelled on the great Almohad Tour Hassan in Rabat

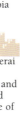

Bottom right: The intricate *pisé* decoration of the kasbah reflects traditional Berber motifs

Agadir

The *agadir or irherm*, such as Irherm n'Ougdal (➤ 172) built in elaborate *pisé* work (see below), looks like a kasbah but is used as a communal fortified granary in southern villages.

Djamaa (mosque)

With a couple of exceptions, Morocco's most obvious Islamic monuments are closed to non-Muslims. Built in Moorish style, and modelled on the 8th-century Grand Mosque of Córdoba in Spain, most Moroccan mosques have simple exteriors, with only the minaret and ornate entrance gate attracting attention. The mosque always has a *sahn* (courtyard) with an ablution fountain and at least one prayer room along one of its sides, with a *mihrab* or *qibla* (niche facing Mecca). The *muezzin* calls believers to prayer from the top of the minarets, most of which are modelled on the great Almohad minarets of Spain's Giralda mosque in Seville, Tour Hassan in Rabat (➤ 78) and the Koutoubia Mosque in Marrakech (➤ 61).

Fondouk

The *fondouk* or caravanserai are where travelling merchants used to sleep and eat, store their wares and stable their animals. One of the most impressive surviving examples is the restored 18th-century *fondouk* Nejjarine in Fès (➤ 124).

Hammam (steam bath)

Physical purity is fundamental to Islam. As prayers should always be preceded by ablutions, *hammams* were usually built near mosques and supervised by them. As well as being practical (private bathrooms are comparatively recent), they were also popular meeting places. Men and women are always kept separate. One enters *a hammam* covered by a towel, moving from the cold room to the tepid room and the hot room. The restored Hammam Mounia in Essaouira is a good place to be tempted by the pleasures of steam.

Ksar/Kasbah

The *ksar* (plural: *ksour*) is a fortified tribal village mostly occupied by Berbers. Every *ksar* used to have its own decorative patterns,

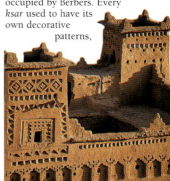

the magazine 23

festivals, traditions and costumes. A kasbah, similar to a *ksar*, traditionally belongs to just one important family. Kasbahs and *ksour* are often incredibly grand and monumental, despite the fact that their *pisé* work (see below) just "melts" back into the sand during the seasonal rains. When the *pisé* walls began to disintegrate, the community would simply abandon the complex and built another one, so you often see a cluster of *ksour* in various states of ruin. The Route des Kasbahs (➤ 148–149) is lined with impressive examples, as in the south they are spectacularly decorated with bold Berber motifs, particularly at Aït Benhaddou (➤ 150).

Medersa

Medersas (Koranic schools) played an important role in old Morocco, as an education based on Islamic theology, law and rhetoric led to higher political, judicial or religious careers. The *medersa* attracted students from outside the city, so it had to provide lodging and the isolation needed for their work. The

Above: Elegant calligraphy, mainly of Koranic verses, intricately decorates the inside of religious monuments

Below: The flaming colours of Taourirt Kasbah in Ouarzazate at sunset

24 *the magazine*

Medersa Bou Inania in Fes (▶ 122) follows the archetypal plan: built around a central courtyard are a prayer room and several classrooms, with the cells or bedrooms looking over the courtyard.

Marabout

Cities and countryside alike are strewn with small *marabouts* or *koubbas* – domed, square tombs, usually whitewashed – where saints are buried. In cities, these tombs can be very elaborate, as in the Saadian Tombs in Marrakech (▶ 62), while in rural areas they tend to be more basic like Sidi Chamarouche in the High Atlas (▶ 169).

Medina

The medina is the old part of a city, a labyrinth of narrow alleys enclosed within thick ramparts. Its main arteries are clogged with souks, workshops and sacred buildings and bustle with noise and energy, while the quieter residential back streets provide its inhabitants with a sense of calm and safety. The medina of Fes el-Bali (▶ 122–124) is a perfect example of the classic medina: every quarter has its main mosque, hammam,

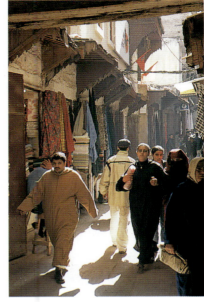

Traditional values are more persistent in the warren of alleys and souks that form the medina

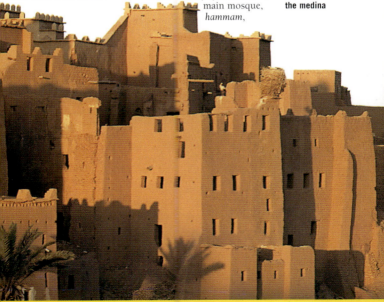

the magazine 25

bakery, market and school. The word "medina" comes from the place in Saudi Arabia where the Prophet Mohammed fled after his persecution in Mecca.

Pisé

Pisé, packed clay found in riverbeds and dried in the sun, is the cheapest and very often the only available building material. It is often used to build kasbahs and *ksour* (see above).

Riad

The hip place to stay in Morocco is the *riad* hotel. *Riad* literally means an enclosed garden, but now also refers to the house it surrounds. Most rooms overlook the garden and may only have small windows facing the outside of the building. *Riads* once housed extended families, each with their own apartment. These structures have been converted into small, often luxurious hotels in the heart of the medina. Marrakech in particular has many *riad* hotels (► 64–65) or restaurants (► 66–67), although more are opening in places such as Essaouira and Fes.

Souk

Souks (market and shopping streets) are some of the main attractions of Moroccan cities. Often pedestrianised and sometimes covered, souks are arranged by speciality, so there are souks for carpets, spices, vegetables or wool, and for blacksmiths, leatherworkers, dyers and so on. The result is an exotic riot of colours, smells and noises, offering the pleasure of bargaining. Watch out if you hear the word "*balek!*" as you might be about to be hit by a passing donkey or porter. Marrakech has some of Morocco's largest souks (► 52–53) and Fes (► 122–125) some of the finest, but for more relaxed trading try Essaouira (► 81–83) or Rabat (► 76–78).

Zellij

Every courtyard in Morocco is decorated with *zellij*, a mosaic work of small coloured ceramic fragments arranged in geometric patterns.

Zellij, multi-coloured mosaics arranged in geometric patterns, add colour to *riads*

26 *the magazine*

Berbers, Morocco's original inhabitants, still form more than half of the population. The Romans called these fierce and wild tribes "the Barbarus", which became "Berbers", but they themselves prefer to be called "Amaziah".

Keeping the Amaziah Language Alive

The Berbers are a proud race and consider themselves Berber before Moroccan. Their most identifiable feature is their language, the country's second after Arabic and before French. Berber belongs to the same family of languages as Arabic and Hebrew, and is believed to be the oldest language in North Africa. It's mostly a spoken language and, although an ancient alphabet – the *tifinagh* – is still used by the Tuareg Berbers of the western and central Sahara, it's now usually written by slightly adapting Latin or Arabic script.

Morocco has three main Amaziah

Berber First, Moroccan Second

A New Tradition

Raï music was created in neighbouring Algeria, but soon became popular with Moroccan youth. Although it has its roots in traditional Berber music, it has also been influenced by Western music, particularly in the use of synthesizers and rhythm guitars. The word *Raï* means "opinion" and the songs express concerns of youths, often with one foot in Africa and one in Europe, such as sex, drugs, alcohol, emigration and cars.

the magazine 27

dialects Riffi in the north, Tashilhait or Chleuh in the High Atlas and south, and Tamazight in the Middle Atlas and central Morocco. A growing cultural awareness among Berbers, supported by King Hassan II, has given greater importance to the Berber language, which can now be studied at universities and regularly heard on Moroccan television and radio.

The tea ceremony is important to Berber families

Berber women are renowned for their excellent weaving skills

Magical Carpets

Many Moroccan carpets are woven by the Berber tribes of the Middle Atlas. It's an ancient family activity whose traditions are strictly respected in the schools and co-operatives. The background is usually a warm orange-red, a natural colour made from madder root, although there are many variations now that chemical pigments are also used. Designs are always geometric; a good carpet will show a variety of patterns. As with all Berber art, carpets are woven for practical rather than decorative purposes, for use in the house or tent, or as saddlebags.

The Sound of the Berbers

- The music of the Berbers, like their language, differs from region to region.
- **Village music** is a communal affair. People, gathered for a harvest or religious festival, dance around the musicians who sing and play flutes and drums.
- **Itinerant musicians** are professionals who travel in groups often comprising a singer-poet, a violinist, a flautist and a tambourine player. They sing about heroism and impossible love.
- The two most famous groups are the spiritual **Daqqa** from Marrakech and **Jajouka** from the Djebala, who were recorded by the Rolling Stones and who perform a sort of pagan ritual music invoking Pan, their god of fertility.

Berber Life and People

In the mountains, the Berbers live in stone houses perched on rocky slopes, overlooking their cultivated terraced fields. Some Berbers, like the Aït Atta of Jebel Sahro and the Draa plains, are still nomadic, living in low tents made of goat skins and camel hair.

Berber women are unveiled and more open in public than women in the cities and plains of the north. They herd and graze goats and cattle, and carry huge loads of firewood or provisions on their heads. The weekly souks, often established on tribal borders, are a central part of their lives, particularly for the nomads, because as well as produce, this is where news and views are exchanged. Berbers in the plains built *ksour* (➤ 23–24), fortified villages, as protection against surrounding tribes, but in the hills, where they were more able to defend themselves, they only protected their *agadirs* or *irherms* (granaries).

Berber woman with typical face tattooos

Giggling Berber girls from Asilah

the magazine **29**

Pirates & Corsairs

When, in 1610, the devout Catholic king Philip III expelled all Muslims and Jews from Spain, many headed for nearby Morocco. Some were skilled craftsmen who applied their art to the construction of elegant monuments, but others took their revenge against Christians by becoming pirates or corsairs. The corsairs of Tetouan and Bou Regreg were much feared, venturing as far north as England and Iceland. Piracy continued in Morocco until bombardment by Austria, in revenge for the loss of one of their ships, seriously damaged Rabat and other coastal settlements in 1829.

The Salée Rovers

The richest of the corsair states was the Republic of Bou Regreg. Over 300,000 Moriscos (Muslims expelled from Spain) settled on either side of the Bou Regreg river, in Rabat and Salé. Many of them took to piracy, mainly against Spanish ships. The notorious Salée Rovers, as they became known, soon also attracted European adventurers and renegades. Their language was a *lingua franca*, a mixture of Spanish, Italian, French and Portuguese. They specialised in plundering ships returning to Europe from West Africa and the Spanish Americas. One of the most successful Rovers was Mourad Reis, a German originally called Jan Janz who converted to Islam. Mourad Reis attacked villages in Cornwall (England), Ireland and Iceland, taking hundreds of captives who were sold in slave markets in North Africa.

The Pirate Queen of Tetouan

Like Salé and Rabat, the city of Tetouan saw an influx of Moriscos from Spain and soon the city grew rich on

Sir Henry Mainwaring

The 16th-century Englishman Henry Mainwaring worked for all the big pirate bosses, including the Sultan of Morocco, the Bey of Tunis and the Duke of Tuscany. Based in Mehdiya (► 84), he looted ships and sold his captives in slave markets in France and North Africa. Later in his life he returned to England, where he became a naval officer and eventually a politician, arguably not much of a career change.

the profits of their piracy. In 1512, upon the death of Tetouan's founder el-Mandari, his dynamic 20-year-old wife, Fatima, assumed power and became the corsair queen. Her corsairs were much feared, and she even had alliances with the fearsome Ottoman pirates of Barbarossa. Fatima ruled for more than 30 years and used her wealth to patronise artists and intellectuals at her court.

Built with corsair money

Under the rule of the Alaouite sultan Moulay Rashid, and his successor Moulay Ismail (► 128–130), the corsairs of Tetouan and Salé were encouraged to attack Christian ships. Many of the captives were forced to help build Moulay Ismail's new capital at Meknes. As the sultan took about 60 per cent of this profitable business, the corsair republic soon went into decline.

Pirates attack the boat of the famous Arab traveller Ibn Battutah

the magazine 31

The American writer, translator and composer Paul Bowles dominated Tangier's post-war artistic and intellectual life. His novels, short stories and translations have shaped Western notions of Tangier and other Moroccan cities.

Paul Bowles's Morocco

After studying music in Paris, Bowles headed for Tangier in 1931 and was immediately enchanted, though he didn't come to live in Morocco until several years later. Unlike many foreigners, Bowles was self-effacing and fascinated by his new environment. Although he and his artistic friends were at the heart of the foreign expat community, his real interest lay in Moroccan life and culture, and he befriended many local people.

Bowles was married to the writer Jane Auer, but spent his early years in Tangier living with the Moroccan painter Ahmed Yacoubi. He was later close friends with the author Mohammed Mrabet, whose work he translated (▶ 21).

Paul Bowles' best-known work, *The Sheltering Sky*, is a popular film

Brief Bibliography
The Sheltering Sky (1949)
Let It Come Down (1952)
The Spider's House (1955)
Up Above the World (1966)
Without Stopping (autobiography, 1972)

His evocative first book, *The Sheltering Sky*, attracted many visitors to the country, including the surreal author William Burroughs and assorted hippies. The story was filmed by Bernardo Bertolucci in 1989, starring Debra Winger and John Malkovich, with Bowles himself as narrator, and the movie attracted a new wave of visitors to the country.

Although Bowles is mostly known for his literary work, he spent the 1930s and 1940s composing music. He also recorded traditional Moroccan music – some compilations are available on CD.

Paul Bowles died in 1999 in Tangier but his influential works still offer an insight into aspects of Morocco that are usually hidden from foreigners.

the magazine

Finding Your Feet

34 Finding Your Feet

First Two Hours

Morocco has 12 international airports, the most important of which are
Casablanca, Marrakech, Agadir and, to a lesser extent, Tangier. The Straits
of Gibraltar (14km wide) separate Morocco from Europe. Regular ferries
operate from Algeciras and Tarifa (Spain) to Tangier or Ceuta, from Sète
(France) to Tangier, Almeria and Málaga (Spain) to Melilla.

Aéroport Mohammed V, Casablanca
- Morocco's largest airport for domestic and international flights is **30km from town**.
- **Trains** to the Gare des Voyageurs and Gare du Port in the centre run every hour between 6 am and 10:45 pm and cost 25dh, and there's also a shuttle bus (about 30dh) to the main bus station (*gare routière*).
- A *grand taxi* to the centre costs about 200dh.

Marrakech Airport
- The airport is only **5km from town**. Bus 11 runs to Djemaa el-Fna, but services can be erratic.
- *Grands taxis* are about 50–60dh to Guéliz (the new town).
- There's a *bureau de change* and several *car-hire* desks.

Agadir al-Massira Airport
- Agadir's airport is **25km east of the city**.
- There is no public transport, but *grands taxis* charge a fixed rate (150dh) into town, taking six people.
- The airport's bank is usually open 24 hours, and there are several **car-hire** agencies.

Fes Airport
- The small airport at Saïs, **15km south of the city**, only handles international flights from Paris.
- **Bus 16** goes to the railway station or a *grand taxi* should cost about 100dh.

Tangier Airport
- The airport is **15km from the centre**.
- Local **buses 17** and **70** to Grand Socco in the centre leave from the main road, 2km away from the airport. Otherwise try to negotiate a price for a *grand taxi*; the official charge is 100dh per car for up to six people, but drivers often try to charge per person, and will ask for extra money if you're carrying luggage.
- The **car-hire desks in the arrivals hall** don't offer the best deal in town.

Tangier Port
- Passport control in Tangier Port is notoriously slow, so **expect a long queue**. Make sure you get a departure card on the boat and have your passport stamped before getting off, or the wait will be even longer.
- There are *bureaux de change* inside and outside the port.
- Tangier centre is within walking distance, but if you have a lot of luggage take a *petit taxi* (10dh per person).
- The port area is notorious for its **hustlers**, who may tell you that you need a guide because the city is dangerous, or that your hotel is full. It's best to ignore them.

First Two Hours 35

Tourist Information Offices

While tourist offices in Morocco are not always very helpful, they can provide you with a few (often ancient and very general) leaflets and sometimes maps. They can also help with dates of festivals, addresses or put you in touch with official guides. All staff speak Arabic, French and very often also English.

Agadir
+ 184 A3
✉ Immeuble A, place Prince-Héritier-Sidi-Mohamed
☎ (04) 8846379
(Syndicat d'Initiative) ✉ boulevard Mohammed V
☎ (04) 8840307

Casablanca
+ 182 C3
✉ 55 rue Omar Slaoui
☎ (02) 2271177
(Syndicat d'Initiative) ✉ boulevard Mohammed V
☎ (02) 2221524

Fes
+ 183 F4
✉ Immeuble Bennani, place de la Résistance
☎ (05) 5623460

Marrakech
+ 182 C1
✉ place Abdelmoumen ben Ali, Gueliz
☎ (04) 8872911

Meknes
+ 183 E3
✉ place Administrative
☎ (05) 5524426

Rabat
+ 183 D3
✉ 22 avenue d'Alger
☎ (03) 7739562
(ONMT) ✉ corner of avenue al Abtal and rue Oued Fes
☎ 03 768 1531

Safi
+ 182 B2
✉ rue Imam Malek
☎ (04) 4622496

Tangier
+ 183 E5
✉ 29 boulevard Pasteur
☎ (03) 9948050

Tetouan
+ 183 E5
✉ 30 avenue Mohammed V
☎ (03) 9961915

Faux Guides

- Hustlers and *faux guides* can be a problem for the first time visitor, mainly in the medinas of tourist cities, but also at airports and, particularly, in Tangier port. The authorities have dealt with most of them, but some remain and should be avoided.
- They may tell you that there is no public transport into town in the hope that you take their car, or that your hotel has recently closed so you can go and stay at their "cousin's" hotel, where they get a percentage of the cost. They may also tell you (wrongly) that medinas are dangerous places where you will get lost. They will then offer to guide you around and lead you to shops where they will receive a commission on whatever you buy. If you try to shake them off they will often accuse you of being racist or a paranoid tourist, but just ignore all that.
- If you do want assistance, look for the officially accredited guides recommended by your hotel or by the tourist office.
- One drawback of the clampdown is that it has now become more difficult to walk around town with a Moroccan friend, as this may attract police attention.

36 Finding Your Feet

Drugs

- The Rif Mountains are a pretty lawless region, as their main crop is *kif* (cannabis). Although its cultivation is legal, it's strictly illegal to buy, sell or be in possession of cannabis or hashish.
- Many foreigners are in Moroccan jails for getting involved in the business, so beware. Local gangsters, particularly around Ketama, often target vehicles passing through, especially foreign or rented cars.
- Visitors are likely to come across marijuana in various forms and in related traditional by-products such as *majoun* and honey. Beware, however, that you are more likely to find yourself in trouble for buying some than the locals.

Admission Charges

The cost of admission to museums and places of interest mentioned in the text is indicated by the following price categories:

Inexpensive under 20dh
Moderate 20–30dh
Expensive over 30dh

Getting Around

Generally, the public transport system works well in Morocco. An efficient train service links the main towns in the north with Casablanca, Rabat and Marrakech; elsewhere you can travel by bus, *grand taxi* or communal taxi.

Urban Transport

- The best, and often the only, way to **explore the medina is on foot**, but you may need some transport to visit sights further away.
- *Petits taxis* can only travel within the city, and carry no more than three people. They are relatively cheap and all have meters, but do insist that the driver switches it on after departure. The normal rate doubles after 8 pm. It is standard practice, particularly with a single passenger, for the driver to pick up more passengers on the way.
- *Grands taxis* (see below) operate in cities like normal taxis but, as they have no meters, you need to negotiate the price before you set off.
- Tourists rarely use local buses because **taxis are inexpensive** and you can do most things on foot. Where a bus is useful it has been indicated in the text.

Trains

- The network only covers a small part of the country, but there it is usually the **best way to travel**. Trains are comfortable, reliable and efficient.
- **Two main lines** run from Tangier to Marrakech and from Oujda to Marrakech, joining the Tangier line at Sidi Kacem.
- **Timetables** are available at main stations and tourist offices or online at www.oncf.org.ma.
- It's best to **book tickets in advance**, but very often you can just turn up and get a seat, as there are frequent trains.
- **Second-class tickets** usually cost a little more (just over 3dh per 10km) than a similar journey by bus, while **first class** (air-conditioned) costs more but is still very reasonable.

First Two Hours/Getting Around

Buses
- The **bus service is very good**, and slightly cheaper than *grands taxis*, at around 2dh per 10km.
- The national bus company **CTM** has the fastest and most reliable buses with fixed departure times, numbered seats and loud videos on the longer routes.
- All major towns have a *gare routière* (bus station), but **CTM buses leave from their own offices**, which are not necessarily near by. For longer journeys and CTM buses try buying tickets in advance.
- In summer you might consider taking **night buses** for longer journeys to avoid the midday heat.
- Services run by some of the **smaller companies** only leave when they are full up, and they stop when flagged down.
- The train company ONCF also runs fast and efficient **Supratour Express** buses to connect larger cities like Essaouira, Agadir and Tetouan with their rail network.

Grands Taxis
- Collective *grands taxis* (service taxis) operate almost everywhere in Morocco, and they are the **fastest way to get around**. Big Peugeot or Mercedes cars will carry up to six passengers and operate all day, particularly on popular routes, departing as soon as they are full.
- Just turn up at the *grands taxis* terminal and **state your destination** to get a seat in a car.
- **Prices are fixed per seat**; just ask the other passengers. If you do not want to wait you can pay the price of all six seats.

Sample Journey Times
- **Marrakech–Casablanca**: 3 hours (train)
  3 hours 30 min (CTM bus)
  2 hours 30 min (*grand taxi*)
- **Tangier–Casablanca**: 6 hours (train/bus)
- **Fes–Casablanca**: 4 hours 10 min (train)
  5 hours 30 min (bus)
  3 hours (*grand taxi*)
- **Agadir–Casablanca**: 9 hours (bus)
- **Essaouira–Casablanca**: 5 hours (bus)
- **Essaouira–Marrakech**: 3 hours 30 min (bus)

Domestic Flights
- **Royal Air Maroc** (RAM) operates from Casablanca to the major cities in Morocco (tel: 0900 0800/(02) 2538080; www.royalairmaroc.com). For most flights you have to change in Casablanca.
- **Book all domestic flights in advance** and make sure you reconfirm them 72 hours before departure.
- For anything other than long distances, such as from Laayoune or Dakhla in the far south, **it may be faster by train or car**.

Driving
- Driving is fairly easy in Morocco, but **accidents are quite frequent**, particularly because people often walk in the road without looking out for traffic. Always watch out for pedestrians or cyclists, particularly in villages or towns.
- **Roads are generally good and well kept**, and there is relatively little traffic out of urban areas.
- **Police checks are frequent**, especially for speed offences.

38 Finding Your Feet

- **Driving in the dark is dangerous** as many people cycle or walk in the middle of the road, or even drive without lights.
- To drive on **pistes or unsurfaced roads** – in remote areas or in the desert – you need an appropriate vehicle (preferably four-wheel-drive) and some experience of similar environments.

Driving Essentials

- The **minimum age** for drivers is 21 years.
- **Speed limits**: on motorways 120kph
  on main roads 100kph
  on urban roads 40kph.
- Drive on the **right**.
- **Seatbelts** are compulsory for drivers and passengers, and you may be fined if caught not wearing one.
- **Petrol stations** are common in and around towns, but there are fewer in rural areas and in the south, so always fill up when you can.
- **Premium** is the standard brand of petrol for cars, and unleaded petrol is available at most stations. Prices are similar to those in Europe, but the duty-free fuel in Melilla and Ceuta is less expensive.

Car Hire

- A car is especially rewarding in the **south of Morocco**, where there is less public transport, and the traffic is light.
- **Hiring a car is easy** as there are many agencies in Morocco, but it is generally expensive. International agencies tend to be more expensive than local ones, but are cheaper when booked before arrival or with a flight. With local firms you can usually bargain a little over the fare, but you should ensure that you check the quality of the vehicle before use.
- To hire a car you must be **over 21**, and you need a **passport** and **driving licence**. An international licence is not required but can be useful if your normal one does not carry a photograph.

Breakdowns

- **Moroccan mechanics are usually good** and very resourceful. Most small towns have a garage but, as most spare parts are for French makes such as Peugeot or Renault, it may take a while to order anything else.
- If you break down far from a garage **you may have to pay a truck driver to tow you** to the garage.

Parking

- In almost every town centre or at every sight someone will offer to be a *gardien de voitures*, sometimes officially, but very often self-appointed. In either case you should offer them a few dirhams for looking after your car before driving off.

Police Checks

- As a result of the large number of deaths on Moroccan roads, the police have become increasingly vigilant and there are often **checks** outside cities. Foreigners are usually flagged through, though you may be asked to show your papers.
- If you are stopped for **speeding** or for some other reason, always remain calm and polite. A quick apology may get you off a fine of up to 450dh.
- Major roads have **radars** to check speed – but drivers coming in the opposite direction will usually warn others by flashing their lights.

Getting Around/Accommodation

Accommodation

This guide includes a wide though carefully selected choice of places to stay, ranging from simple but charming bed and breakfasts to sumptuous royal palaces. Coastal areas are busiest in summer, while Marrakech is now busy almost all year round, and particularly during the school holidays.

Hotels
- Moroccan hotels are usually either **classified**, with tourist board star-ratings, or **unclassified**, less expensive places with very few comforts.
- Morocco has been criticised for not using international ratings for its hotels. But, although in the past many of its "five-star" hotels were not up to standard, they now have improved services and amenities. Many new hotels have been built, and medinas all over the country also have some **excellent *riad* hotels**.
- Morocco has a fair number of luxurious palace hotels, as well as numerous well-kept and friendly budget hotels, but the middle categories can be quite grim.

Riads
- For an authentic Moroccan experience, the best place to stay is a ***riad*** (➤ 26), which is often hidden in the medina. These large old houses or palaces are increasingly being converted into restaurants, bed and breakfasts or luxurious hotels.
- *Riads* are smaller and more intimate than ordinary hotels, with only with a few rooms, usually centred around a tranquil, leafy courtyard – often just a step away from the exotic markets and intriguing alleys of the medina.
- Prices vary from budget to very expensive, and the decorations and facilities vary accordingly.

Youth Hostels
- Morocco has 11 quite **well-run and clean youth hostels** (*Auberges de Jeunesse*) in the major cities.
- A membership card is not required, although members get a reduced rate. Prices range from about 25 to 50dh per person per night in a dormitory.
- Information is available from Fédération Royale Marocaine des Auberges de Jeunesse, Parc de la Ligue Arabe, PO Box 15998, Casa Principale, Casablanca 21000; tel: (02) 2470952; fax: (02) 2227677.

Camping
- There are very basic and inexpensive (about 10–20dh per person) **campsites** (*muhayyem* in Arabic) in all major cities and along the coast. Most have fairly rudimentary washing and toilet facilities, but a few are well kept and some upmarket ones even have swimming pools.
- **Security is not a priority** at most sites, so do not leave anything valuable in your tent.
- Camping outside sites is not illegal, but it's not advisable unless you're looking for adventure.

Booking Accommodation
It's usually best to fax and ask the hotel to fax back your confirmation, as phone bookings are not always secure.

40 Finding Your Feet

Useful websites for information and bookings include:
www.hotelstravel.com/morocco.html Details of mainly high-class hotels
www.riadomaroc.com Offers authentic *riad* apartments for rent
www.riad2000.com *Riads* and guest houses in southern Morocco
www.fesmedina.com Historic properties for rent in Fes medina.

Accommodation Prices
In many hotels, particularly out of season and if you are staying a
few days, it is possible to negotiate room rates. The price categories
indicated in this guide are for a double room per night, including
breakfast and taxes:
£ under 640dh   **££** 640–1,600dh   **£££** over 1,600dh

Food and Drink

You can eat well in Morocco. Every city has a choice of restaurants to suit
all tastes and budgets. If you are looking for something exotic, then head
for the medina, where restaurants are usually less expensive. In general,
Moroccans are a lot better at their own cuisine than at international cooking. Moroccan food is traditionally prepared by women to recipes handed
down from mother to daughter. Men traditionally make the tea and are not
often allowed near the stove. The best food is eaten at home, but if you are
not lucky enough to be invited, the nearest thing to Moroccan home-cooking
is one of the *riad* restaurants.

Eating Out
- During **Ramadan** many restaurants in tourist areas remain open, but
  visitors should be discreet when eating or drinking during the day.
- **Breakfast** is usually from 7:30 to 10 am, **lunch** from noon to 2:30 pm
  and **dinner** from 8 to 11 pm, although opening hours are vague.
- A **meal** usually starts with raw or cooked salads, followed by a tagine
  (stew of vegetables or fruits with meat, chicken or fish) or couscous.
  Dessert is usually fresh fruit, or Moroccan pastries with mint tea.
- **Some Moroccan food takes a long time to prepare** and so needs to be
  ordered well in advance, when you book the table.
- In most places **the dress code is relaxed**, although in more upmarket
  places in Marrakech and Casablanca it is a good idea to dress up for
  the occasion.
- **Menus** are generally written in French and Arabic, and in English at
  more touristy places.
- Traditionally a Moroccan meal is eaten with two fingers and the thumb
  of the **right hand**. Bread is served in large quantities and is often used
  as cutlery to scoop up food.

Moroccan Restaurants
- Most **upmarket hotels** have both an international and a Moroccan
  restaurant (usually better), decorated in traditional style with
  banquettes around low, round tables.
- Moroccan restaurants are usually the precinct of **tourists**, as locals
  prefer to eat Moroccan food at home, and French or Italian food when
  they go out. A meal in these places is often accompanied by a floor-
  show with musicians and a belly dancer.

Accommodation/Food and Drink 41

■ Some *riad* restaurants in Marrakech charge a **fixed price** for an evening of delights, which include a steady flow of culinary pleasures, wine, an exotic décor and a warm ambience, with live traditional music and dancing shows.

International Cuisine

The French legacy is still strong, usually in the *Villes Nouvelles* (new towns), and French eateries range from old-style colonial dives to upmarket restaurants, often run by expatriots.

Vegetarian Cuisine

■ Vegetarians can have a **hard time eating in Morocco**, where many people find it hard to comprehend the concept.
■ Most **salads** are based on vegetables only, but there is a wide choice. **Tagines** can be served without meat, but are often cooked in meat stock or meat fat.
■ If you are eating in someone's home, **your hosts will usually serve you meat** even if you have told them you do not eat it, as they will assume that you do not eat meat because you cannot afford it. Leave the meat if you must, but eat something so as not to offend your hosts.
■ **Markets** have plenty of fresh fruits and vegetables, as well as excellent **yoghurt** to supplement your diet.

Street Food

■ Moroccans like to eat at *gargottes*: street stalls and small cafés that sell inexpensive and often excellent snacks such as harira soup, salads and brochettes (skewers of meat), merguez (spicy sausages) and simple tagines (➤ 17).
■ The most obvious place to sample street food is on **Djemaa el-Fna in Marrakech** (➤ 50) or the stalls outside **Essaouira harbour** (➤ 81).
■ Tourists are often wary of the **hygiene standards** in these places, but if it's popular with the locals then the food is usually fresh.

Drinks, Wine and Beer

■ **Green tea** with mint is the national drink, but Arabic coffee is also served. Morocco has wonderful oranges so most places sell fresh **orange juice** in season. **Almond milk** and **banana with milk** are also popular.
■ **Soft drinks** and bottled **mineral water** are available everywhere.
■ Morocco is a Muslim country so, while **alcohol** is widely available in tourist hotels, restaurants and bars, it is generally not easy to buy it in medinas or in rural areas.
■ Moroccans who do drink alcohol often prefer a cool **local beer**, either Stork or Flag. Hotels usually have **imported beers**, though at double the price of the local brew.
■ Moroccan **wines**, mostly from the Meknes region or from Haha near Essaouira, are a little heavy but quite drinkable. The most common wines are the red Cabernet, Ksar, Siraoua, the rosé Gris de Boulaoune and the dry white Special Coquillages. The red Clairet de Meknès is quite rare but excellent.

Restaurant Prices

Price guides are for a three-course meal per person, excluding drinks but including taxes and service:

£ under 160dh   **££** 160–350dh   **£££** over 350dh

42 Finding Your Feet

Shopping

Morocco is a shopper's delight, with a variety of good-quality crafts at
reasonable prices. There is only one rule in the souks: bargain hard. Almost
every city and large town has an *ensemble artisanal* (government shop) that
makes and sells regional crafts at fixed prices. The prices tend to be a bit
higher than in the souks, but these shops are perfect places for those who
hate bargaining, as you can get an idea of the sort of prices you'll expect to
pay, before venturing into the souks.

Shopping Hours
- **Shops in the *Ville Nouvelles*** (new town areas) usually open Mon–Sat
  8:30 am–noon and 2–6:30 pm; in the summer they may close for
  longer during the afternoon and stay open later; during Ramadan they
  don't close for lunch, but do close earlier in the afternoon.
- **Shops in the medinas** tend to be open from 8 or 9 am to around 8 pm or
  even later in tourist areas. Many shops are closed on Friday for prayers
  at the mosque.
- **Souks** usually start at around 6 am.

Bargaining
Bargaining in Morocco is as normal as saying hello, and is expected
wherever you shop. There are no real rules about how much of the initial
price you should pay as some vendors start with ridiculous mark-ups,
while others stay close to their final price. It's often a good idea to check
out prices before you start buying. The main rule is to take your time and
not be intimidated: it can be a fun game! But never mention a price you
are not prepared to pay. If you go shopping with a guide he will take you
to shops where he will earn a percentage of your purchases, which will be
added to your bill.

Souk Days
- Many villages are named after their weekly market day.
- There are no markets on Friday as it's a day for rest and prayers.
- Arrive early in the morning when the market is in full flow, as it usually
  finishes by lunchtime.

Souk el-Had	Sunday market
Souk el-Tnine	Monday market
Souk el-Tleta	Tuesday market
Souk el-Arba	Wednesday market
Souk el-Khamees	Thursday market
Souk es Sebt	Saturday market

Spices and Toiletries
- Spices and natural toiletries are plentiful and make good, **inexpensive
  presents** or souvenirs.
- The most common **spices** are cinnamon sticks or powder, nutmeg,
  powdered ginger, paprika, curcuma, cumin, *ras el hanout* (➤ 17) and
  saffron. The best and most genuine strands of saffron come from
  Taliouine; often the powder is fake.
- **Toiletries** sold in the spice market include kohl (black eye make-up also
  used to protect the eyes), *ghassoul* (clay to wash the hair or skin),
  henna (to dye hair), small clay pots imbued with poppies (lipstick),
  amber and musk (perfume).

Shopping 43

- **Honey** is widely produced and is often found in village souks, but also in specialised shops in Essaouira and Agadir.
- Essaouira is also famous for its rich and sweet nutty **oil** pressed from argan nuts (► 93).

Minerals and Fossils
- Everywhere in the Atlas you will come across stalls selling minerals and fossils at very tempting prices; but **beware of fakes**, particularly the brightly coloured ones.
- Often these fossils are just found in the desert, riverbeds or mountains, and so their trade is **not harmful to the environment**.

Jewellery
- When most of the Jewish population left the country, they took a lot of authentic Moroccan silver jewellery with them. As a result, the majority of the jewellery found on sale in Morocco today comes from **India, Indonesia and Niger**.
- The **best jewellery souks** are in Essaouira, Tiznit and Marrakech. Silver jewellery is sold by weight, except for very rare old pieces. Many craftsmen reproduce some antique designs beautifully, particularly in the Tiznit region, but do not be tempted to pay antique-level prices for them.
- Most genuine **Berber jewellery** is very heavy and chunky.

Crafts
- **Craft traditions are still going strong** in Morocco, and even a lot of tourist tat is still pretty tasteful and well made.
- Among the main tourist souvenirs are *babouches* (slippers), the traditional footwear in Morocco, made by craftsmen who pass their skills from father to son.
- Moroccans excel at **woodwork**, especially in Essaouira, where beautiful thuya or cedar inlay work is produced.
- Fes is famous for its blue-and-white designs of **pottery**, while Safi, Morocco's major ceramic centre, produces colourful pottery houseware, as does Salé.
- **Leather** is also an excellent buy, typically as *babouches* or pouffes, although places like Marrakech also have good-quality leather clothing and handbags.
- **Carpets** tend to be expensive in Morocco, but good-quality rugs and kelims (flat-woven carpets and rugs) are more reasonable. The best kelims are made by the Berbers of the Middle and High Atlas, and are available in village souks such as Midelt, Azrou or Asni near Marrakech. Berbers (particularly in the Rif mountains) also weave beautiful *fouta*, woollen blankets in natural or bright colours.

10 Best Buys from Marrakech
- **Spices** (Marché Central or Rahba Qedima)
- **Slippers** (souk des Babouches)
- Moroccan **teapots and tea glasses** (off souk des Babouches)
- **Shopping baskets** with leather handles (Marché Central, Guéliz)
- Thick felt-wool **handbags**, dyed with saffron (souk des Babouches)
- **Fabric man with fez** to handle a hot teapot (Maison d'Été)
- **Iron lanterns** (Souk des Haddadine)
- **Love potion** (Rahba Qedima)
- **Moroccan music cassettes** (off Djemaa el-Fna, Marrakech)
- **Mejdoul dates** from the oases (markets)

44 Finding Your Feet

Entertainment

Cities in Morocco have a few bars, mostly for men, and discos (often in tourist hotels), but the main entertainment is a meal and a good show in a wonderful Moroccan restaurant. There are few spectator sports, but the country offers a wide range of outdoor activities.

Sport
- **Golf** was made popular by King Hassan II, and Morocco now boasts spectacular courses near every major city. For more details, contact **Royal Moroccan Golf Federation**: Dar es Salaam Golf Club, Rabat; tel: (03) 7755960; fax: (03) 7751026.
- The Atlantic coast is usually good for **surfing**, and spots like Sidi Kaouki near Essaouira and Dar-Bouazza near Casablanca are especially popular. **Royal Moroccan Surfing Federation**: tel: (02) 2259530; fax: (02) 2236385.
- During the winter it is usually possible to **ski** near Oukaïmeden in the High Atlas or near Fes and Meknes in the Middle Atlas. You can cross-country ski in the High and Middle Atlas, as well as in the Rif Mountains. Contact **Royal Moroccan Ski and Mountaineering Federation**: tel: (02) 2203798; fax: (02) 2474979; email: frmsm@hotmail.com.
- Moroccan horses are superb and, with wonderful landscapes to explore, **riding** here can be very rewarding. The Atlas Mountains in particular are an impressive place to ride (► 162).
- **Hiking** is popular all over the country, but particularly in the Atlas range around Mount Toubkal. Contact **Club Alpin Français**: tel: (02) 2270090; fax: (02) 2297292 or **Royal Moroccan Ski and Mountaineering Federation** (see above).
- In the toughest **long-distance run** in the world, competitors in the annual Marathon des Sables cover 250km of sand dunes and rocky desert terrain in a week – while carrying all their supplies. If this appeals to you, contact **Cimbaly**: PO Box 58 10002, Troyes, Cedex, France; tel: 25 82 01 28; fax: 25 82 07 23.
- **Hunting** is a popular activity, particularly with the Moroccans and the French, and mainly in the Middle Atlas. The season for wild boar and for birds such as quail, pigeons, partridges and ducks runs from the first Sunday in October until early spring, every Sunday and on public holidays. Licensing is strictly controlled. Contact **Royal Moroccan Hunting Federation**: tel and fax: (03) 7707835.
- Deep-sea **fishing** is popular in the Atlantic, with trips available from Essaouira, Safi and Asilah, and for wilder shores from Dakhla and Laayoune. Trout and other freshwater fish can be found in the lakes of the Middle Atlas, near Azrou, Ifrane, Beni Mellal and Ouirgane. Contact **National Fisheries Office**: tel: (02) 22405; fax: (02) 224 2305.

Traditional Music and Dance
Major hotels and restaurants may host traditional music and belly dancing. Don't miss the spectacular parties known as *fantasias*, traditionally held at Berber *moussems*, but also staged for tourists in Marrakech.

Festivals
Religious festivals are movable occasions according to the Islamic lunar calendar, but popular annual events include the Moulay-Idriss *moussem* (► 131), the Wedding Festival in Imilchil (► 133), Erfoud's Date Festival (► 155) and the Festival of Sacred Music in Fes (► 138).

Marrakech

Getting Your Bearings 46 – 47
In Three Days 48 – 49
Don't Miss 50 – 60
At Your Leisure 61 – 63
Where to... 64 – 70

46 Marrakech

Getting Your Bearings

The Red City of Marrakech gave its name to the country and, if you only see one part of Morocco, it should be this. The "Pearl of the South" offers a vast array of exotic colours, smells, sounds, people and experiences. It can also be a delightful place to hide away and relax, in great gardens, sumptuous *riad* restaurants and some of Africa's best hotels.

Above and previous page: The red *pisé* ramparts encircle the city for 16km, and are mostly well preserved

Marrakech is set spectacularly against the High Atlas Mountains. At its heart is Djemaa el-Fna, a hub of entertainment for tourists and Marrakchis (or Marrakechis) alike, particularly at dusk. Behind it lies the medina, an intriguing maze of alleys and souks enclosed by thick mudbrick walls.

The Almoravid conqueror Youssef ben Tachfine founded Marrakech around 1070. Legend has it that he ate so many dates that he created a large palm grove, the Palmeraie, and Marrakech still boasts many fine gardens.

The city can be overwhelming at first but staying in a *riad* in the medina, wandering around the streets, sipping mint tea and chatting to the friendly locals can be incredibly rewarding.

Left: Medicine men claim to have a cure for almost any ailment. Right: Brass on sale in the craft souk

Getting Your Bearings

★ Don't Miss
1. Djemaa el-Fna ➤ 50
2. Souks ➤ 52
3. Ben Youssef Medersa ➤ 54
4. The Ramparts and Gates ➤ 56
5. Gardens of Marrakech ➤ 58

At Your Leisure
6. Koutoubia Mosque ➤ 61
7. Koubba Ba'adiyin ➤ 61
8. Dar Menebhi ➤ 62
9. Saadian Tombs ➤ 62
10. El-Badi Palace ➤ 62
11. El-Bahia Palace and Museum ➤ 63
12. Maison Tiskiwin ➤ 63
13. Dar Si Said Museum ➤ 63
14. Guéliz ➤ 63

Marrakech

One of the great pleasures of Marrakech is to stroll through the souks, bargaining and watching the people. The medina and Djemaa el-Fna change throughout the day so it's worth passing through at different times.

Marrakech in Three Days

Day One

Morning
Start at the **6 Koutoubia Mosque** (Mosquée de la Koutoubia, right; ➤ 61) and then stroll over to **1 Djemaa el-Fna** (➤ 50–51) for refreshments. Head for the northern medina via **souk Smarine** (➤ 52), which turns into **souk Chaaria**, with **8 Dar Menebhi** (➤ 62) on the right. Further along the street is the **9 Ben Youssef Medersa** (➤ 54–55) and near by is the **7 Koubba Ba'adiyin** (➤ 61). Return through the souks to Djemaa el-Fna for lunch at the Argana (➤ 66).

Afternoon
For some proper shopping, take in some of the **2 souks**, such as **des Babouches** and **des Teinturiers**, the **kissarias** and the **Rahba Qedima** (handmade hat seller, left; ➤ 52). Return to Djemaa el-Fna, which by now will be packed with performers and food stalls, and watch the sun set behind the mountains from the roof terrace of the Café de France at the entrance to the souks.

Evening
Spend time in an exotic and magnificent *riad* (mansion) restaurant in the medina, such as Dar Marjana or Le Tobsil (➤ 67), where the set price often includes wine and a belly dancing show.

In Three Days 49

Day Two

Morning
Walk from the gate of **Bab Agnaou** (➤ 57) to the **9 Saadian tombs** (Tombeaux Saadiens, ➤ 62), then continue to the **10 el-Badi Palace** (Palais el-Badi, ➤ 62). Note place des Ferblantiers, the main square of the *mellah* (Jewish quarter). North of the square follow Riad Zitoun Djedid, a street of large mansions, including the palace and museum of **11 el-Bahia** (Palais el-Bahia, ➤ 63). Lunch at a *riad* restaurant such as Dar Douirya (14 Derb Djedid) or Palais Gharnatta (5/6 Derb al Arsa, off Riad Zitoun Djedid).

Afternoon
Visit the nearby **12 Maison Tiskiwin** (➤ 63) and **13 Dar Si Said Museum** (➤ 63). In the late afternoon, take a caleche tour of the **4 ramparts** (➤ 56–57, 164–166).

Evening
Dress for a drink and dinner at the **Hotel La Mamounia** (pictured above) and take a stroll through its magnificent gardens (➤ 59, 65).

Day Three

Morning
Visit the **Jardin Majorelle** (pictured right), one of the **5 gardens of Marrakech** (➤ 58–60), and take a taxi or caleche to **14 Guéliz** (➤ 63) for a walk and coffee in Café des Négociants on avenue Mohammed V (➤ 66). Buy picnic provisions from the nearby Marché Central, or have lunch in Catanzaro behind the market or in al-Fassia (➤ 67).

Afternoon
Around 4 pm, rent a bike or take a caleche to the **Ménara Gardens** (Jardin de la Menara, ➤ 59) before strolling back through Djemaa el-Fna.

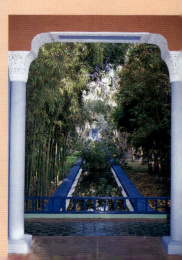

50 Marrakech

Djemaa el-Fna

It all happens in the Djemaa el-Fna, one of the world's most extraordinary meeting places, and the living heart of the city. By day it's a sleepy transit towards the souks. At dusk the spectacle starts as locals and visitors gather to hear ancient tales from storytellers, have their fortune told or get a recipe for a magic potion from the herbalists.

Above: At night Djemaa el-Fna becomes an open-air restaurant, theatre, circus and hospital. Below: Snake charmers also charm tourists into giving money

"Without the Djemaa el-Fna Marrakech would just be a city like any other." There is perhaps some truth in the words of the writer Paul Bowles (➤ 32).

The open-air theatre and restaurant that is Djemaa el-Fna is so unique that Unesco had to create a new category – it's the first to be recognised as "Immaterial Heritage of Mankind". Nobody is sure how it all started, or where its name came from. But, sitting just at the entrance to the medina, it seems always to have been the city's focal point, a place of spectacle, trade, encounter and even execution – heads rolled here until well into the 19th century.

The square reverberates with the overwhelming sounds of snake charmers, water carriers, dancers, singers, acrobats, and the enthusiastic reactions of their audience. It disappears under the smoke from the many food stalls that entice passers-by to eat freshly prepared snail soup, sheeps' brains, fried sole or grilled sausages.

TAKING A BREAK
The food here is freshly prepared and well worth trying. **Juice stalls** set up early in the

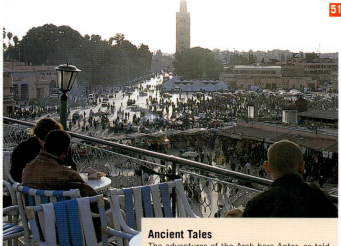

The best view over the square is from the rooftop terrace of the Café de France

morning, **al-Baraka** and **Argana** (► 66) are good places for lunch, while the rooftop of the **Café de France** is recommended for refreshments including mint tea, especially at sunset, when there are great views over the medina and the High Atlas Mountains.

🏠 182 C1
🕘 Daily 8 am–2 pm
🚌 1, 3, 5, 7, 8, 9, 10, 11, 15, 23

Ancient Tales

The adventures of the Arab hero Antar, as told by a storyteller in the Djemaa el-Fna, begin:

"From the story of the black knight, the lion with pennant and standards, with the flag and the horse, defender of the Bani Abs Adnane, from Fizara and Dibane, intrepid knight with the reckless heart, snake in the river bed, burning without fire, the one for whom the bravest heroes bowed down, in full battle, courageous conqueror of the grandest warrior, and of Noujeir the son of Giants, master of Mourad and Zaid, Antara ibn Chaddad…"

DJEMAA EL-FNA: INSIDE INFO

Top tips Bring plenty of **loose change** for the street entertainers, especially if you want to photograph the colourful performers. The snake charmers in particular can be quite aggressive and ask for exorbitant amounts if you take a picture, but how much you pay is up to you.
• If you have any trouble with **hustlers** go to the tourist police on the square.
• **Beware of pickpockets** in the crowds, particularly after dark.

One to miss Definitely the **dentists** who pull out teeth in the square.

In more depth If you want to take some of the sounds home, head for the **cassette stalls** on the edge of the square.

2 Souks

The souks of Marrakech are a feast for the senses: the labyrinth of alleys, the mixture of people, the variety of wares, the colours, the smells and the play of light and shadow through the roof can be overwhelming. Take it slowly on your first visit, starting with the main drag. When you return, remember that one of the attractions is to get lost, so wander into side alleys where craftsmen make and sell their traditional wares in small workshops.

Above: Carpets cover the Criée Berbère, where carpet auctions take place in the afternoon

The easiest way into the souks is through the alley opposite the Café de France on **Djemaa el-Fna** (➤ 50–51). Stalls in the first covered part of the souk sell nuts, dried fruits and hand-woven baskets. At the end of this is the main arched entrance to rue **Souk Smarine**, the area's principal artery. Souk Smarine is broad and dominated by merchants selling fabrics, kaftans and circumcision outfits for boys, though this is also a good place for upmarket antiques and serious carpets. Some 200m down on the right, two alleys lead into the **Rahba Qedima**, an open square lined with spice and apothecary stalls. At the end a passage leads into the **Criée Berbère**, the Berber market where slaves were sold until 1912. Now you can buy carpets from all over Morocco at auctions held around 4–6 pm.

Souks 53

For live chameleons, magic potions, tagine spices and baskets head for the Rahba Qedima

🚏 182 C1
🕙 Shops/stalls: daily 9–7 or 8; many closed Fri 11–4 and public holidays

Craft Souks

Beyond the market, Souk Smarine forks in two: to the right **Souk el-Kebir** leads through the leather souk to the **Ben Youssef Medersa** (➤ 54–55). The left fork **Souk el-Attarin** leads through the **Souk des Babouches** (slippers) to the **Souk des Teinturiers**, where dyers hang colourful wool to dry, the **Souk Chouari** (carpenters) and the smoky **Souk el-Haddadine**, where blacksmiths forge iron. The area between the two streets is known as the **Kissaria**, a covered market that may be locked, as this is traditionally where more expensive goods such as fine cloth and jewellery are sold.

TAKING A BREAK

The obvious place to stop for a drink or a snack is on **Djemaa el-Fna** (➤ 50–51), where there is plenty of refreshment choice. If you are already in the souks then go for tea in the wonderful *riad* hotels, such as **Riad Tamsna** (➤ 65) or the **Dar Cherifa** (Derb Chorfa Lakbir, Mouassine, tel: (04) 4426463).

SOUKS: INSIDE INFO

Top tips The souks are **liveliest around 4–5 pm** as the temperature cools, tourists finish sightseeing and Marrakchis go for their early evening stroll.
• Marrakech can be an expensive place for crafts, so visit the **Ensemble Artisanal** (avenue Mohammed V, daily 9 am–1 pm, 3–7 pm) for an idea of the top prices before some hard bargaining in the souks.
• Until recently it took some skill to **enter the souks on your own**, but now with the tourist police at the gates it's much easier. Bear in mind that whilst you don't need one, if you take a guide or *faux-guide* into the souk then prices will be higher to include the guide's commission on everything you buy.

In more depth To see an authentic souk where Marrakchis shop, take a *petit taxi* to **Bab Ailen**. No one will try to sell you anything aggressively, but instead stroll through stalls of fishmongers, butchers and greengrocers, past tiny cafés, women catching up on the news and children playing in the streets.

54 Marrakech

3 Ben Youssef Medersa

The largest Koranic school in Morocco rivals the *medersa* in Fes in splendour. Its perfectly proportioned courtyard is a marvel of Moorish architecture, striking an amazing balance between plain surfaces and elaborate decoration.

The splendid medersa, built around 1570, was used as a Koranic school and hostel until 1962

The school took its name from the nearby Mosque of Ben Youssef, which was built in the 12th century, but almost entirely rebuilt in the 19th century at half its original size. The *medersa* was part of the Merenid Sultan Abou Hassan's extensive educational plan, which included the Fes *medersas*

Ben Youssef Medersa

(➤ 122), but in 1564 it was completely restored by the Saadian Sultan Abdullah el-Ghalib. It follows the traditional plan with its central courtyard and a prayer hall, but unlike other *medersas*, Ben Youssef's is entered via an inconspicuous portal and a long, dark corridor. This undoubtedly heightens the pleasure of discovering the large courtyard bathed in sunlight at the end of the passage. The space, centred on a large fountain pool and flanked by two rows of pillars, is intended to inspire a sense of peacefulness. Although rich and elaborate, with colourful *zellij* mosaic, stucco and cedar carving, the decoration never disturbs the tranquillity.

> ### Not Dead But Sleeping
> All Morocco's historic cities have one or more patron saints, often connected with the creation of the city. The saint is called *moul lablad*, the "master of the place", and his tomb is a place of pilgrimage. Moroccans often use the patron saint's name when referring to a particular city – Marrakech is also Sab'at Rijal (Seven Saints). Tradition has it that they are not dead but asleep, and many Muslims come to the city on a pilgrimage to the seven mausoleums spread all over the medina.

At the back, a beautiful ornamental portal gives way to the prayer hall. Divided into three aisles by fine marble columns, the room is covered by a cedar dome surrounded by 24 small windows with detailed stucco work. The *mihrab* is decorated with lace-like sculpted plaster.

The *medersa* was built to house more than 900 students in 150 or so spartan cells on its first floor. Most cells were grouped around smaller interior courtyards, lit purely by skylights, but the favourite or most promising students were treated to the best rooms, overlooking the magnificent central courtyard.

Above: Intricate carved calligraphy. Left: Fine cedarwood screens cover windows overlooking the courtyard

> ### TAKING A BREAK
> Have a fresh juice or a mint tea with Moroccan sweets at the stylish cafeteria in the courtyard of the nearby **Dar Menebhi** (➤ 62).

🕂 182 C1
✉ place Ben Youssef, turn left at the end of Souk el-Kebir
🕐 Daily 9–6
💰 Moderate

BEN YOUSSEF MEDERSA: INSIDE INFO

Top tips You can keep your shoes on during the visit, but **wear modest clothing** out of respect.

• At the time of writing the *medersa* was undergoing **major restoration work** that could continue for some time. As a result, some parts of the monument may be under scaffolding, but it's even a pleasure to see the craftsmen at work.

Hidden gems Don't forget to have a look at **the toilets** at the end of the corridor opposite the entrance: master craftsmen were employed even here.

4 The Ramparts and Gates

A tour of the city's 16km of ramparts reveals the superb, well-preserved *babs* (gates) and *pisé* walls and also offers glimpses of the real, less familiar Marrakech. Some stretches of wall run through a cemetery, while others cut through a busy souk or a crowded public square. The colours of the mud walls change with the light of day, from light pink to ochre to red to deep purple.

In 1126, the Almoravid sultan Ali ben Youssef began the magnificent walls, which were 10km long and 9m high, with 200 defence towers and 20 entrance gates. Within a year his workmen had finished them. The walls were frequently restored and enlarged by the Almohads and Saadians, but they still basically follow the 12th-century plan.

The massive square towers of **Bab Doukkala** are no longer used to enter the medina since a modern gate was built beside them. These gates once guarded the road to Doukkala, the Berber region between el-Jadida and Safi, but now the area is dominated by a busy bus station. Near by is the **cemetery of el-Hara** with the **Koubba (tomb) of Sidi Bennour**. Behind the gate rises the elegant minaret of the **Bab Doukkala Mosque**, built in the 16th century by Lalla Messouada, the mother of Ahmed el-Mansour (► 20).

The essence of Marrakech: The red *pisé* of the walls, the palm trees and gardens, and always the beautiful backdrop of the High Atlas Mountains

The Ramparts and Gates

Past the small gate of **Bab Moussoufa** is the **palm grove of Sidi Bel Abbès**. On the other side of the wall is the **Zaouia of Sidi Bel Abbès**, containing the tomb of the city's great 12th-century patron saint, who is particularly venerated by merchants, farmers and blind people.

There is a daily market at **Bab el-Khemis** that is especially lively on Thursday mornings when livestock is sold. Just before the gate is the **Koubba of Sidi el-Babouchis**, patron saint of slippers. Beneath the Almoravid towers of **Bab Debbarh** is the entrance to the **Tanners' Quarters**, but beware – the smell can be overwhelming in the afternoon. Inside **Bab Ailen** is the shrine and mosque of **Qadi Ayad**, another of the city's seven patron saints. Further along you'll find the vast **cemetery of Bab Rhemat and Bab Ahmar** with the Aguedal Gardens (Jardin Agdal) to the south (➤ 58).

The most elegant gate in Marrakech is Bab Agnaou, which leads into the Imperial City

Go through Bab Ahmar to **Bab Irhli**, passing several grand *mechouars* – processional squares where festivals were celebrated. **Bab er Rob** has a good food and pottery souk, behind which is **Bab Agnaou**, the gate to the imperial city. In the cemetery beyond Bab er Rob is the tomb of **Sidi es Soheili**, another of the Seven Saints. The tour ends at **Bab Jdid** with the wall surrounding the Hotel La Mamounia.

TAKING A BREAK

End the tour with a picnic in the **Menara Gardens** (Jardin de la Menara, ➤ 59), or with a drink on the lovely terrace of **Hotel La Mamounia** (➤ 59, 61), admiring the gardens.

✚ 182 C1
✉ Start at Djemaa el-Fna
🚖 Rented bike, caleche or taxi

RAMPARTS AND GATES: INSIDE INFO

Top tips Although it is possible to walk around the walls in about 4–5 hours, it's **not advisable because of the heat**.
• The most pleasant way is to **rent a caleche** (horse-drawn cab) from the stand in Djemaa el-Fna (➤ 164–166).
• You can rent bikes from the **Hotel de Foucauld** (place de Foucauld; tel: (04) 4445499) at about 70dh for half a day.
• Do the tour in the **late afternoon** when it's cooler.
• The **best-preserved stretches** are between Bab Ailen and Bab Rhemat, and near l'Hivernage.

58 Marrakech

5 Gardens of Marrakech

Hail a caleche and enjoy the peace and soft afternoon light in one of several gardens, which say as much about the city's history as its monuments do. The city's gardens may not be as splendid as they were 100 years ago, but they still offer a great escape from the bustle of the medina.

From its creation by the Almohades in the 11th century until the 1920s, Marrakech was a garden city – two-thirds of the medina was given over to gardens and orchards. Some olive and fig trees and vines have survived the spread of the medina, but street names are often the only reminder of former green spaces. However, the future looks greener as new owners are restoring the gardens of many *riads*, while Moroccan and foreign organisations are revamping and replanting the gardens.

Marrakchis tend to be particularly fond of gardens with perfumed flowers, fruit trees, water and shade, as they see gardens as an earthly reflection of paradise. In summer, many families shelter from the relentless midday sun in one of the gardens, or head for their relative cool in the evening.

Tranquil Waters

Outside the city walls, some splendid gardens and green spaces have survived. Largest of all is the **Aguedal Garden** (Jardin Agdal), created by the 12th-century Almohad sultan Abd el-Moumen and enlarged by the Saadians. The kings and their court held lavish parties in the shade of these huge olive groves and near the large, tranquil tanks (reservoirs) filled with

Above: Colourful flowers in the Hotel Mamounia gardens. **Left:** The Jardin Majorelle is a beautifully manicured oasis garden

Gardens of Marrakech

water from the Ourika River. The main reservoir is Sahaj el-Hana (Tank of Health), beside the beautiful 19th-century pavilion of Dar el-Hana with superb views from the terrace over the Atlas Mountains. It is hard to believe that, in 1873, Sultan Mohammed IV drowned in this tank when his boat capsized. Another pavilion is the Dar el-Beida, a royal palace that's closed when the king is in residence (this is usually during the winter).

Pavilioned in Splendour

Also built by the Almohads, but rebuilt by the Alaouites in the 19th century, are the **Menara Gardens** (Jardin de la Menara). Mohammed IV constructed an elegant green-tiled pavilion overlooking the large water basin and set in a cypress garden surrounded by olive groves. Walk around the reservoir to see the great reflection of the pavilion in the water, or stroll in the shade of the endless olive groves.

Swaying Branches

The Almoravids established the vast palm grove of the **Palmeraie**, originally covering 13,000ha and planted with more than 150,000 trees. The circuit (22km) in the groves was a popular excursion from the centre but, although it is still well worth seeing, the grove has seriously dwindled – partly due to disease, but mainly because land has been developed for hotels and villas.

Rooms With a View

Another well-established garden is the **Jardin de la Mamounia**, now part of the Hotel La Mamounia (► 65). The park belonged to the 18th-century Prince Moulay Mamoun

Above: The vibrant blue of Majorelle's house was inspired by the French workers' overalls

Marrakech

and flaunts splendid palm, guava, orange and lemon trees, as well lush bougainvillea, olive trees and a rose garden.

French Fancies

No less impressive is the Jardin Majorelle, planted between 1922 and 1962 by the French painter Jacques Majorelle (1886–1962). Against a background of bright blue walls he created a fabulous, unusual garden of cacti, giant bamboos and slender palms. After his death the garden was neglected until it was bought and restored by the French fashion designer Yves Saint Laurent, who lives next door.

Well-tended flowerbeds in Hotel Mamounia's gardens

TAKING A BREAK

The **Hotel La Mamounia's** terrace is ideal for a drink or dinner. Less expensive is the small cafeteria of the **Menara Gardens**, or you could bring a **picnic**.

Jardin Agdal
- 182 C1
- Bab Irhli and Bab Ahmar
- Check with tourist office
- Rented bike, caleche or taxi Free

Jardin Majorelle
- 182 C1
- avenue Yaqoub el-Mansour
- (04) 4301852
- Daily summer 9–12, 2–7; winter 8–12, 2–6
- Bus 4 from Djemaa el-Fna
- Moderate

Jardin de la Menara
- 182 C1
- 2km west of Bab Jdid
- All the time
- Bus 11 from Djemaa el-Fna
- Free

Hotel La Mamounia
- 182 C1
- avenue Bab Jdid
- (04) 4444409
- Restricted to hotel residents, but possible if you dress up and have a drink on the terrace Free

La Palmeraie
- 182 C1
- 8km from town on the Fes road
- All the time
- Bus 1 from Djemaa el-Fna
- Free

GARDENS OF MARRAKECH: INSIDE INFO

Top tips The best time to visit is **late afternoon** when the air is cooler and the light warmer.
• The best and most pleasant way to get to and around the gardens is by **caleche or rented bike** (➤ 57 for rental information).

Hidden gem Jacques Majorelle's house has been turned into a beautifully arranged museum containing some of his colourful paintings, and Yves Saint Laurent's collection of traditional Moroccan crafts.

At Your Leisure

At Your Leisure

6 Koutoubia Mosque (Mosquée de la Koutoubia)

Towering above the medina and the new town is Marrakech's main landmark, whose stunning 70m minaret was finished by Sultan Yacoub el-Mansour during the late 12th century. It's the oldest and most complete Almohad tower and served as a model for the classic Moroccan minaret that's still visible in the country's mosques. Legend has it that the three golden balls on the top were made from the jewellery of one of el-Mansour's wives, donated and melted down as penance because she had broken her fast during Ramadan by eating three grapes.

✚ 182 C1 ✉ place Youssef ben Tachfine ⊘ Closed to non-Muslims

Wherever you are in Marrakech you can see the minaret of Koutoubia Mosque

7 Koubba Ba'adiyin

It might not be obvious from the outside, but this small two-storey kiosk – the only surviving Almoravid monument in town – is one of the highlights of Islamic art. The 12th-century ablution hall, with its variety of arches and exquisite interior decoration, is the earliest known example of the typical Moorish style that later became so popular in Andalucía and North Africa.

✚ 182 C1 ✉ Off place Ben Youssef ⊘ All the time

62 Marrakech

8 Dar Menebhi (Le Musée de Marrakech)

This large, late 19th-century palace built by Menebhi, defence minister during the reign of Moulay Abdelaziz, is a perfect example of the Arab-Moorish style. It was a school for many years, until it was restored in the late 1990s by the collector Omar Benjelloun and it's now a gallery for contemporary art and a space for exhibitions from private collections of Islamic and Moroccan art. Happy with its success, the Omar Benjelloun Foundation is now also funding other restoration projects in the medina.

182 C1 place Ben Youssef
(04) 4390911 Daily 9:30–6
Moderate

The Tombeaux Saadiens were there long before the Saadians arrived in Marrakech

9 Saadian Tombs (Tombeaux Saadiens)

The Saadian kings were buried in these splendid mausolea, built during the late 16th century by Ahmed el-Mansour. Moulay Ismail built a large wall around them a century later and eventually they were "lost" until the French rediscovered them by accident in 1917. The flower-filled cemetery has several *koubbas*, but the first one, containing the tomb of Ahmed el-Mansour, is the most remarkable. He was buried in its magnificent central hall, surrounded by his sons. A diffuse light filters onto the tombs beneath a marvellous cedar ceiling supported by 12 marble columns. El-Mansour also built a mausoleum for his mother Lalla Messaouda.

182 C1 Bab Agnaou
Wed–Mon 9–11:45 am, 2:30–7 (6 in winter) Inexpensive

10 El-Badi Palace (Palais el-Badi)

When this 16th-century palace – "the Incomparable" – was built by the Saadian sultan Ahmed el-Mansour, it became the marvel of the Muslim world. Workmen from all over the country took part in its construction; the marble came from Italy, and the walls and ceilings were decorated with mosaics, stucco work and gold leaf. A hundred years later, it took Moulay Ismail (➤ 128) 10 years to strip its splendour in order to build Meknes. Nonetheless, the *pisé* walls, vast pools, sunken gardens and summer pavilions that are open to visitors today remain impressive sights. The palace is most beautiful in June, when it becomes the main venue for the Festival National des Arts Populaires, a large folklore and music festival.

182 C1 Bab Berrima, near place des Ferblantiers Daily 9–11:45, 2:30–5:45 Inexpensive

Only the vast spaces within the walls today suggest how grand el-Badi palace once was

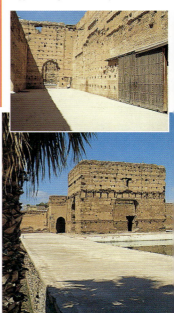

At Your Leisure

11 El-Bahia Palace and Museum (Palais el-Bahia)

This lavish royal palace, whose name means "the Brilliance", was built in the late 19th century by the vizier Bou Ahmed, a slave who had come up in the world. He is said to have lived here with four wives and 24 concubines.

Covering over 8ha, the richly decorated apartments are built around flower-filled courtyards but, compared to the exquisite style of the nearby Saadian Tombs (➤ 62) and the el-Badi Palace (➤ 62), some of the decoration may appear vulgar and over the top. The guided tour takes in vast reception rooms with sculpted and painted ceilings, the harem and a garden planted with orange, lemon and banana trees, jasmine and date palms.

🔳 182 C1 ✉ rue Bab Rhemat ⏰ Daily 8:30–11:45, 2:30–5:45; closed when the royal family is in residence 💰 Moderate plus tip for obligatory tour guide

12 Maison Tiskiwin

The beautiful town house of Maison Tiskiwin, worth a visit in its own right, was named after a Berber dance from the High Atlas. It contains a fine collection of Moroccan crafts, lovingly collected by the Dutch art historian Bert Flint. He has lived in Morocco since the 1950s and his aim is to explain the enormous variety of shapes, materials and techniques used in the popular arts of the country. Well arranged, with each room devoted to the carpets, jewellery, pottery or textiles of one particular region or city, it gives an excellent overview of Morocco's traditional crafts.

🔳 182 C1 ✉ 8 rue de la Bahia, off Riad Zitoun Djedid ☎ (04) 4443335 ⏰ Daily 9:30–12:30, 4–6:30 (knock for entry) 💰 Moderate

13 Dar Si Said Museum

The pleasant palace of the Dar Si Said, a smaller version of el-Bahia (➤ left), was also built by the vizier Bou Ahmed, but this time for his brother. Today it houses the superb Museum of Moroccan Arts, with a particularly good collection of Berber jewellery, fine carpets, intricately carved woodwork taken from the kasbahs and a beautiful marble basin from the Ben Youssef Medersa (➤ 54–55).

🔳 182 C1 ✉ off Riad Zitoun Djedid near Maison Tiskiwin ⏰ Wed–Mon 9–12, 2:30–5:45 💰 Moderate

14 Guéliz

Guéliz is another name for the Ville Nouvelle (new town), created during the French Protectorate. The main avenue Mohammed V connects Guéliz with the medina and is lined with airline offices, café-terraces, restaurants and shops. Also on this avenue is the Marché Central, the best food market in town (open mornings only). The residential area, l'Hivernage, which has many hotels and sumptuous villas, is perfect for a quiet stroll.

🔳 182 C1 ✉ Tourist office: corner of avenue Mohammed V and place Abd el-Moumen ben Ali ☎ (04) 4436131 🚌 Buses 1, 1 from Djemaa el-Fna; 14, 28 from the train station

64 Marrakech

Where to... Stay

Prices

Expect to pay for a double room, including breakfast and taxes
£ under 640dh **££** 640–1,600dh **£££** over 1,600dh

Marrakech's hotels range from the new, luxurious Amanjena to the fleapits that were popular with hippies in the 1960s and 70s. During high season, Easter and autumn holidays, the best hotels get booked up quickly, so plan ahead. The streets off avenue Mohammed V in Guéliz have plenty of mid-range hotels – and package tourists – while most of the upmarket places are in l'Hivernage. Several agencies now rent out *riads* in the medina, including:

• **Marrakech Riads:** tel: (04) 4385858; dzillije@iam.net.ma

• **Riads au Maroc:** tel: (04) 431900; riadomaroc@cybernet.net.ma; www.riadomaroc.com
• **Marrakech-Medina:** tel: (04) 442448; rak.medina@cybernet.net.ma; www.marrakech-medina.com

Amanjena £££

Part of a super-luxurious chain, the Amanjena, styled on a traditional Moroccan palace, opened outside town in 2000. Forty sumptuous pavilions, each with up to three large and beautifully decorated bedrooms, are set in lush gardens with a superb swimming pool.

⊞ 182 C1 ⊠ 7km north of Marrakech ☎ (04) 440353; fax: (04) 4403471; www.amanjena.com

Dar Mouassine £–££

This small *riad*, run by a chic French couple, has five rooms and a courtyard with a plunge pool in the shade of palm trees. The neat and peacefully uncluttered rooms feature antique Indian beds, colourful silk cushions and Moroccan pottery. There's also a pleasant shaded roof terrace and two cosy sitting rooms, one with an extensive video library, the other with an open fire.

⊞ 182 C1 ⊠ 148 derb Snane, medina ☎ and fax: (04) 4445287

Dar Sara £

One of the simpler *riad* B&Bs, Dar Sara's six rooms have whitewashed walls and bright blue shutters, and are simply decorated with locally made furniture and colourful rugs. There are plenty of corners to relax with a book, or try the roof terrace, where children can play happily without fear of breaking something.

⊞ 182 C1 ⊠ 120 derb Arset Aouzal, Bab Doukkala ☎ (04) 4385858

Les Deux Tours £££

Away from the hubbub of the medina, in the heart of olive and orange groves in the Palmeraie, is this charming hotel. It was designed by Charles Boccara, Morocco's most famous architect, who also designed Marrakech Opera House. The complex consists of six villas, each set in its own garden with terraces and a beautiful pool. You can either rent a whole villa or an individually decorated *en suite* room, some with a real fire and most with a balcony or patio. The food, served on the terrace in good weather, is excellent too.

⊞ 182 C1 ⊠ Douar Abiad, Palmeraie ☎ (04) 4329527; fax: (04) 4329523

Galia £

This wonderful little hotel in two *riad* houses has been run by the same French family since 1929. It's in a quiet alley near place Djemaa el-Fna, and has a rooftop terrace overlooking the area. The rooms are simple but spotless, and breakfast is served in a simple courtyard with a fountain, birdsong and tortoises dawdling under the greenery. Make sure you book well in advance.

☐ 182 C1 ☒ 30 rue de la Recette, 500m from place Djemaa el-Fna ☎ (04) 445913; fax: (04) 444853

Farouk £

The welcome is always friendly at this excellent budget hotel near the train station in the Guéliz area. The simple rooms are clean, the showers are hot and the food in the restaurant is very good.

☐ 182 C1 ☒ 66 avenue Hassan II, Guéliz ☎ (04) 4431989; fax: (04) 4440522

Hotel de Foucauld £

Centrally located in a dusty, neo-Moorish building, this hotel has a slightly faded interior. But the rooms are comfortable, the patron speaks English and there's a small pool on the roof terrace. If you want to trek in the Atlas, then organise a trip here, as experienced guides tend to hang out in the bar.

☐ 182 C1 ☒ avenue el-Mouahidine, near Djemaa el-Fna ☎ (04) 4445499; fax: (04) 4441344

Hotel La Mamounia £££

This old hotel remains the haunt of celebrities and it's easy to see why. It has the air of an elegant, sumptuous palace. Although it lacks the intimacy of the *riad* hotels, it offers its own tranquil world, with a fabulous swimming pool, Jacuzzi, health centre, Andalucian garden (▶ 59), bars and Morocco's best hotel-restaurants – including Le Marocain (▶ 67). The high prices match the facilities, but rates can be cheaper through a travel agent.

☐ 182 C1 ☒ avenue Bab Jdid, just outside the medina ☎ (04) 4444940; resa@mamounia.com; www.mamounia.com

Riad Enija £££

Just a short walk from Djemaa el-Fna, the Riad Enija offers peace and quiet, and also serves excellent light meals. There are nine suites, each a riot of colour and fitted with huge beds, luxurious bathrooms and private verandas overlooking a pretty garden.

☐ 182 C1 ☒ Rahba Laktima, 9 derb Mesfiou ☎ (04) 4440926; fax: (04) 4442700; riadenija@hotmail.com

Riad Tamsna £££

The innovative owner Meryanne Loum-Martin wanted people to see what goes on behind the high walls of the houses in the medina, so she converted a gorgeous *riad* into a hotel, restaurant, tea room and gallery. It's decorated in contemporary Marrakchi style and has become an extremely popular hotel.

☐ 182 C1 ☒ riad Zitoun Jdid, 23 derb Zanka Daika ☎ (04) 4385272; fax: (04) 4385271; tamsna@cybernet. net.ma

Es Saadi ££–£££

The Saadi is a quiet resort hotel in the heart of the l'Hivernage garden quarter. It's managed by a French woman, and the long-serving staff are friendly and efficient. The spacious and stylish rooms feature old French furniture, and many overlook the wonderful garden and swimming pool. It's pleasantly old-fashioned with its 1970s décor, but it is the calm and the welcome that draws guests back each year.

☐ 182 C1 ☒ avenue el-Quadissa, l'Hivernage ☎ (04) 448811; fax: (04) 447644

Sherazade £–££

You'll have to book well in advance for this delightful budget hotel in a renovated *riad* near Djemaa el-Fna. The comfortable, spotless rooms, some with private bathroom, open onto two courtyards painted in white and blue. The roof terrace, where breakfast is served, has great views over the medina. Rooms on the first floor are lighter and quieter.

☐ 182 C1 ☒ 3 derb Jemaa, riad Zitoun el-Kedim ☎ and fax: (04) 4429305

Where to...
Eat and Drink

Prices
Expect to pay for a three-course meal, excluding drinks but including taxes and service
£ under 160dh ££ 160-350dh £££ over 350dh

Marrakech's wide range of restaurants and bars perhaps reflects the wealth of its expat community, who live in the medina and l'Hivernage. Booking is essential in all top restaurants, particularly those in the medina: note that most upmarket options close in August. From 6 pm, the square of Djemaa el-Fna turns into a huge open-air restaurant – a great spectacle and perfect for people-watching over a snack or casual dinner. Rue Bani Marine, south of Djemaa el-Fna between the post office and the Bank al Maghrib, has several excellent budget cafés that are good for a snack.

Argana £
The Argana is undoubtedly the best place to eat around this great square. The food is simple but good, offering both Moroccan and international dishes, including pastas and salads. Even better than the food is the view from the first-floor terrace, from where you can watch the sunset and the crowds below over a snack or a mint tea.

✉ place Djemaa el-Fna ☎ no phone ⏰ Daily 8 am-late

Bagatelle ££
A friendly Provencal couple run this excellent restaurant, which features a pleasant vine-shaded garden for summer dining. On offer is well-prepared, traditional French brasserie food, including frogs' legs, steak frites and chocolate mousse.

✉ 101 rue Yougoslavie, behind the Marché Central, Guéliz ☎ (04) 4430274 ⏰ Thu–Tue lunch and dinner

Café des Négociants £
This café in the heart of Guéliz has a large terrace overlooking the busy crossroads. In addition to the usual mint tea and soft drinks it also serves cold beers and an excellent breakfast. On the opposite side of the roundabout, the similar Café de la Renaissance has great views over the city from its roof terrace.

✉ avenue Mohammed V, Guéliz ⏰ Daily 8 am-late

Le Catanzaro ££
This extremely popular, French-run Italian restaurant specialises in grilled meats and pizzas baked in a wood oven, but is also renowned for its excellent pasta. The décor – rustic Italian with beams – is rather kitsch, but service is swift and the food great, so it's never empty.

✉ rue Tarik Ibn Ziyad ☎ (04) 4433731 ⏰ Mon–Sat lunch and dinner

Chez Bij Guinni £
The appeal of this small but very popular restaurant lies in the friendly service and lively atmosphere. It serves good grills with fresh salads, but no alcohol. There's no sign outside, but it's sandwiched between two other eateries; if in doubt, just ask – everyone knows it.

✉ rue Mohammed el-Begal, near avenue Mohammed V, Guéliz ⏰ Daily 10 am–11 pm

Dar el Yaqout £££
Designed by the American interior designer Bill Willis and run by Britain's honorary consul in the city, Dar el Yaqout is one of Marrakech's top restaurants. Classic Moroccan

Where to... 67

specialities, prepared with devotion, are served in an exquisitely decorated room. For a fixed price of 600dh, which includes everything from food and drinks to music, Dar el-Yaqout offers an unforgettable evening. Start with an aperitif in the first-floor salon, followed by dinner and excellent Andalucian music, performed on the ground floor or in the courtyard in summer.

🗺 79 Sidi Ahmed Soussi, medina
☎ (04) 4382929 🕐 Tue–Sun dinner; by reservation only

Dar Marjana (House of Coral) £££

For a fixed price of 600dh this excellent *riad* restaurant offers a wonderful night in spectacular surroundings. After a drink in the gorgeous courtyard, go into the splendid 19th-century salons for a delicious series of classic dishes. Specialities include couscous with seven vegetables or chicken tagine in a sweet tomato sauce. The resident musician plays beautiful Andalucian music, but the belly dancer can be a little wild.

🗺 15 derb Sidi Ali Taïr, Bab Doukkala
☎ (04) 4385110 🕐 Wed–Mon dinner; by reservation only

Al-Fassia ££

Run by an all-female staff, this is a wonderful and popular Moroccan restaurant. The lunchtime set menu is a perfect introduction to the delights of Moroccan cuisine.
At night the menu is à la carte and offers some of the best couscous in Morocco, great tagines, unforgettable *pastilla* stuffed with pigeon and golden roast shoulder of lamb. Food is served in two ornate Moroccan salons or in a small garden in summer.

🗺 232 avenue Mohammed V, Guéliz ☎ (04) 4434060 🕐 Daily noon–2.30, 7–11

Liberty's £

This pleasant budget restaurant contains both European and low Moroccan tables. It's a lively place with friendly staff who welcome children. Specialities are pizzas and fresh pasta, with a large salad to start. No alcohol is allowed, and credit cards are not accepted.

🗺 23 rue de la Liberté, Guéliz
☎ (04) 4436416 🕐 Daily 6:30 am–midnight

Le Marocain £££

Hotel La Mamounia's (▶ 65) superb, stylish restaurant offers the ultimate Moroccan dining experience. The décor is ornate and seating is on soft, low banquettes. No less attention has been paid to the delicious food, which includes all the national classics. The charming staff enjoy delighting guests with their flair – opening the lids of steaming tagines with a flourish, or carrying aloft shoulders of lamb, huge salads and tiered trays of desserts. The authentic musical show is also superlative.

🗺 Hotel La Mamounia, avenue Bab Jdid, just outside the medina
☎ (04) 4444409 🕐 Daily dinner only

The Pavillion £££

At the end of an alley in a magnificent *riad*, the Pavillion is the best French restaurant in town. Several small salons surround a beautiful courtyard with a fountain and orange trees. The menu varies from day to day, but each dish is exquisitely prepared. The wine list is also one of the best in Marrakech. Booking is essential.

🗺 47 derb Zaouia, Bab Doukkala, medina ☎ (04) 4387040 🕐 Wed–Mon dinner only

Le Tobsil £££

This trendy place serves excellent Moroccan *nouvelle cuisine*, accompanied by Gnaoua music. Le Tobsil is young, lively and decorated in a contemporary fusion of Moroccan and Western styles. No one ever seems to leave early and everyone ends up dancing so as a result it's extremely popular: book in advance.

🗺 22 derb Moulay Abdallah ben Hezzaïen, Ksour ☎ (04) 444052 🕐 Daily dinner only; closed Aug

Where to... Shop

MEDINA

You'll find some of the medina's best **antiques** dealers at the beginning of **Souk Smarine**, including **El-Abidi Nasser Eddine** at No 9 (tel: (04) 4441066), who has a great collection of old jewellery, amber, hands of Fatma and heavy Berber necklaces.

The intriguing **La Lampe d'Aladin** at No 99 and 70bis (tel: (04) 444 3484) has good pictures, carpets, old jewellery and *objets d'art*. But don't expect to find any bargains here.

Rahba Qedima, an open square lined with spice and apothecary stalls, is the place to pick up spices, perfumes, toiletries and love potions, particularly at **Herboriste Avicenne** at No 172–174, which

claims to have a cure for everything, including a "pick-me-up" potion for men.

La Criée Berbère (where slaves were auctioned off to the highest bidder until 1912) is a carpet souk (though *faux guides* will tell you it's a weekly Berber market) which has auctions late in the afternoon.

Back on the main street is **Souk des Babouches** (slippers), where you can find typical Moroccan slippers in almost every colour.

Souk el-Haddadine, in a narrow, dark alley, is where the blacksmiths work and where you can buy some pretty wild and unusual lanterns or candelabra. **Souk des Teinturiers** (dyers' souk) has several good junk stores, as well as a few shops selling roughly spun wool in amazing colours. This is where you'll also find one of the medina's few surviving fez makers.

Rue Mouassine, the other main street through the medina, is much calmer and has a range of upmarket tourist bazaars and antiques shops.

Back on Djemaa el-Fna, the alley near the Argana café leads to picturesque place Bab Fteuh. Have a look for a sign announcing **Bab Fteuh Fondouk**, an area where some of the souk's wholesalers trade from *fondouks* (caravanserais). Two southerners here deal in good-quality daggers, boxes and Tuareg jewellery at **Chez Touareg** (Alfatni No 37, Boutique 22) and **Ettari el-Bachir** (Ouarzazi, Boutique 24 and 27).

A world apart from the rest of the medina shops is **Ministro del Gusto** (derb Azouz 22 el-Mouassine; tel: (04) 4426455), a gallery owned by a fashion editor turned interior designer. This is one of the city's best-kept secrets, where you'll find funky wooden furniture, the best local crafts and great *objets d'art*, mostly designed by the owner and made in town. Call first to make an appointment, or just ring the bell if you're passing.

The **Riad Tamsna** hotel and restaurant (▶ 65) often has good

exhibitions of jewellery, paintings, contemporary design and furniture by young Moroccan designers.

VILLE NOUVELLE

Some say the best antiques are to be found in Guéliz, and **Al-Badii** (55 boulevard Moulay Rachid) is a good place to start. The shop is run by Mohamed Bouzekri and his wife, and sells high-quality pictures, furniture, jewellery and an excellent selection of tribal carpets in the basement. This is the shop where visiting VIPs are brought (Mohamed Bouzekri acts as their guide), so prices tend to be high. It's almost like visiting a museum, and the owners are always happy to explain their stock, even if you're just browsing.

Marco Polo (55 boulevard Zerktouni) and **De Velasco** (26 boulevard Mohammed V and at the Hotel La Mamounia) are also worth searching out for antiques and fine art.

In **l'Orientaliste** (15 rue de la Liberté; tel: (04) 4434074), Madame Amzallag sells old embroideries, textiles, fine craftwork and quirky antiques, as well as pictures and old books.

Le Comptoir (avenue Echouada, l'Hivernage; tel: (04) 443702), the sister branch of the popular outlet in Paris, has become something of a cult address in Marrakech. The bar-restaurant in this beautiful villa serves juices, ice-cream and light but delicious snacks, while the shop sells a select range of furniture and the best Moroccan crafts.

Maison d'Été at 17 rue de Yougoslavie (tel: (04) 436061) sells a good combination of traditional and contemporary housewares in Moroccan style.

At **Intensité Nomade** (139 boulevard Mohammed V; tel: (04) 431333) you'll find a good selection of leather goods on the ground floor, but the basement is worth checking out for elaborately embroidered kaftans and jellabas.

The shop also sells amazing creations by the young Moroccan fashion designer Noureddine Amir – sculptural Moroccan-influenced clothes in fine woven linen, cotton, wool and silk, which are timeless and at the same time, contemporary. This is also a good place to have a jellaba or kaftan designed just for you and you can choose from the simplest to the most elaborate embroidery. The work is exquisite but expensive.

FOOD

The **Marché Central** on avenue Mohammed V is the best place to buy ingredients, spices, dried fruits and fresh oysters from Oualidia. As well as food, the market also has a good selection of pottery, crafts and hand-made baskets in all colours and sizes.

Patisserie Belkabir at 25 rue el-Houria (corner of rue Tarik ibn Ziad; no phone) sells some of the best Moroccan sweets in town. In the medina the street leading from Djemaa el-Fna to Souk Smarine is lined with wonderful stalls selling a wide selection of fresh dates, figs, dried apricots and nuts at reasonable prices. There is another good covered food market in the medina, between avenue Houmane el-Fetouaki and Arset el-Maash.

Hakima Alami at **Al-Jawda** (11 rue de la Liberté) has been making traditional cakes according to her mother's recipe for the last 15 years – try gazelle horns, almond macaroons and fresh cream *faqqas*.

BOOKS/NEWSPAPERS

The **Dar Menebhi Museum** in place Ben Youssef in the medina (▶ 62) contains an excellent bookshop with titles on Marrakech, Moroccan history and local crafts.

The **American Bookstore** (3 Impasse du Moulin, off boulevard Mohammed Zerktouni) stocks a good selection of English-language books, as does the kiosk in front of the Hotel La Mamounia (▶ 65). At the **Librairie d'Art** in the Résidence Taïb (55 boulevard Mohammed Zerktouni) you'll find glossy coffee-table books on Morocco, mainly in French.

The largest selection of foreign English-language newspapers is available from the bookshop at the **Hotel La Mamounia**, and from the newsagent outside the **Tourist Office** on avenue Mohammed V in Guéliz.

ENSEMBLE ARTISANAL

The government shop on avenue Mohammed V (open 10–7) features several workshops where all the traditional crafts are made and sold.

Behind the shops are the workshops where young people learn about the craft. Prices are often fixed and quite reasonable. Look out for the carpet weavers, wood carving, marquetry, silver jewellery, different styles of pottery, and leather goods.

Where to...
Be Entertained

NIGHTLIFE

Most entertainment in the medina revolves around **Djemaa el-Fna** (▶ 50), where stalls and cafés are open until after midnight and there is an audience. Most **discos** are found in hotels and can get very crowded at weekends. The best are **Paradise** at the Hotel Pullman Mansour el-Dahabi (avenue de France; tel: (04) 448222) and **Le Diamant Noir** at the nearby Hotel Marrakech, which attracts a mainly gay crowd during the week and a more mixed clientele at weekends. Sleazier, and perhaps not to everyone's taste, is **Shéhérazade** at the Kenzi Hotel (avenue Yaqoub el-Mansour). It's popular with locals drinking and smoking *kif*, who often let loose when the live band plays. Lone women are likely to attract attention, but if you're in a group it's a great place to get some Moroccan atmosphere.

Marrakech has two **casinos**, for which you need to dress up a little. The most sumptuous is in the **Hotel La Mamounia** (▶ 65). The other is the **Casino de Marrakech** at the Saadi hotel (▶ 65).

CINEMA, THEATRE AND MUSIC

The best cinema, the **Colisée** (boulevard Mohammed Zerktouni, Guéliz; tel: (04) 444 8893), shows good recent films, mostly uncensored. Other cinemas show Arab or Hindi films, or Western films cut so extensively that they're almost unrecognisable, although the experience itself can be fun. Try also **Cinema Mabrouka** (rue Bab Agnaou, medina). The **Institut Français de Marrakech** (route de la Targa, Jebel Guéliz, tel: (04) 444 6930) has a varied programme of theatre, cinema and exhibitions.

Many of the *riad* restaurants (▶ 66–67) offer evening musical performances or folklore shows with dinner. Worth checking out is the **Riad Tamsna** (▶ 65), which also organises regular exhibitions.

FANTASIAS

Fantasias – big folkloric parties held in the open air or in Berber tents – usually include musicians and dancers, fireworks and spectacular displays by Arab horsemen. These well-organised shows are traditionally staged at Berber *moussems*, but in Marrakech they are also staged for tourists to accompany a traditional Moroccan dinner in large, torch-lit tents outside the city. One of the most popular is **Chez Ali** in the Palmeraie (tel: (04) 4307730).

SPORT

The large **swimming pool** in the **Moulay Abdessalaam Garden** (off avenue Mohammed V) is popular with young Marrakechi boys. Many hotels allow non-residents to use their pools for a fee. The nearest pool to the medina is at the **Grand Hotel Tazi**.

Marrakech has three superb **golf** courses: the **Marrakech Royal Golf Club** (tel: (04) 404705); the **Palmeraie Golf Club** (tel: (04) 4301010) and the **Amelkis Golf Club** (tel: (04) 404414).

There are **tennis** courts at many hotels or at the **Royal Tennis Club** (rue Ouadi el-Makhazine, Guéliz; tel: (04) 4431902).

Horse-riding is on offer at **Club de l'Atlas** near the Menara Gardens (tel: (04) 4431301) and **Club Equitage** (tel: (04) 4301010).

The Atlantic Coast

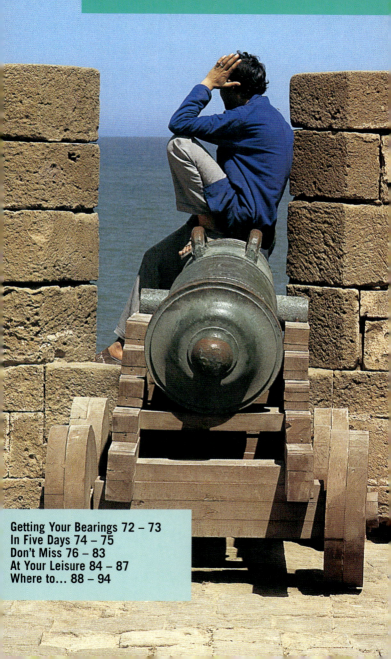

Getting Your Bearings 72 – 73
In Five Days 74 – 75
Don't Miss 76 – 83
At Your Leisure 84 – 87
Where to... 88 – 94

72 The Atlantic Coast

Getting Your Bearings

The Atlantic coast is Morocco's economic and political nerve centre. The 500km from Kenitra to Essaouira alone, including the cities of Rabat and Casablanca, are home to over 5 million people, a fifth of the country's population. Less exotic and perhaps less obvious at first as a tourist destination, the coast has more to offer than its beaches: impressive Portuguese fortresses, colonial architecture, good surf, plenty of seafood and some less-visited monuments.

Rabat, the country's charming capital, has a relaxed, provincial air and some great monuments, including a splendid kasbah. Its neighbour and former rival, Salé, is not as well preserved, except for its wonderful white medina. Casablanca, the country's economic capital, prides itself on having the largest port in North Africa and substantial industrial activities, but it also offers stately colonial architecture, busy cafés, relaxed souks, nearby beaches and excellent restaurants. Smaller cities such as Essaouira are even more laid back and have plenty of character. Agadir, the country's most popular beach resort, boasts pleasant year-round temperatures, but is also the least Moroccan of all the coastal towns. For a more authentic beach holiday try nearby Tarhazoute, the lagoon town of Oualidia or, if you are looking for good surfing waves, go to Sidi Kaouki, south of Essaouira, or Dar-Bouazza near Casablanca.

Previous page: Dreaming on Essaouira's Skala du Port ramparts

Left: The garb of the Royal Guards in Rabat

Azem

El-Jadida **7**

Sidi-Smail

Oualidia **8**

Cap Beddouza

Khémis-des-Zememra

Be

(P8)

Safi **9**

Tleta-Sidi-Bouguedra

(P12)

Chen

Dar-Caïd-Hadji

Moulay-Bouzerktoun

Talmest

Tensift

Essaouira

Ile de Mogador **3**

Tleta-Henchane

Chichaoua

Sidi-Kaouki (P8)

Imi-n-Tanoute

Tamanar

(P40)

Jebel Touchka

3555m
▲ Jebel Aoulime

Tamri

10

Taghazout

Imouzzer des Ida Outanane

Agadir **11**

Taroudannt

Souss

Inezgane

(P32)

Biougra

Getting Your Bearings 73

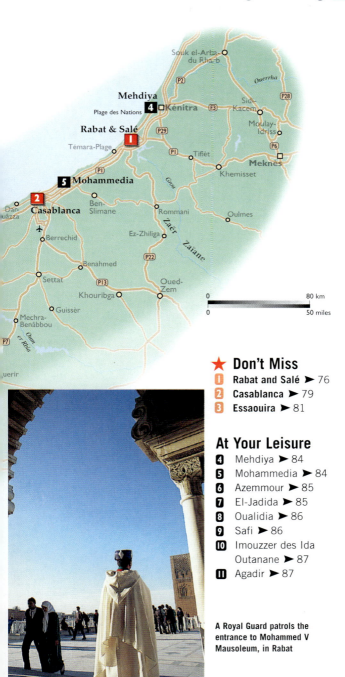

★ Don't Miss
- **1** Rabat and Salé ➤ 76
- **2** Casablanca ➤ 79
- **3** Essaouira ➤ 81

At Your Leisure
- **4** Mehdiya ➤ 84
- **5** Mohammedia ➤ 84
- **6** Azemmour ➤ 85
- **7** El-Jadida ➤ 85
- **8** Oualidia ➤ 86
- **9** Safi ➤ 86
- **10** Imouzzer des Ida Outanane ➤ 87
- **11** Agadir ➤ 87

A Royal Guard patrols the entrance to Mohammed V Mausoleum, in Rabat

74 The Atlantic Coast

With its moderate climate and Western-orientated cities, this region offers a gentle introduction to Morocco.

The Atlantic Coast in Five Days

Day One

Morning
Start in ❶ Rabat (➤ 76–78) with a stroll through the medina, including **rue des Consuls**, the **Kasbah des Oudaïas** and the nearby **Oudaïa Museum**. Stop for a mint tea in Café Maure, in the Andalucian garden, or head to the beach for lunch at the Restaurant de la Plage (➤ 92).

Afternoon
Take a taxi to **Bab er Rouah** and then walk to the **Archaeological Museum**. Continue downtown to the **Hassan Tower**, the **Mausoleum of King Mohammed V** (left) and the **Hassan Mosque** in time for the daily changing of the guard at 5 pm.

Evening
Enjoy an apéritif at the Hotel Balima on avenue Mohammed V, then dinner in a downtown restaurant such as Zerda (➤ 92).

Day Two

Morning
Take a boat to **Salé** (➤ 78) and visit the main sights, including the **Souk el Ghezel** and the **Grande Mosquée**. Return by *grand taxi* for lunch at the atmospheric Koutoubia (➤ 91).

Afternoon
Visit the picturesque Roman ruins and Muslim cemetery of **Chellah**. If you're driving, head to Témara beach (about 15km south of Rabat) for a swim before continuing to Casablanca, otherwise take the train to Casablanca for dinner at A Ma Bretagne (➤ 90).

In Five Days

Day Three

Morning
Start your visit to **2 Casablanca** (➤ 79–80) with a tour of the **Mosque of Hassan II** (right), then return to the centre to explore the magnificent colonial architecture. Have lunch in a restaurant in the Marché Central.

Afternoon
Take a taxi to the **Quartier Habous** for some shopping, a pastry from Bennis (➤ 93) and a mint tea in the café on the square. Head for the old medina for a more Moroccan shopping experience before dinner back at Le Port de Pêche (➤ 91).

Day Four

Morning
Start early for the drive to Essaouira, and in just over an hour you'll reach the Portuguese town of **7 El-Jadida** (➤ 85–86). After refreshments on place Mohammed ben Allah, continue for 80km to **8 Oualidia** (➤ 86) for lunch at a seafood restaurant on the beach.

Afternoon
Have a swim in the lagoon if the tide is in, before continuing for another 65km to the pottery town of **9 Safi** (➤ 86). Follow the coast road through windswept villages to the attractive city of **4 Essaouira** (➤ 81–83), and stroll across the main square to Chez Sam for dinner (➤ 90).

Day Five

Morning
Have breakfast in place Moulay Hassan before walking along the old walls to **Skala de la Ville**, the **woodworkers' souk** (artisan pictured below), the small **Musée Sidi Mohammed ben Allah** and through the old *mellah* (Jewish quarter). Return through the souks towards the clock tower for lunch.

Afternoon
Visit the galleries on avenue Mohammed Zerktouni, and go for a long walk along the beach, returning around dusk to see the fishing boats. End with dinner at Le Riad Bleu Mogador (➤ 92).

The Atlantic Coast

Rabat and Salé

Rabat is Morocco's capital and its second imperial city. With its tree-lined avenues, public gardens and peaceful residential areas, the city exudes an air of elegance and good living. Less dramatic than Fes, less exotic than Marrakech and less turbulent than Casablanca, it is calm and airy, with a provincial feel.

The Hassan Tower was to be as grand as the Koutoubia minaret in Marrakech, but it was never finished

The Phoenicians, like the Romans and their successors, were attracted by Rabat's safe harbour in the estuary of the Bou Regreg. The Almohad Sultan Yacoub el-Mansour made the city his capital in 1184, ringing it with 6km of walls with five monumental gates, expanding the kasbah and building the colossal mosque of Hassan, its minaret even taller than the grand Giralda Mosque in Seville, Spain.

Soon after his death, however, the city he called "Rabat el-Fath" (Rabat of Victory) went into decline until the 17th century and the arrival of the *mariscos* (Moors expelled from Spain). Both Rabat and neighbouring Salé then flourished from a new source of income: piracy (▶ 30–31).

The New Town
In 1912 the French made Rabat their colonial capital. They left the medina alone, but built a **Ville Nouvelle** (new town)

Rabat and Salé

of broad avenues and residential quarters. This area's main artery is palm-lined **avenue Mohammed V**, between the royal palace and the medina, with shops, a theatre and cinemas. One of the chief sights is the surviving Almohad wall and gates running parallel to the avenue. Near the splendid Almohad gate of **Bab er-Rouah** (Gate of the Wind), the **Archaeological Museum** houses excellent Roman bronzes from Volubilis (➤ 126–127) and Chellah. These include the fine figure of the attacking *Dog of Volubilis* and superb busts of Cato the Younger of Uttica – an orator who died for the freedom of the republic rather than live under Roman rule – and of the Berber king Juba II.

The main thoroughfare then becomes avenue Yacoub el-Mansour, leading to the romantic ruins of **Chellah**. This long-deserted Roman city became a burial ground during the 13th century under the Merenids. The entrance to the walled site is a stunning Merenid gateway flanked by two towers. The Roman ruins are to the left, while a path to the right leads to Muslim tombs and mosques in an overgrown garden of fig trees, olive branches and wild flowers.

This fine bronze is thought to represent the Berber king Juba II

The 17th-century Spanish immigrants responsible for the **medina** also built the **Andalucian wall** that runs along avenue Hassan II. The heart of the medina is **rue des Consuls**, lined with good craft shops and running into **Souk el-Ghezel**, the wool souk and former slave market. The **Kasbah des Oudaïas**, named after the tribe installed here by the Alaouites, was built in the 10th century.

The Kasbah

The entrance to the kasbah is through the splendid and well-proportioned **Porte des Oudaïas**, built in the late 12th century by Yacoub el-Mansour. In the middle of this whitewashed village, in the 17th-century palace built by Moulay Ismail (➤ 128), is the **Oudaïa Museum**, containing a wonderful collection of Moroccan art and crafts. Equally delightful is the palace's **Andalucian garden**, filled with lemon and cypress trees, date palms and flowers.

A field of columns and an unfinished minaret is all that remains of Yacoub el-Mansour's enormous **Mosque of Hassan**. The mosque

The walls of Oudaïa Kasbah have been constantly reinforced since it was built by the Almohad Sultans

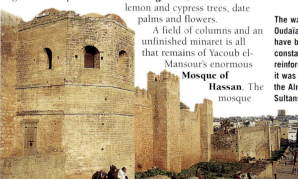

The Atlantic Coast

was never finished and later rulers used the stones to restore the kasbah. The 44m minaret, the **Tour Hassan**, has different decoration on each face. Mohammed V chose this spectacular background for his traditional **mausoleum**, where he is buried with his two sons.

Bab Mrissa entices you into Salé's old medina

Salé

The area across the river has less to show for its illustrious past, but its whitewashed medina is much more picturesque and characterful than the one in Rabat, and makes for a pleasant stroll. From **Bab Mrissa** walk to the picturesque **Souk el-Ghezel**, the wool souk, and then towards the **Grande Mosquée**. Near by is a beautiful 14th-century **Merenid Medersa** with superb views from the terrace over Salé and the river, and the *marabout* (tomb) of Sidi Abdallah ben Hassoun, the city's patron saint of travellers. Further on, the northwest tower houses a charming little ceramics museum and has great views over Rabat.

TAKING A BREAK

The tranquil Moorish **Café Maure** in the Andalucian garden of Kasbah des Oudaïas is an enchanting place for sipping mint tea in beautiful surroundings.

Rabat
🏠 183 D3
🚌 Buses from Casablanca, Tangier, Marrakech, Fes and Meknes
🚆 Trains from Tangier, Fes, Meknes, Casablanca and Marrakech
✈ Flights from Casablanca

Archaeological Museum
✉ 23 rue el Brihi, near the es Souna Grand Mosque
🕐 Wed–Mon 9–11:30, 2:30–5:30 (6:30 in summer); Wed–Mon 10–5:30 during Ramadan
💰 Moderate

Chellah
✉ 2km from the centre
🕐 Daily 8:30–6:30
💰 Inexpensive

Oudaïa Museum
🕐 Wed–Mon 9–11:30, 3–5:30; closed public holidays
💰 Moderate

Mohammed V Mausoleum
✉ Near boulevard abi Regreg
🕐 Open access; dress modestly
💰 Free

Salé
🏠 183 D4
✉ 3km from central Rabat
🚌 Bus 6 or 12 from boulevard Hassan II; *grand taxi* or rowing boat from near Kasbah des Oudaïas (inexpensive)

Merenid Medersa
✉ Opposite the Grande Mosqueé
🕐 The caretaker will open it on demand
💰 Inexpensive

RABAT AND SALÉ: INSIDE INFO

Top tips The **view over the river from Café Maure** in the grounds of Kasbah des Oudaïas is particularly beautiful at sunset.

• Salé is **accessible by boat, bus or *grand taxi***. Otherwise, it's about 30 minutes' walk across Pont Moulay Hassan.

2 Casablanca

Unlike most Moroccan cities, Casablanca (Dar el-Beida) is modern. Most visitors inevitably pass through "Casa", as Moroccans affectionately call the city, and it is a delightful place to spend a day or two. The souks are more hassle-free than most, it is easy to get around and there is plenty of art deco and art nouveau architecture along the broad boulevards. But don't come looking for the Casablanca of Humphrey Bogart and Ingrid Bergman – the film was shot entirely in Hollywood.

North Africa's largest port, Casablanca was built by the French and modelled on Marseille. The city looks and feels very European, but in places it even has a touch of Miami. Women are rarely veiled and beach clubs are often throbbing with a cosmopolitan crowd.

The most obvious and only "real" monument in town is the gigantic **Mosque of Hassan II**, finished in 1993. King Hassan II wanted to build a mosque on the water, so the French architect Michel Pinseau designed the vast complex on reclaimed land. Its 200m minaret, a beacon of Islam, is the tallest in the country. Up to 25,000 worshippers can pray inside, some kneeling on a glass floor that reveals the ocean

Above: The spectacularly floodlit Hassan II Mosque rises like a beacon in the night

The Atlantic Coast

Casablanca by Numbers
- It's the fourth largest city in Africa.
- Its 4 million inhabitants represent about 10 per cent of Morocco's total population.
- With 60 per cent of the country's industry, Casa uses 30 per cent of the electricity supply and phone lines.
- Its inhabitants pay more than half of the nation's taxes.

below. The courtyard can hold another 80,000. More than 2,500 of Morocco's master craftsmen worked day and night on the mosque's decoration, and the enormous cost of the building, an estimated £500 million, was financed purely by donations.

Most of the grand colonial buildings, built in a French interpretation of Moorish style, are grouped around **place Mohammed V** (formerly place des Nations Unies) and **boulevard Mohammed V**, where the **Marché Central** offers the country's best selection of fruit and vegetables. At the end of boulevard Mohammed V is the current **place des Nations Unies** (confusingly, the former place Mohammed V) with café-terraces, the Hyatt Regency Hotel (➤ 88) and the entrance to the **old medina** and souks. The palm-lined boulevard Félix Houphouet leads to the **port**. The French-built new medina, **Quartier Habous,** is opposite the royal palace.

The entrance gates of Hassan II Mosque surpass those of any mosque in Morocco

TAKING A BREAK
Oliveri (132 avenue Hassan II) is the most popular ice-cream parlour in town. Café terraces on **place des Nations Unies** are buzzing in the afternoon, while several reasonably priced restaurants in the **Marché Central** sell fresh fish snacks.

✚ 182 C3

Ain Diab Beach
✉ 3km from the port
🚌 9

Hassan II Mosque
✉ boulevard de la Corniche
☎ (02) 2302001
🕐 Obligatory guided tours
Sat–Thu 9, 10, 11, 2

💰 Expensive

Quartier Habous
✉ 1km southwest of town
🚌 81

CASABLANCA: INSIDE INFO

Top tips Parc de la Ligue Arabe is a wonderful place to relax among the palm trees and exotic flowers.
- Locals hang out in the beach clubs on **Ain Diab beach**.

One to miss Avoid going to the old medina at night; it can be dangerous.

3 Essaouira

This charming blue-and-white city is where Arab, Berber, African and European influences merge happily. It is a place out of time, seemingly running its own course at its own rhythm. The frantic bustle of the fishing harbour contrasts starkly with the laid-back atmosphere in the medina. Essaouira's beauty has long attracted and inspired writers and artists. Add to this the *alizee*, a forceful wind blowing from the Atlantic (Sawiris, the city's inhabitants, say that it blows away the bad spirits and also crowds of tourists) and it is hard not to fall in love with Essaouira.

Formerly called Mogador, Essaouira looks older than it is. Although originally settled by Phoenicians, today's city was built in 1764 by Sultan Mohammed ben Abdallah. Designed by French architect Théodore Cornut, it was called "es Saouira", the "well drawn".

Out to Sea
The liveliest part of town is the **fishing harbour**, especially in the late afternoon when the boats come back. The fishermen's wives have the first pick; the rest of the incredible variety of fish is then sold by auction – a colourful spectacle. On the south side of the port is a shipyard where boats are constructed in the traditional way.

A Dramatic Setting
The port is reached from the city through the 18th-century **Porte de la Marine**, whose stairway leading up the walls of the **Skala du Port** offers great views over the town. The American actor and director Orson Welles filmed several scenes of his acclaimed *Othello* (1952) here. The **Skala de la Ville** is an impressive sea bastion with a collection of

Top: Lovely Essaouira has inspired many writers and artists. Above: Blue is the dominant colour in town

The Atlantic Coast

The harbour is protected by the L-shaped Skala du Port, the port bastion with two towers

European bronze cannons on the top, and wide views of the ocean crashing into the rocks. Underneath are the workshops of the carpenters who work mainly with *thuja* (thuya) wood from evergreen coniferous trees. Near by, the small **Musée Sidi Mohammed ben Abdallah** has pictures of old Essaouira and displays of marquetry and costumes.

The Gnaoua

Traditionally, the Gnaoua people, descendants of slaves from Mali and Senegal, were healers and musicians, whose music was reputed to exorcise evil spirits. On religious festivals they hold a *lila*, when their drums, castanets and flutes send participants into a trance. Nowadays you are more likely to see them performing on café-terraces, with swirling strings of cowrie shells on their hats. In Essaouira several Gnaoua draw on these traditions as subjects for their colourful, almost naive paintings. The most famous Gnaouan painter is Mohammed Tabal, whose works are on show in Galerie Frederic Damgaard.

Lovingly Crafted

The souks, with some excellent crafts (➤ 93), spread from here to the **mellah** (Jewish quarter). The town always had a large Jewish community who acted as intermediaries between the Muslim sultan and foreign powers. Only a dozen or so members of the community still live here, a far cry from 8,000 to 9,000 in the 19th century.

On either side of avenue Mohammed Zerktouni is the new **Souk Djedid**, with the spice and fish market on one

Essaouira 83

side and the grain and jewellery market on the other. At the harbour end of the same street, several galleries sell the work of Essaouiri artists, the best of which is **Galerie Frederic Damgaard**, owned by a Danish expat who encourages Gnaoua painters (see box and ➤ 93).

Windy City

The city's splendid beach stretches for several kilometres, but the constant wind makes it better for windsurfing than swimming or sunbathing.

Opposite town are the **Îles Purpuaires**, named after the purple dye – the colour of choice of Roman emperors – made from the shells of the native murex (a tropical marine mollusc). The largest island, Île de Mogador, has a small harbour, fort and mosque. The islands were declared a nature reserve as they are the only breeding ground of Eleonora's falcon (*Falco eleonorae*).

TAKING A BREAK

Have a mint tea **in place Moulay el-Hassan** or in the **Hotel Riad el-Medina** (➤ 89). For lunch try **Taros** (➤ 92), with views over the harbour from its terrace, or browse in its library. Or be adventurous and have a **grilled fish snack** (left) at the stalls just outside the harbour.

Essaouira
🕂 182 A1
✉ Tourist office: Syndicat d'Initiative, rue du Caire
☎ (04) 4475080
🚌 Regular buses from Marrakech, Casablanca and Agadir

Musée Sidi Mohammed ben Abdallah
✉ derb Laalouj
🕐 Wed–Thu, Sat–Mon 8:30–noon, 2:30–6:30; Fri 8:30–11:30, 3–6:30
💰 Moderate

Galerie Frederic Damgaard
✉ avenue Oqba ibn Nafii
☎ (04) 4784446
🕐 Daily 9–1, 3–7

ESSAOUIRA: INSIDE INFO

Top tips The best way to get to know Essaouira is to **stroll around** looking for secret passages, gorgeous gateways, picturesque alleys and amazing *riads* and houses.
• Spend some time in **place Moulay el-Hassan** watching the constant passage of Sawiris and visitors.
• Stroll along the **windswept beach** in the late afternoon.
• The **best surfing beach** is Sidi Kaouki, 25km south of town.

The Atlantic Coast

At Your Leisure

4 Mehdiya

Although founded by the Carthaginians, Mehdiya's only historic monument, the **kasbah**, dates from the

16th century. By then, the town had become a corsair stronghold from where pirates attacked passing ships. The kasbah, built by the Spanish to protect their interests along the coast, is fronted by an impressive gateway added by Moulay Ismail (➤ 128). Inside the kasbah are the ruins of a 17th-century mosque, the souks, the governor's palace and the northwest bastion with ship's cannons and views over the Sebou River. During the summer, Mehdiya Plage is a busy beach resort, as is the Plage des Nations, 9km away. Near this is the wonderful little **Musée Dar Beghazi**, which houses a private collection of Moroccan crafts and Islamic art gathered by the Fassi artist and antiques dealer Abdallah Beghazi.

Near by are the delightful **Jardins Exotiques de Sidi Bouknadel**, planted in the 1950s by the French horticulturist Marcel François. The gardens are divided into three main sections: a splendid Andalucian garden, an area of Moroccan indigenous plants and a park with Asian plants, including huge bamboos.

🚩 183 D4 ✉ 40km north of Rabat
🚌 Buses from Rabat and Salé

Musée Dar Beghazi
✉ Near Plage des Nations ☎ (03) 7822178
🕘 Daily 8–5 🚌 Bus 28 from Salé 💰 Expensive

Jardins Exotiques de Sidi Bouknadel
✉ 9km from Plage des Nations, on the west side of the Rabat road
🕘 Daily 9–6 💰 Inexpensive

5 Mohammedia

Mohammedia is Morocco's second port and the centre of its oil industry, and is also a popular summer resort with a long sandy beach. The oil industry is fairly recent, but the town was already a significant port and

The beach of el-Jadida is quiet out of season, but is very busy in the summer

At Your Leisure

trading post in the 16th century, when the Portuguese built the kasbah. The old fortified town has been restored, and the alleys of its quiet residential quarter make for a pleasant stroll.

🚪 182 C3 ✉ 28km north of Casablanca 🚌 Train and bus from Rabat and Casablanca

❻ Azemmour

This picturesque little white village is built on a cliff over the estuary of the poetically named river Umm er Rbia (Mother of Spring). The Portuguese occupied the ancient river port of Azama for only 30 years (from 1510), but their colonial architecture has lasted much longer. A walk on the well-preserved ramparts around the 16th-century **Portuguese kasbah**, including the arsenal of **Dar al-Baroud**, is a great way to start exploring the town. The Moroccan medina is delightful, its souks and alleys filled with bougainvillea. The best views are from the bridge on the northeastern side of the medina. About 2km away is the popular resort of **Haouzia**, but the beach stretches all the way to el-Jadida.

🚪 182 C3 ✉ 17km north of el-Jadida 🚌 Daily buses from el-Jadida and Casablanca

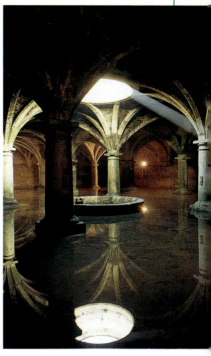

The vast Portuguese cistern in el-Jadida is an amazing sight, particularly when it's lit by the strong midday sun

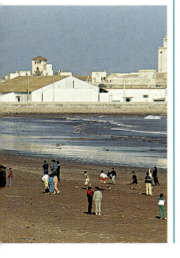

❼ El-Jadida

El-Jadida is a summer resort popular with young Moroccans for its great sports facilities and mild climate. As it is mainly an industrial town, you may prefer to walk around the old Portuguese quarter, following in Orson Welles's footsteps, than hang out on the beach. The well-preserved **Portuguese garrison**, known as Mazagan, was built in 1502 and has four surviving bastions; **Bastion de l'Ange** offers fine views over the old town. The Muslims turned the area into the *mellah* in 1815, hence the large Jewish cemetery just outside the walls. On the main axis of the citadel is the **Portuguese Cistern**, a vast, spectacular, underground cellar. It so impressed Welles that he filmed part of *Othello* here in 1952. The

The Atlantic Coast

light streams in through a small skylight in the vault, supported by 25 massive columns. The beach of Sidi Bouzid is 7km to the south.

🚩 182 B3 ⊠ 89km south of Casablanca ☎ Tourist office, avenue el Jaich el-Malaki: (02) 3344788 🚌 Daily buses from Casablanca, Essaouira and Agadir

Portuguese Cistern
⊠ rue Mohammed el-Hachmi Bahbah
🕐 Daily 9–1, 3–6 💵 Inexpensive

8 Oualidia

Famous for its excellent Japanese oysters, Oualidia sits above a fine lagoon beach protected from the Atlantic surf by a barrier of little islands, which makes it the calmest beach along this stretch of coast. Little more than a village, it was named after the Saadian sultan el-Oualid, who built a kasbah to defend himself from the Portuguese in el-Jadida. Overlooking the vast beach is Mohammed V's picturesque, but now abandoned, royal villa. Unspoilt Oualidia is a great place to relax for a few days and try some fresh fish and shellfish. You can also visit the oyster banks at Parc Ostréole 007, north of town.

For the Kids

- Bigger kids will appreciate the surf along most of the Atlantic coast, but smaller ones may prefer the calmer waters of Agadir, Tarhazoute and the lagoon in Oualidia (➤ above).
- Check out **Sindbad**, the small amusement park on the Corniche in Casablanca (➤ 94).
- The park at **Vallée des Oiseaux** in Agadir has a little zoo and playground (➤ opposite).

🚩 182 B2 ⊠ 80km south of el-Jadida 🚌 Bus from Casablanca, Essaouira and Safi

9 Safi

This industrial town is not an obvious stop, but its charming old medina and pottery industry flourish beside the phosphate factories. The Portuguese also built a fortress here in the 16th century – **Dar el-Bahar**, overlooking the port.

Near by is the **Kechla**, another Portuguese fortress, which served as a prison until 1990 and is now a small **Ceramics Museum**. The souks in the medina culminate with the Souk des Poteries, a showcase for work made on the nearby Colline des Potiers. The colourful plates that you'll see on sale across the country, and most of the green tiles used for the roofs of Morocco's mosques and palaces, are produced in these potters' quarters.

🚩 182 B2 ⊠ 66km south of Oualidia ☎ Tourist office, rue Iman Malek: (04) 4622496 🚌 Buses from Casablanca, Essaouira and Marrakech 🚆 Train from Benguerir on the Casablanca–Marrakech line

Dar el-Bahar
⊠ place de l'Indépendance
🕐 Daily 8:30–noon, 2:30–6
💵 Inexpensive

Ceramics Museum
⊠ off avenue Moulay Youssef
🕐 Wed–Mon 8:30–noon, 2–6
💵 Inexpensive

The vast stretch of beach in Agadir during a quiet moment

🔟 Imouzzer des Ida Outanane

Reached via the lush Vallée du Paradis, this popular spot for a weekend picnic offers a great escape from the beaches. The small village of white houses overlooking a beautiful palm grove lies at the foot of the High Atlas, at 1,250m. This is the administrative centre of the Ida Outanane, a Berber tribe that occupies the whole area from the lower mountain slopes to the Atlantic Ocean. The Thursday souk is a popular affair, noted for its medicinal (but illegal) mountain honey made from marjoram and marijuana. Only 2km away are the pleasant **Imouzzèr Falls**, with some great rock formations and a deep-green natural water pool into which locals dive from dangerous heights.

🟥 184 A3 ✉ 60km north of Agadir
🚌 Daily bus from Agadir

---

5 Best Seafood Restaurants on Morocco's Atlantic Coast
- **Chez Sam**, at the harbour in Essaouira (➤ 90)
- **Restaurant du Port**, fishing-boat shaped eaterie, Casablanca (➤ 92)
- **L'Hippocampe**, hotel with excellent restaurant, Oualidia (➤ 88)
- **Le Goéland** French-style fish (➤ 91)
- **A l'Araignée Gourmande**, for a seafood feast (➤ 88)

⓫ Agadir

The holiday resort of Agadir has two main attractions: a splendid beach and a superb climate, with over 300 sunny days a year. As a modern city – the old one was destroyed by an earthquake in 1960 – it has little obvious charm, but it offers a wide choice of hotels catering mainly to northern European package tourists. It is worth visiting the largest **fishing port** in the country, the **new medina** and souks and the reconstructed **Portuguese Fortress**, which has been turned into a graveyard for those who died in the earthquake. The **Musée Municipal** has a great collection of Berber jewellery, and children will like the small zoo, **Vallée des Oiseaux**. For a less crowded beach take a bus to Taghazout, 19km further north.

🟥 184 A3 ✉ 225km southwest of Marrakech ☎ Tourist office: Immeuble A, place Prince Héritier Sidi Mohammed: (04) 8846379 🚌 Buses from Marrakech, Essaouira, Casablanca, Taroudannt, Ouarzazate, Tiznit 🚆 Trains from Marrakech ✈ Flights from Casablanca and Marrakech

Musée Municipal
✉ Pedestrian street behind theatre on avenue Mohammed V ☎ (04) 8224909 🕘 Daily 8–5:30 💰 Moderate

Vallée des Oiseaux
✉ Corner of boulevards du 20 Août and Hassan II 🕘 Wed–Sun 9:30–12:30, 2:30–6:30, Tue 2:30–6:30 💰 Inexpensive

88 The Atlantic Coast

Where to... Stay

Prices
Expect to pay for a double room, including breakfast and taxes
£ under 640dh ££ 640–1,600dh £££ over 1,600dh

A l'Araignée Gourmande £
This charming hotel with large, clean rooms is situated right on the beach. Half board is compulsory, but the restaurant, like most in Oualidia, is famed for its seafood. Sit on the pretty terrace and try the "Festival of Seafood", as amazing an array as you may ever see – an enormous platter of lobster, oysters and crevettes. Start early to finish eating before midnight.

➕ 182 B2 ✉ Oualidia beach, near the campsite ☎ (02) 3356144; fax: (02) 3366447

Astrid £
In a side street off rue Prince Moulay Abdallah, this very central but quiet little hotel offers pleasant, comfortable rooms with bright and cheerful bathrooms. A large breakfast is served in the tea room.

➕ 182 C3 ✉ 12 rue du 6 Novembre, Casablanca ☎ (02) 2277803; fax: (02) 2293372

El-Bahia £
At this friendly place offering excellent value for money the sunny and airy bedrooms are spotless, and the more expensive ones have TV and private bathroom. Breakfast is served in a shaded courtyard filled with flowers.

➕ 184 A3 ✉ rue el-Mehdi ben Toumert, Agadir ☎ (04) 8822724; fax: (04) 8824515

Balima ££
This huge 1920s building with a 1950s interior was once the smartest hotel in town, but has now faded in a dignified way. The rooms are vast and comfortable, and those on the top floor command excellent views over Rabat. The restaurant food is rather mediocre, but the terrace and garden are popular meeting places, and pleasant for a drink or two.

➕ 183 D3 ✉ avenue Mohammed V, Rabat ☎ (03) 7707755; fax: (03) 7707450

L'Hippocampe ££
The Hippocampe is a well-kept secret – a wonderful, reasonably priced place to relax for a few days. Its comfortable bungalows are set in a beautiful garden, there's a good swimming pool, and the hotel and restaurant on the beach boast spectacular views over the lagoon. Half board is compulsory, but the food is excellent, particularly fresh oysters caught from the bay. It's a popular place, so make sure you book in advance.

➕ 182 B2 ✉ Oualidia beach ☎ (02) 3366108; fax: (02) 3366461

Hyatt Regency £££
The centrally located Hyatt gives you everything you could want from a luxury city hotel. Rooms are large and tastefully decorated, with superb views over the town, the old medina and the harbour. Rick's Bar, where Humphrey Bogart and Ingrid Bergman hung out in the 1942 film Casablanca, is represented by the hotel's Casablanca Bar, with pictures from the movie and staffed by costumed waiters. The hotel also has several excellent restaurants.

➕ 182 C3 ✉ place des Nations Unies, Casablanca ☎ (02) 2261234; fax: (02) 2220180

Ibis Moussafir ££
This mid-range hotel next to the train station is handy for an early departure or late arrival, but the lower-floor rooms are quite noisy.

Part of a national chain, it has attractive rooms, a beautiful garden and a tiny swimming pool.

➕ 182 C3 ⊠ place de la Gare Casa Voyageurs, Casablanca ☎ (02) 2401984; fax: (02) 2400799

Le Marrakech £

Painted in sugary pink and electric blue, this basic, well-located and friendly hotel has rooms that overlook a courtyard. Note, however, that the ground-floor rooms have no windows.

➕ 183 D3 ⊠ 10 rue Sebbahi, medina, Rabat ☎ (03) 7727703

Le Palais Andalou ££

Located in a palace built during the 1940s, this features large rooms decorated with Moorish arches and lots of mosaics, surrounding a courtyard with fountains. Although the rooms are lovely, with huge beds – some so high you need steps to climb into them – the service could be better and the food is mediocre. However, the Andalou is

a good place for a drink in the evening. No credit cards are accepted.

➕ 182 B3 ⊠ boulevard Docteur de Lanoë, next to Hospital Mohammed V, el-Jadida ☎ (02) 3343745; fax: (02) 3351690

Résidence Le Kaouki £

This blissful, simple little hotel overlooks the countryside and a large surfing beach. The white and electric-blue building has communal hot showers but has not installed electric lights; instead, it's romantically lit by candles. Half board is compulsory in the summer, but Myriem, the chef, prepares excellent Moroccan meals. If you're looking for a hotel with character to hide in, this is ideal, but book in advance.

➕ 184 A4 ⊠ 500m from the marabout at Sidi Kaouki ☎ (04) 4783206; fax: (04) 4475447; info@sidikaouki.com

Résidence Yasmina ££

If you feel like staying a few days, then try renting a small flat away

from the hotels full of beach-bound tourists. These flats are comfortable and well decorated, each with balcony, small kitchen and satellite TV. The complex also has two swimming pools and a sun terrace.

➕ 184 A3 ⊠ rue de la Jeunesse, Agadir ☎ (04) 842660; fax: (04) 8845657

Riad el-Medina ££

A former hippy hang-out, this gorgeous 19th-century riad has been transformed into one of Essaouira's most attractive hotels. Individual rooms feature inventive and colourful décor inspired by local traditions. Upstairs rooms have windows and/or terraces overlooking the market streets. Public rooms, surrounding a stunning courtyard, are lit by candles at night and sun in the daytime. Here you can have a leisurely breakfast, a mint tea or dinner.

➕ 184 A4 ⊠ 9 rue el-Attarine, Essaouira ☎ (04) 4475727; fax: (04) 4476695

La Tour Hassan £££

This beautiful hotel, built in 1914, is in the heart of town. Its 139 large, air-conditioned rooms are comfortable, luxurious and tastefully decorated, and there's also a gym and swimming pool. The Andalucian garden is superb, as are the Moroccan restaurant La Maison Arabe and the popular Pasha Bar.

➕ 183 D3 ⊠ 26 rue Chellah, Rabat ☎ (03) 7732535; fax: (03) 7725408

Villa Maroc ££

One of the first riad hotels, Villa Maroc is relaxed and charming. Two 18th-century houses have been converted into a small hotel where every room is different. The walls are whitewashed, but elsewhere the main colour is blue, with plenty of colourful details. Rooms are decorated with beautiful finds and paintings by local artists.

➕ 184 A4 ⊠ 10 rue Abdallah ben Yassin, Essaouira ☎ (04) 4476147; fax: (04) 4475806; villamaroc@casanet.net.ma

90 The Atlantic Coast

Where to...
Eat and Drink

Prices
Expect to pay for a three-course meal, excluding drinks but including taxes and service
£ under 160dh **££** 160–350dh **£££** over 350dh

À Ma Bretagne £££
Reputed to be the best French restaurant in Casablanca (and arguably the best in Africa), you'll find this in a modernist building overlooking the sea and the shrine of Sidi Abder Rahmane. The classic food, impeccably prepared by the French chef, includes excellent duck and some great fish dishes, such as steamed fillet of sole. The equally impressive wine list features the best of French and Moroccan offerings. The service is attentive and the sumptuous, bright décor is delightful, particularly on the terrace.

➕ 182 C3 ☒ Boulevard Sidi Abder Rahmane, Casablanca; 5km from town along the Corniche ☎ (02) 2362112 ⏱ Mon–Sat lunch and dinner

Les Chandeliers ££
Despite its French owners and chef, this wonderful restaurant specialises in fresh pastas and other Mediterranean specialities. It is also renowned for its superb thin-crust pizzas baked in a traditional wood oven. The décor is rustic, with whitewashed walls, locally made wooden furniture and Provençal-style tablecloths. As an added bonus, the service is very friendly.

➕ 184 A4 ☒ 14 rue Laalouj, Essaouira ☎ and fax: (04) 4476450 ⏱ Daily lunch and dinner

Chez Sam ££
With its red gingham tablecloths, large candlesticks, plenty of woodwork and even some atmosphere, Chez Sam is an old favourite. The dishes, including oysters and fish tagine, are excellent value, but the à la carte menu is more expensive. You can watch developments in the harbour from the window tables.

➕ 184 A4 ☒ At the end of the harbour, Essaouira ☎ (04) 4476513 ⏱ Daily lunch and dinner

La Clef £
This is a good budget restaurant serving Moroccan and French specialities, particularly excellent tagines and grilled meats, as well as one of the best *pastillas* with pigeon in town. The downstairs bar is the preserve of serious drinkers, so you may want to head straight for the popular dining room upstairs, or

the pleasant shaded terrace on a balmy evening.

➕ 183 D3 ☒ End of rue al-Matini, near the train station, Rabat ☎ (03) 7701972 ⏱ Daily 7 pm–late

De Provence Hotel-Restaurant £–££
The restaurant of this central but quiet hotel with comfortable and well-kept rooms is generally considered the best in town. The mainly French menu with some Moroccan influences is excellent, as is the wine list. Dining is in the atmospheric restaurant or on the beautiful terrace.

➕ 182 B3 ☒ 42 avenue Fquih Mhammed er Rafdi, el-Jadida ☎ (02) 3342347; fax: (02) 3352115 ⏱ Daily breakfast, lunch and dinner

Dinarjat £££
The best Moroccan food in Rabat comes at a price, but the experience will surely be memorable. The restaurant is set in a splendidly lit "1,001 Nights" palace and offers

Where to... 91

food to match the surroundings – several different couscous dishes and tagines, including a sweet one that's famous for satisfying the cravings of pregnant women. No alcohol.

✚ 183 D3 ⊠ 6 rue Belgnaoui, Rabat, opposite the kasbah; a caretaker can take you by candlelight from the car park on avenue el-Alou ☎ (03) 7704239 ◉ Daily lunch and dinner

Le Goéland £££

Located not very far from the sea, this restaurant specialises in fish and shellfish prepared in traditional French or Mediterranean style. The dining room is large, white and airy and the charming staff are efficient.

✚ 183 D3 ⊠ 9 rue Moulay Ali Cherif, Rabat ☎ (03) 7768885 ◉ Mon–Sat lunch and dinner

Koutoubia ££

The Koutoubia is an old-style Moroccan restaurant that's been run by the same family since the 1950s and who have not changed the colourful décor since then. Kings Mohammed V and Hassan II were regular patrons, and it's easy to see why because the traditional food, particularly the tagines, couscous and roast shoulder of lamb, is still utterly superb.

✚ 183 D3 ⊠ 10 rue Pierre Parent, off rue Moulay Abdelaziz, Rabat ☎ (03) 7760125 ◉ Daily lunch and dinner

Lina £

This elegant and fashionable Franco-Belgian patisserie serves excellent pastries in a European-style tea room. There is no smoking inside and mint tea is not available – a rarity in Morocco – so it's a perfect for a relaxed breakfast or afternoon tea.

✚ 183 D3 ⊠ 45 avenue Allal ben Abdallah, Rabat (next to the French consulate) ◉ Daily breakfast–9 pm

Mimi la Brochette £

This is a good place to enjoy sea views and savour brochettes of meat and fish, freshly grilled over charcoal, and tagines that come with with crispbread – and they're all served with a smile.

✚ 184 A3 ⊠ The Promenade near the beach, Agadir ☎ (04) 8840387 ◉ Daily lunch and dinner (closed Fri dinner, Sat lunch)

Le Miramar ££–£££

The Italian manager Renato Rattazi is quite a character – charming, a born raconteur and very funny – and he's worth the visit alone, although the food will also satisfy, especially the fish and shellfish, served in a large room with a beautiful fireplace.

✚ 184 A3 ⊠ Boulevard Mohammed V, Agadir ☎ (04) 8840770 ◉ Daily lunch and dinner

Oliveri £

This Casablanca institution has sold the best ice-cream cones in town for many years. The queue in the evenings shows its popularity, despite the limited flavours, which include the usual vanilla, chocolate, strawberry, mocha and praline.

✚ 182 C3 ⊠ 132 avenue Hassan II, Casablanca ◉ Daily until 1 am

La Pergola ££

The atmosphere here is more rural France than Morocco, but the food is excellent, with different lunch and dinner menus. The speciality is fish cooked in a crust of salt, but there's also a wide choice of good meat dishes. The Pergola also has a few rooms, which are comfortable.

✚ 184 A3 ⊠ 8km from Agadir, on the road to Inezgane ☎ (04) 8330841 ◉ Daily lunch and dinner

Le Port de Pêche ££

The name speaks for itself at this wonderful establishment for fans of fish and shellfish. This restaurant, with red-and-white gingham tablecloths and fishing nets on the walls, is a local family favourite. If you have not booked in advance you'll have to join the long queue, but the food is worth the wait. The soupe de

The Atlantic Coast

poison is legendary, and freshly caught fish comes cooked in every possible way: tagine, fried, baked and in filo pastry.

➕ 182 C3 ✉ Casablanca harbour (turn left at customs) ☎ (02) 2318561 🕐 Daily lunch and dinner

Refuge Sidi Bouzid £–££

This popular restaurant is very simple but totally charming, and people travel a long way to savour its fresh seafood. While watching the boats on the sea from the terrace, you can enjoy a copious platter of seafood, a lobster or delicious fresh shrimps with a glass of chilled wine.

➕ 182 B3 ✉ 4km from Safi, coast road to el-Jadida ☎ (04) 4464354 🕐 Tue–Sun lunch and dinner

Restaurant de la Plage ££

The menu at this excellent fish restaurant, frequented by a wealthy crowd from Rabat, includes fresh oysters from Oualidia, lobster, grilled fish and squid, and also several meat dishes. The spacious and airy dining room is elegantly decorated in light tones and the sheltered terrace, with lovely views, is particularly pleasant.

➕ 183 D3 ✉ On the beach below the kasbah, Rabat ☎ (03) 7707586 🕐 Daily lunch and dinner

Restaurant du Port ££

This harbour restaurant, with its boat shape and nautical theme, is the most famous place for fish in town. People come from Rabat and beyond to sample the excellent menu, particularly the lobster. The simple interior is very cosy but you can also eat in the beautiful garden courtyard if you wish.

➕ 182 C3 ✉ 1 rue du Port, Mohammedia ☎ (02) 3324447 🕐 Daily lunch and dinner

Le Riad Bleu Mogador ££–£££

Housed in a restored *riad* in the heart of the medina, its spectacular, brightly coloured interior makes this one of the most attractive restaurants in town. It offers superb varied, inventive and contemporary cooking, including both Western cuisine based on local ingredients and excellent Moroccan specialities. Staples include a delicious salad selection and very tempting couscous. Booking is recommended.

➕ 184 A4 ✉ 23 rue Bouchentouf, off rue Mohammed el-Gorry, Essaouira ☎ (04) 4784128 🕐 Daily lunch and dinner

Riad Zitoun ££

Located in a quiet corner of the town centre, this good Moroccan restaurant has a loyal following, attracted by its excellent specialities, including couscous with pigeon and a delicious fish tagine.

➕ 182 C3 ✉ 31 boulevard Rachidi, Casablanca ☎ (02) 2223927 🕐 Sun–Fri lunch and dinner

Taros £££

Taros features several attractions in one big house: a terrace on the square – a wonderful, sunny roof terrace with views over the port and the town – and several rooms inside the house, which also has an extensive library on Morocco. This is a calm place where you could easily spend an afternoon dining, browsing or relaxing with a pot of mint tea and some pastries in simple Moroccan surroundings.

➕ 184 A4 ✉ 2 rue Scala, place Moulay Hassan, Essaouira ☎ (04) 4476407 🕐 Daily breakfast–late

Zerda (Chez Michel) ££

Zerda is a small restaurant with a great atmosphere, where live music – ranging from traditional *oud* to Moroccan raï or even jazz – accompanies well-prepared Jewish-Moroccan food. Specialities include spicy boiled aubergine salad, chicken stuffed with couscous and nuts, and *kamfounata* – a Moroccan version of ratatouille. Advance booking is essential.

➕ 183 D3 ✉ rue Patrice Lumumba, Rabat ☎ (03) 7730912 🕐 Daily lunch and dinner

Where to...
Shop

SOUKS

In **Rabat**, the main market street is **rue Souika** and its continuation **Souk es Sebbat**, where shops sell textiles, silverware, *babouches* and the usual tourist fare. The best place to shop, however, is **rue des Consuls**, with its carpet shops and a carpet souk on Thursday morning. The **Ensemble Artisanal** near the Kasbah des Oudaia is also good for crafts. A daily *joutia* (flea market) takes place in the *mellah* below Souk es Sebbat towards Bab el-Bahr, and there's a daily flower market on **place Moulay Hassan**.

Casablanca's medina sells more clothes and tapes than crafts. Locals shop at **Centre 2000**, a vast modern mall near Casa Port train station.

ARTS AND CRAFTS

At the **Oulja** Complexe des Potiers, 2km from Salé, look out for master potters **Tarfaya** at stall No 9 and **Hariky** at No 10, who make some of the finest pottery in Morocco. In **Casablanca** many craft shops are concentrated on **boulevard Felix Houphouët-Boigny**, but the relaxed **Quartier Habous** also offers reasonable prices.

Essaouira's pedestrianised medina offers some of the most interesting shopping in Morocco, as the town has long inspired writers and artists, and has a deep-rooted tradition of decent crafts. Traders are also more relaxed than elsewhere. The town is especially famous for its woodwork and, at the workshops under the **Skala de la Ville**, craftsmen make big bowls, furniture and picture frames in woods that include argan, which only grows in Morocco.

The best place to look for paintings in Essaouira is **Galerie**

Frederic Damgaard (avenue Oqba ibn Nafiaa, tel: (04) 4784446), which represents the widest range of Gnaoua artists. The eponymous Danish owner is passionate about this art and has done much to bring it to international notice (▶ 82).

GIFTS

Argan oil from the indigenous tree contains a lot of vitamins and is used against burns and rheumatism as well as for cooking. You can buy it in Essaouira at **Produits Naturels** (rue Sidi Mohammed ben Abdallah, left of Hotel Central), which also sells natural honey. A women's co-operative produces the argan oil on sale at **Chez Aicha** (place aux Grains), which also stocks extremely fine Berber pottery.

Near Essaouira's fish and spices souk is a **weavers' workshop** where you can buy traditional *haiks* (veils) that work well as throws or tablecloths. In the street off the fish market, shops sell typical Gnaoua

musical instruments such as *gimbris* (long-necked lutes) and *garagabs* (metal castanets).

JEWELLERY AND FASHION

Essaouira is also known for its raffia shoes, sold hand-made to measure. The best of these is **Rafia Craft** (82 rue d'Agadir, tel: (04) 4783632; rafiacraft@yahoo.fr), where designer Miro adds contemporary touches to traditional styles, all of which are stunning and perfectly made.

For ethnic jewellery, check out **Tazra**, which is next to the hotel Riad el-Medina (▶ 89).

FOOD

While in Casablanca stop at **Patisserie Bennis** (2 rue Fquih el-Gabbas) for the best Moroccan sweets in town, such as honey biscuits and *cornes de gazelles*, (pastries shaped like gazelle horns and stuffed with almond paste).

The Atlantic Coast

Where to...
Be Entertained

NIGHTLIFE

Most of Casablanca's larger hotels have **nightclubs**, but the atmosphere is usually pretty sedate. For something livelier check out **Le Village** (boulevard de la Corniche, near the hotel Riad es Salam), a large complex with a restaurant, bars and a disco. Also on the Corniche is the popular and trendy **Armstrong jazz bar**.

Agadir has a lively nightlife with many clubs and hotel discos open until early morning. The best of these are **Tan Tan** in the Hotel des Almohades (tel: (04) 8840233) and **Jimmy's** in the Hotel Melia (boulevard du 20 Août). The most fashionable nightclub in Rabat is **Amnesia** (rue Monastir, tel: (03) 7701860), while **l'Arc en Ciel**

(avenue Mohammed V, next to the Balima Hotel) alternates disco with live Moroccan music.

CINEMA AND THEATRE

Most cinemas in Rabat show films in French, except for the small art house **Salle du 7ième Art** (avenue Allal ben Abdallah), **Atelier** (16 rue Annaba) and **Marsam** (6 rue Usqufiah). The **Théâtre National Mohammed V** (avenue el-Mansour ed Dahabi; tel: (03) 7707528) has concerts and films. Casablanca has several cinemas – listings are in the free magazine *7 jours à Casa* – and most films are dubbed into French. Agadir's **Théâtre Municipal** (boulevard Mohammed V, tel: (04) 8840784) schedules regular concerts and shows all year.

SPORT AND LEISURE

Golfers are well catered for and the **Dar es Salaam Golf Club** in Rabat (tel: (03) 7755864), with both 9- and 18-hole courses, is Morocco's best. Agadir also has three courses: the **Royal Golf Club** (tel: (04) 8831278), **Dunes** (tel: (04) 8834690) and **Golf du Soleil** (tel: (04) 8337329). There's also a 9-hole course in Anfa, Casablanca (tel: (02) 2365355) and an 18-hole course at **Mohammedia** (tel: (02) 3324656).

The beaches in and around Essaouira – "Windy City Africa" – are popular with **windsurfers**, particularly at **Moulay Bouzerktoun**, 26km north of town, and **Sidi Kaouki**, 20km to the south. Information and equipment hire is available at **Club Nautique** on Essaouira beach and from the **African Waveriders Connection** at Hotel Poisson Volant (rue Labbane; tel and fax: (04) 4472152). Surfers and bodyboarders could also head

for the beach of **Dar-Bouazza** in Casablanca.

If your hotel in Casablanca does not have a **swimming pool** you can try the **Piscine Océanique** at Aïn Sebaa or the Corniche beach clubs.

Casablanca is the best place to watch **football** as the city has two major teams: RAJA and WYDAD (check the local papers for fixtures), and **horse-racing** takes place some Sundays at the Hippodrome in Anfa.

Horse-riding can be organised at **Ranch REHA**, 17km from Agadir on the road to Essaouira (tel: (04) 8847549).

For total relaxation, the **Centre de Thalassothérapie d'Agadir** on Tikida Beach (tel: (04) 8842120) offers hydro massages, algae therapy and aqua-stretching, among other treatments.

You can take your kids to **Sindbad** on Casablanca's Corniche, a small complex that gets very crowded at weekends – one of the few **amusement parks** in Morocco

The North

Getting Your Bearings 96 – 97
In Five Days 98 – 99
Don't Miss 100 – 107
At Your Leisure 108 – 110
Where to… 111 – 116

96 The North

Getting Your Bearings

Northern Morocco is where Europe meets Africa or, more precisely, where Andalucian culture meets Berber traditions. Between the Atlantic and the Mediterranean coast, the Hispanic-influenced cities contrast starkly with the wild landscapes of the Rif Mountains. In the towns, stylish urbanites mix in markets and squares with the more traditional Rifians who come to sell their produce.

Tangier is a place all its own, with memories of intrigue and dreams. Its stories and scandals involving bad boys and *femme fatales*, lawlessness and beauty, inspired many writers, filmmakers and artists. Elegant Tetouan and attractive Chefchaouen have preserved their Andalucian heritage, as have the seaside towns of Asilah and Larache. And Spain still holds five enclaves along the Rif coast: Ceuta, Melilla and three small, uninhabited islets.

The Rif Mountains form a barrier between the Mediterranean world and central Moroccan culture. The ruined settlements of many foreign powers, from Phoenicians and Romans to Arabs and Spaniards, are scattered along the coastline – but the Rif only ever belonged to the Berbers. Very few Moroccan sultans succeeded in conquering the region and even today it remains troublesome. The eastern mountains are remarkably beautiful, but something of a no-go area because of the flourishing cannabis trade. However, King Mohammed VI's plans for the area have resulted in the development of tourist resorts.

Previous page: A musical moment in Tetouan. Right: Carved plaster with floral motives, calligraphy and zellij in spectacular geometric compositions all vie to capture the attention

Getting Your Bearings 97

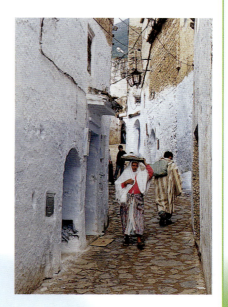

★ Don't Miss
1. Tangier ➤ 100
2. Tetouan ➤ 104
3. Chefchaouen ➤ 106

At Your Leisure
4. Larache ➤ 108
5. Asilah ➤ 108
6. Ceuta ➤ 109
7. Rif Coast ➤ 109
8. Ouezzane ➤ 110
9. Al-Hoceima ➤ 110
10. Oujda ➤ 111

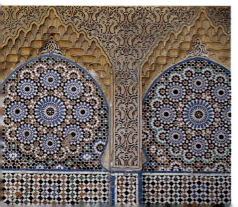

Above:
Traditions are important in the blue-washed streets of Chefchaouen

The North

Explore the area where Europe merges with Africa, taking in fascinating cities and some dramatic natural scenery.

The North in Five Days

Day One

Morning
Start your tour in Tangier (➤ 100–103) at the **Grand Socco** square, then visit the **Mendoubia Gardens**, **La Légation des États-Unis** and the **Musée d'Art Contemporain de la Ville de Tanger**. Have a drink at the Gran Café de Paris (➤ 103) on place de France before lunch at the San Remo restaurant (15 rue Ahmed Chaouki; tel: (03) 9938451) a few blocks away.

Afternoon
Returning to the **Grand Socco**, enter the **medina** and head towards the **Petit Socco**, the **kasbah** and **Dar el-Makhzen**. Later, relax on the terrace of the Café Hafa (➤ 113), the Gran Café de Paris (pictured above) or the Hotel Continental (➤ 111) before dinner in the El-Minzah hotel's splendid Moroccan restaurant (➤ 112).

Day Two

Morning
Leave town along Zankat Belgika and follow signs west to **La Montagne** for spectacular views over Tangier and the Mediterranean, then continue to **Cap Spartel**. Walk towards the lighthouse (closed; pictured right), and then walk or drive 3km to the **Grottes d'Hercule** before having a drink on the nearby panoramic terrace of the Hotel Mirage (➤ 111). Drive back to Tangier and follow the road out towards Ceuta, passing **Cap Malabata** and more good views over the city. Have lunch at Laachiri (near the river), a fish restaurant in Ksar es Seghir.

Afternoon
Continue on the spectacular road to Ceuta along the **Rif coast** (➤ 109), then turn south and stop at one of the beaches near **Cabo Negro** for a swim before heading to Tetouan for dinner at the Palais Bouhlal restaurant (➤ 114).

In Five Days

Day Three

Morning
Start your exploration of ❷Tetouan (➤ 104–105) at place Hassan II and visit the medina and the souks. Have lunch at Le Restinga (➤ 114).

Afternoon
After a visit to the **Musée Archéologique**, walk through the Jewish quarter to the **Musée d'Art Marocain** and the **École des Métiers** craft school on the other side of the Bab el-Okla.

Day Four

Morning
It's a two-hour drive to ❸**Chefchaouen** (➤ 106–107) for a stroll round the sights of **place Uta el-Hammam** before lunch at a restaurant on the square.

Afternoon
Visit the **Musée Artisanal** and then stroll through the souks (crafts shop in the medina; left), maybe stopping for a *hammam* (Turkish bath). Drive out of town towards the Hotel Asmaa for great views over the Jebala Mountains and Chefchaouen, and then dinner at the Tissemlal restaurant in Casa Hassan (➤ 111).

Day Five

Morning
From Chefchaouen drive 3km south for a dip and a stroll at **Ras el-Maa**, a charming river with small pools and waterfalls. Continue through the **Jebala Mountains** to ❽**Ouezzane** (local children pictured right; ➤ 110) for lunch.

Afternoon
Visit the **medina** and **souks** of Ouezzane, stopping for a drink at the terrace under the vines on rue Nejjarine before heading back to Chefchaouen for dinner.

The North

Tangier

Tangier (also known as Tanger or Tanja) looks splendid from the sea, an amphitheatre of blue-and-white houses overlooking the bay, interspersed with minarets and palm trees. Gone are its golden days as the "International City", when it attracted millionaires and inspired artists. The Tangier-born writer Tahar ben Jelloun compares his city to "a lady who no longer dares to look at herself in the mirror". But Tangier has kept an air of individuality, if not eccentricity, and has plenty to offer, from its medina and evocative bars to the beautiful landscape around it.

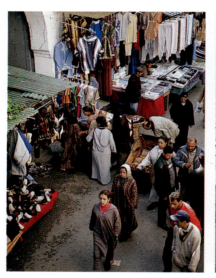

The Petit Socco was the centre of nightlife at the time of the "International City"

Looking over the Strait of Gibraltar, controlling the entrance to the Mediterranean and the easiest crossing from Europe to Africa, Tangier was always of great strategic importance. From the 1920s until Morocco's independence in 1956, it flourished under its special designation of "International City". Its easy tax laws and free-port status attracted banks and other businesses, and in turn an influx of foreigners. Most of the city's income now comes from the passenger port and, less officially, from the Rif cannabis trade.

The **Grand Socco** (place du 9 Avril 1947) links old and new Tangier. Flanking the square are the **Mendoubia Gardens** – look for the beautiful banyan tree that's said to be more than 800 years old. On nearby Zankat Salaheddine and Zankat el-Oualili is a food market where Rifians sell their

Tangier

produce. The 19th-century **Church of St Andrew** on rue d'Angleterre reveals a blend of Moorish and English styles. The American journalist Walter Harris is buried in its cemetery alongside many other foreigners who made the city their home, including the British eccentric David Herbert whose tombstone, in contrast to his flamboyant lifestyle, reads simply "He loved Morocco". Along the same street, the small **Musée d'Art Contemporain de la Ville de Tanger** fills the former British consulate with Moroccan art.

The US created its first embassy back in 1777 in **La Légation des États-Unis** (Old American Legation), a fascinating palace containing historical exhibits of the city as well as paintings by Americans in Morocco, including James McBey and

A carpet representing Rifian women on show at the American Legation

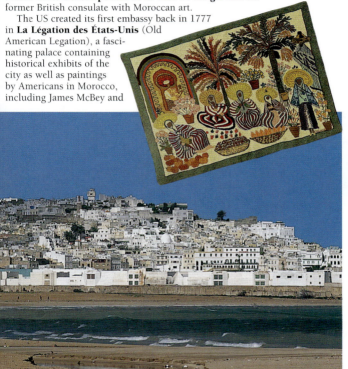

Oscar Kokoshka, plus works by Morocco's first painter, Mohamed ben Ali Rbati. The **Bab Fahs** leads from the Grand Socco into **rue des Siaghin** (silversmiths' souk) and the **Petit Socco**, once a centre of prostitution and intrigue, but now much quieter with jewellers' shops and café terraces. A stroll through picturesque alleys and streets leads to **place de la Kasbah**, offering panoramas over the straits and the Moroccan and Spanish coasts.

The **kasbah**, an administrative area and palace since Roman times, rises to the right of the square. It had always been home to royalty, but from the 1920s it became a playground for foreign millionaires attracted by Tangier's decadence, lawlessness, drugs and homosexuality. Among those tempted were the writer Richard Hughes, who built an

The best way to approach Tangier, like any port town, is undoubtedly from the sea

oriental palace within the kasbah, and the Woolworth heiress Barbara Hutton, who flew friends in from around the world to organise lavish parties at her palace.

Dar el-Makhzen, the 17th-century sultan's palace, houses the **Musée de la Kasbah**, divided into the **Ethnographic** and the **Archaeological museums**. At the entrance to the main part of the museum, dedicated to Moroccan arts, is the **Beit el-Mal** (the old treasury). The ethnographic museum has fine ceramics from Fes and Meknes, while the small collection of mosaics and objects from Volubilis (➤ 126–127) dominates the archaeological section.

From the kasbah gate, rue Asad ibn Farrat leads past stunning Moorish villas to the residential area of **Marshan** and the **Palais Mendoub**, a former home of the American publisher Malcolm Forbes (1919–90), which also housed his collection of tin soldiers. The nearby **Café Hafa** (➤ 113), where Paul Bowles (➤ 32) and his friends often hung out, enjoys commanding sea views.

The Bay of Tangier stretches between two capes. To the west is **Cap Spartel**, known to the Romans as "the Cape of Vines". Past the lighthouse, built in 1864, **Robinson beach** overlooks dangerous waters where the Atlantic meets the Med. On the spit are the **Grottes d'Hercule**, natural rock formations enhanced by centuries of quarrying. To the east of Tangier is **Cap Malabata** with many old villas, as well as new

This opening in the Caves d'Hercules resembles Africa

Tangier

Read All About It
Some of the rich literature written about the International City will help enliven it even more. Try:
Let It Come Down by Paul Bowles (1952)
Enderby by Anthony Burgess (1968)
Naked Lunch by William Burroughs (1959)
Tangier, City of the Dream by Ian Finlayson (1992)

hotel complexes. The **Villa Harris**, built by the flamboyant travel writer Walter Harris, can be visited through the Club Med complex. Widely travelled as the Morocco correspondent for the British newspaper *The Times*, he was one of the first foreigners to enter the sacred city of Chefchaouen (➤ 106), as described in his book *Morocco That Was* (1921).

TAKING A BREAK
The terrace of **Gran Café de Paris** on place de France has been popular since the 1940s and is still a great place to see and be seen, particularly in the late afternoon. Near by is the luxury El-Minzah hotel (➤ 112), whose splendid **Caïd Bar** attracts wealthy expats. For sea views head for **Café Hafa** (➤ 113) in the Marshan area.

Above: One of the six entrances to Tangier's kasbah quarter

🚌 183 E5
🚍 Regular buses from all main cities
🚆 Trains from Oujda, Meknes, Fes, Rabat and Casablanca
⛴ Boats from Sète (France) and Algeciras (Spain)

Mendoubia Gardens
✉ Grand Socco
🕐 Open access

Church of St Andrew
✉ Zankat Angleterra
🕐 The caretaker will open it almost any time
💰 Donation

Musée d'Art Contemporain de la Ville de Tanger
✉ rue d'Angleterre
🕐 Tue–Sun 8:30–12, 2:30–6:30
💰 Inexpensive

La Légation des États-Unis
✉ 8 rue d'Amérique
☎ (03) 9935317
🕐 Mon, Wed, Thu

10–1, 3–5, or by appointment
💰 Free

Dar el-Makhzen
✉ Kasbah
🕐 Wed–Mon 8:30–12, 2:30–6:30
💰 Inexpensive

Grottes d'Hercule
🚌 183 E5
✉ 15km west of Tangier
🕐 Daily 9 am–dusk
🚍 17
💰 Inexpensive

TANGIER: INSIDE INFO

Top tips Tangier can be problematic at first, with **persistent hustlers** (*faux-guides*), drug dealers and pickpockets, particularly in and around the port and train station. Otherwise, it's a relaxed and easy place to get around.

One to miss Avoid the beach at night (except for the beach bars) as muggings are quite common, and the water is fairly dirty.

Hidden gem The 1960s **Café Detroit** in the kasbah is where the Rolling Stones met the Master Musicians of Jajouka (traditional Moroccan music), who subsequently appeared on their 1989 album *Steel Wheels*. It's a bit shabby but still has plenty of atmosphere and a splendid view.

Tetouan

The splendid white city of Tetouan, often known as "the Andalucian" or "the daughter of Granada", covers the slopes of Jebel Dersa and overlooks the fertile Martil Valley and the dark rocky mass of the Rif Mountains. The elegant city appears Hispanic at first sight, but it is influenced equally by the traditions and culture of the Berber tribes from the surrounding Rif. Some people claim the name Tetouan comes from the Berber word *Tit'ta'ouin* (the springs), which feed the city's many gardens and fountains.

The elegant mosque of Sidi Saïdi, a 13th-century saint who was buried at the same time as the city was founded

Tetouan was founded in the 15th century by the military commander Sidi el-Mandari and a group of Muslims and Jews who were fleeing Spain after the fall of Granada. Soon after his death, el-Mandari's wife Fatima became the leader of the much-feared corsairs (➤ 30–31), bringing great wealth to the city, and also building most of Tetouan's ramparts in the 17th century. The refugees brought the artistic traditions of el-Andalus, reflected in the fine houses in the medina. When the Spanish occupied this part of Morocco in 1912, they made Tetouan the capital of their protectorate.

The best way into the **medina** is through Bab er Rouah on place el-Feddan (formerly place Hassan II), which is dominated by the royal palace. The first street to the left of this gate leads to the charming **Souk el-Hots**, overlooked by the **Alcazaba fortress**, with stalls selling traditional crafts, and the nearby square of **Guersa el-Kebira**.

The souks around **Souk el-Foki** and **rue de Fes** are some of the nicest in Morocco, famous for jellabas (woollen hooded cloaks), leatherwork and woodcarving. Unesco declared the medina a World

Heritage Site in 1997, to protect its 50 or so mosques and other monuments.

To the right of Bab er Rouah is the *mellah* though, as elsewhere in Morocco, most of Tetouan's Jewish community have emigrated. Towards Bab Okla is the **Musée d'Art Marocain**, an ethnographic museum with a superb collection of textiles and embroidery.

On the other side of the gate, the **École des Métiers** is worth visiting for both the building and the Moorish craft demonstrations. Near Bab Tout is the small **Musée Archéologique** with ceramics from nearby Tamuda, and fine mosaics from Lixus (➤ 108).

The kasbah of Tetouan is still garrisoned and therefore closed to visitors

TAKING A BREAK

Have a drink on the delightful **place de l'Usaa** in the medina, watching the mix of city and country people. **Patisserie Rahmouni** (10 rue Youssef ibn Tachfine, ➤ 114) has excellent Moroccan pastries and sweets, as does **Café-Patisserie Smir** (17 avenue Mohammed V).

183 E5
Buses from Tangier, Chefchaouen, Fes and Meknes
Trains from Tangier, Rabat, Fes and Meknes
Flights from Casablanca, Agadir and Marrakech

Musée d'Art Marocain
Scala, near Bab el-Okla
(03) 9970505
Mon–Fri 8:30–noon, 2:30–6:30
Inexpensive

École des Métiers
Scala, near Bab el-Okla
Mon–Fri 8:30–noon, 2:30–6:30; closed school holidays
Free

Musée Archéologique
2 rue ben Hssain, off place el-Jalaa
(03) 9967303
Mon–Fri 8:30–noon, 2:30–6:30
Moderate

TETOUAN: INSIDE INFO

Top tips In the **late afternoon** join in the *paseo*, when in Spanish tradition everyone comes out for a walk or sits on the terraces of pedestrianised rue Mohammed V.

• **Beware of *faux-guides***, sometimes cannabis dealers from the mountains who are notorious for being the most aggressive in the country. If you want a guide, choose an official one recommended by the tourist office.

Chefchaouen

Chefchaouen (or Chaouen), with its whitewashed houses perched high against the mountains, is one of Morocco's most picturesque towns. The name Chaouen comes from the Berber for "horns", a reference to the shaped rock above the town. This sacred "Blue City" of tranquil alleys and friendly people exudes an air of calm and mystery.

The road from Chaouen to al-Hoceima (➤ 109) is spectacular but wild and dangerous. It takes around five hours to cover the 220km route, which features hairpin bends, steep mountain cliffs and, seasonally, strolling donkeys, mudslides and thick, covering cloud.

The city was founded in the 15th century by Moulay Ali ibn Rachid (a descendant of the Prophet Mohammed) near the tomb of Moulay Abdessalam, the Djebali tribe's patron saint believed to possess strong supernatural powers. This sacred city of many mosques provided a safe haven for many Andalucian Muslims fleeing the Catholic kings of Spain, but for a long time it was closed to non-Muslims. Before the Spanish broke through in 1920 only three Christians had managed to enter and leave with their lives, including Walter Harris in 1889 (➤ 103).

The town is still traditionally divided into quarters, each with four mosques, four *hammams* and four *medersas* (Koranic schools). Elongated **place Uta el-Hammam**, the central square, is dwarfed by the surrounding mountains. On one side of the square are small cafés and restaurants, with crowded cannabis smoking rooms on the upper floor. Although officially illegal, this is very much part of life here. On the other side are the imposing walls of the **kasbah**, and the **Grand Mosque** with a fine octagonal minaret. Inside the kasbah fortress is a wonderful garden with palms, fig trees and

Chefchaouen

flowers, and a small museum containing old photos, musical instruments and crafts. The square is surrounded by *fondouks* (➤ 23), particularly on rue el-Andalous. The light in the medina is extraordinary, reflected on the walls of the houses that glow with a mix of whitewash, blue and ochre. Throughout the medina are workshops where weavers work to designs virtually unchanged over the centuries. Assorted woollen blankets, as well as painted woodwork, are on show in the small **Musée Artisanal** (craft museum) next to the Parador Hotel. **Galerie Hassan** (Tissemlal, ➤ 115) also contains some excellent regional crafts and works by local painters.

On the southeast side of town is a Spanish mosque (open to non-Muslims). A path from here climbs into the mountains, beside small cannabis farms, and offers spectacular views over the town. A short walk from the medina is the small **Ras el-Ma** river, a pleasant place for a dip, whose waters irrigate Chaouen's gardens.

Opposite page: In the maze of the medina, stumble upon beautiful doorways, sacred marabouts and weaving workshops

Below: The café-terraces on Uta el-Hammam offer great views over the imposing kasbah

TAKING A BREAK

Café-terraces on place Uta el-Hammam are the best place to rest, have a snack and watch the people go by.

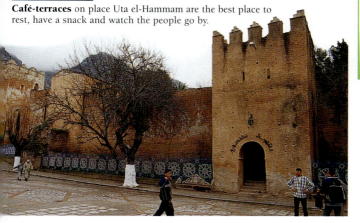

| 182 E5
Souk: Wed, Thu
Bus from Tetouan, Fes and Meknes | **Kasbah/Musée Artisanal**
place Uta el-Hammam
Mon–Sat 9–1, 3–7
Inexpensive | **Galerie Hassan (Tissemlal)**
22 rue Targhi, off place Uta el-Hammam Daily 8 am–10 pm Free |

CHEFCHAOUEN: INSIDE INFO

Top tips Chefchaouen is a centre for the **kif trade**. Smoking cannbis is illegal in Morocco, so steer clear of the dealers.

In more depth As a location of maraboutism (➤ 13), there are a number of important *moussems* in and around Chefchaouen throughout the year, including that of Moulay Abdessalam ben Mchich in May.

The North

At Your Leisure

Part of the ramparts of Château de la Cicogne are now covered by a garden

4 Larache
The pleasant little town of Larache was a Spanish protectorate until 1956 and is still a good place to eat paella and to watch the *paseo*, when the inhabitants go for a walk in the early evening. The medina has retained plenty of character, particularly in streets descending to the sea. Prices in the souks are lower than many places in Morocco, mostly because foreign tourists have not yet arrived in any numbers. The Spanish fortress, the **Château de la Cicogne**, overlooks a fine esplanade. Near the 16th-century **Kebibat fortress** and the lively fishing harbour is the longer esplanade of avenue Moulay Ismail. The French writer Jean Genet is buried in a solitary tomb near the Muslim cemetery.

Near by is **Lixus**, one of the oldest and almost continuously inhabited settlements in Morocco, founded by the Phoenicians in the 12th century BC. The ancient town boasts a Roman theatre and amphitheatre, baths with a beautiful mosaic of Neptune and the oceans, an acropolis and some temple sanctuaries.

🕀 183 E5 ✉ 96km south of Tangier
🚌 Regular buses from Tangier, Asilah, Rabat, Meknes and Ksar el-Kebir

Lixus
✉ 5km north of Larache
🚌 Bus 4 and 5 from Larache
🕐 Open access

Top: Asilah at sunset. Above: Murals in Asilah's medina, a "thank you" from artists who participate in the August festival

5 Asilah
This beautiful, whitewashed beach resort, squeezed within ochre ramparts and reminiscent of a Greek

At Your Leisure 109

island, was in fact a Spanish stronghold for a long time. At the end of the 19th century Asilah was ruled by a local bandit called Raissouli, whose palace, between Bab Homar and the bastion, is open during the international music festival in August. The town is quiet and peaceful now, and the medina – best entered through Bab Homar, part of the Portuguese ramparts – is a pleasant and relaxed place to stroll around. In summer sleepy Asilah comes to life when crowds of Moroccan families descend on its splendid white beach.

+ 183 E5
✉ 45km south of Tangier
🚌 Buses from Tangier, Meknes, Fes and Rabat
🚃 Trains from Tangier, Rabat and Casablanca

6 Ceuta

The Spanish enclave of Ceuta (Sebta) on the peninsula of Monte Acho faces Gibraltar across the strait, with mountains on both sides forming the so-called Pillars of Hercules. Although the town was first occupied by the Phoenicians, it has little to show for its long history. The most obvious reminders are two baroque churches near Plaza de Africa and, further south, the small **Museo de la Legión**, which offers a glimpse into the town's Spanish-African military history. The town's duty-free shops are a major attraction, but land border crossings are slow.

+ 183 E5 **✉** 40km northeast of Tangier **🚌** Buses from Tangier, Casablanca, Tetouan and al-Hoceima

Museo de la Legión
✉ Paseo de Colón
🕐 Daily 10–1:30, 4–6
🎫 Free

7 Rif Coast

The vast, wild and remarkably beautiful Rif Mountains, more than 300km long and 2,500m high, form the border between Europe and Africa, and between central Morocco and the rest of North Africa. The mountain scenery in this lawless region is spectacular, but best enjoyed from the safety of a bus, as passengers in foreign and rented vehicles have been robbed at knife-point or forced to buy drugs, particularly around Ketama.

Shortly after ascending the throne in 1999 King Mohammed VI earmarked the whole Rif for serious attention and development. However, progress has been hampered by limited access, as the mountains are often very close to the shore. Despite this, several tourist resorts with pleasant beaches have already emerged along the stretch of coastline between Ceuta and Tetouan, including **Smir-Restinga**, **Cabo Negro** and **Martil**. Southeast of Tetouan, the coast road climbs into the mountains and, although the few beaches on the way – such as **Oued Laou** and **Kaaseras** – are not as pretty and developed as those further north, they are almost deserted. The road from al-Hoceima (➤ 110) to Cala Iris, dotted with tranquil little fishing villages, is wonderful.

+ 186 A4 **🚌** Regular buses from Tetouan to al-Hoceima and Fnideq; *grands taxis* to Oued Laou, Martil and Cabo Negro

The heart of Ouezzane's medina is home to many workshops of craftsmen and artisans

8 Ouezzane

The town of Ouezzane, on the edge of the Rif Mountains, is twice sacred. It was founded in 1727 and developed around the Zaouia of Moulay Abdallah ben Brahim Cherif – a *sherif* (descendant of the Prophet Mohammed) and founder of the Tabiya Sufi brotherhood. The Sufi influence spread all over North Africa, and the *zaouia* (tomb), with its octagonal minaret, is still an important pilgrimage centre. The brotherhood is now based elsewhere but the founder's *moussem* is still held at his *zaouia* (closed to non-Muslims). The tomb of the pious Rabbi Amrane, renowned for his miracles, also attracts Jewish pilgrims. The old town has much charm, while the souks (Thursday 6 am–1 pm) are famous for woven woollen rugs.

🚼 183 E4 ✉ 60km southwest of Chefchaouen 🚌 Buses from Meknes, Fes and Chefchaouen

9 Al-Hoceima

Tiny and relaxed, this is the best of the Rif coast beach resorts and a pleasant hang-out for a few days. It tends to get overrun by holidaymakers in midsummer, but is very sleepy for the rest of the year. The main attractions are the lovely view over the Spanish islands of Peñon de Alhucemas and the chance to swim at the beach, **plage Quemado**, or nearby **Asfiha** beach. The road between al-Hoceima and Chefchaouen is dramatic but dangerous.

🚼 186 A5 ✉ 325km east of Tangier 🚌 Buses from Chefchaouen, Tetouan, Fes and Nador

10 Oujda

Oujda is important as one of only two border posts between Algeria and Morocco. The country's sixth city has considerable industry and mineral mines and is also a major agricultural centre. The main souks are outside the old city walls, but the **Souk el-Maa**, where water is sold for the gardens, is still held inside the medina. The **Dar es Sebti**, the magnificent mansion of the Sebti family, is now a cultural centre (tel: (05) 5684404). Oujda is the perfect base to explore the spectacular **Beni Snassen Mountains** (Monts de Beni Snassèn), with the **Gorges du Zegzel** and the **Grotte du Chameau**.

🚼 186 C4 ✉ On the Algerian border 🚌 Buses from main towns 🚆 Trains from Casablanca, Rabat, Fes and Meknes ✈ Flights from Casablanca

Where to... Stay

Prices
Expect to pay for a double room, including breakfast and taxes
£ under 640dh **££** 640–1,600dh **£££** over 1,600dh

Tangier has numerous hotels, but very few with any character. Many were built in the 1970s to cater for package tourists, but have suffered from the decline in tourism due to the polluted beach and the city's reputation for crime. However, Tangier's hotels do get crowded with Moroccan families in summer, when you need to book in advance. Apart from the Continental, most of the small hotels in the medina are extremely basic.

Tetouan, despite its many monuments and attractions, as yet has very few tourist facilities, restaurants or hotels.

Casa Hassan (Hotel-Restaurant Tissemlal) £
Decorated with local antiques, the first-floor rooms in this delightful, individual hotel are spotless. They do, however, overlook the courtyard restaurant and can be noisy during the evening. There is a small gallery, which adds to the hotel's liveliness and charm.

➕ 183 E5 ✉ 22 rue Targhi, Chefchaouen; top of the medina in a small street leading to place Uta el-Hammam ☎ (03) 9986153; fax: (03) 9988196

Chams £
Set back from the main road, this pleasant, good-value hotel hides behind an unattractive façade. The large rooms are well decorated and cosy, with clean bathrooms, televisions and air-conditioning, and there's also a good swimming pool to cool off in.

➕ 183 E5 ✉ avenue Abdeljalak Torres, Tetouan, on the road to Ceuta ☎ (03) 9990901; fax: (03) 9990907

Hotel Continental £–££
Tangier's most characterful hotel is set in a colonial and Moorish-style building commanding great views over the medina and the harbour. The refurbished rooms have retained their old-world atmosphere and gained some contemporary touches such as modern artworks and comforts. Many artists and writers have stayed here, including the French painter Edgar Degas (1834–1917). The former British prime minister Sir Winston Churchill (1874–1965) is reputed to have stayed in No 108, a large room with a four-poster bed and old-fashioned furniture.

➕ 183 E5 ✉ 36 rue Dar el-Baroud, medina, Tangier ☎ (03) 9931024

Hotel España £–££
This Spanish-style building is decorated with typical tiling and has spacious rooms with large balconies overlooking the place de la Liberation. This faded beauty can be a wonderful place to stay, though the reception is not always as friendly as it could be.

➕ 183 E5 ✉ 2 avenue Hassan II, Larache ☎ (03) 913195; fax: (03) 9915628

Hotel Mirage £££
A great hotel, built on terraces, with sweeping sea views and surrounded by well-maintained gardens, the Mirage consists of luxurious, very stylish bungalows with flower-filled balconies. Extras include satellite TV, air-conditioning and room service. The restaurant is well worth a visit for its views alone, but the food is also extremely good. Specialities include lobster and fish

112 The North

cooked in a crust of sea salt, but the varied menu ranges from ordinary sardines to more exotic shark and sophisticated sea bass. Leave room for the superb desserts.

☐ 183 E5 ☒ Above the Grottes d'Hercules, Cap Spartel ☎ (03) 933332; fax: (03) 933331

El-Minzah £££

This former villa of an English aristocrat is now one of the country's most interesting luxury hotels. As Tangier's most upmarket place to stay, particularly for those attending the sumptuous parties thrown by local expats, it has seen its fair share of celebrities, including Sir Winston Churchill, King Juan Carlos of Spain and American actors Rita Hayworth and Dustin Hoffman. The swimming pool is shaded by majestic palm trees and surrounded by a garden filled with flowers and bougainvillea. The excellent restaurant serves the sophisticated Fes-style cuisine, while Caid's Bar, with its long list of

cocktails and champagnes, is great for a relaxed drink while you're people-watching.

☐ 183 E5 ☒ 85 rue de la Liberté, Tangier ☎ (03) 935885; fax: (03) 9934546; elminzah@tangeroise.net.ma

Ouad el-Makhazine £

The best budget hotel in town, close to the old city and the beach, has well-kept, airy and spacious rooms, most with *en suite* bath. There's also a small pool and a popular restaurant offering Moroccan specialities and fish dishes.

☐ 183 E5 ☒ Avenue Melilla, Asilah ☎ (03) 9417090; fax: (03) 9417500

Parador ££

On the edge of Chefchaouen's medina you'll find this beautiful and characterful upmarket hotel with small but beautifully decorated rooms. The terrace has a small pool and great views over the mountains. However, the service could be better at times.

☐ 183 E5 ☒ Avenue Hassan II, Chefchaouen ☎ (03) 986136; fax: (03) 9987033

Pension Villa Caruso £

This inexpensive place oozes charm and is very friendly. Housed in a small villa, it has clean (if unremarkable) rooms and is run entirely by women.

☐ 183 E5 ☒ 60 rue du Prince Héritier, Tangier ☎ (03) 9936361

Riad ££

In a mansion that once belonged to a French aristocrat you'll find this grand, peaceful (particularly out of season) hotel, which has large, airy rooms overlooking lovely gardens and a swimming pool (open to non-residents).

☐ 183 E5 ☒ 87 rue Mohammed ben Abdallah ☎ (03) 991262626; fax: (03) 9912629

Tarik ££

This large hotel has 150 spacious and comfortable rooms, all of

which have air-conditioning and good-sized, spotless bathrooms. They overlook either the beach or the swimming pool that's a feature of the large garden. Be aware that the hotel's beach club gets crowded with local families in summer, but out of season it is a pleasant place.

☐ 183 E5 ☒ Route de Malabata, at the end of the Bay of Tangier ☎ (03) 9340949

Zelis ££

The comfortable, refurbished rooms in this handsome hotel – all with pleasant bathroom and some with a small sitting area – have views over the ocean or on to the medina's maze of alleys. There is a beautiful mosaic pool, friendly staff and a restaurant that serves reasonable European-style food and Moroccan dishes if you order in advance.

☐ 183 E5 ☒ 10 avenue Mansour ed Dahabi, Asilah ☎ (03) 9917069; fax: (03) 9917098

Where to...
Eat and Drink

Prices
Expect to pay for a three-course meal, excluding drinks but including taxes and service
£ under 160dh **££** 160–350dh **£££** over 350dh

In Tangier the least expensive eateries are in the medina, but the food tends to be basic and no alcohol is served. For more upmarket restaurants, head for the Ville Nouvelle near place de France or the seafront.

Andaluz £
One of the best café-restaurants in the medina, serving fresh, well-prepared grilled *brochettes* and other snacks, this is a good lunch stop if you are in the area.

➕ **183 E5** ✉ **7 rue de Commerce, off rue de Marine near Petit Socco, Tangier** 🕐 **Daily lunch and dinner**

Café Ahlan £
For breakfast or an afternoon snack try this café specialising in sweet dishes of the north, including little pancakes dipped in honey, *beignets* (sweet dumplings) and cakes.

➕ **183 E5** ✉ **Hotel España (ground floor), 2 avenue Hassan II, Larache** ☎ **(03) 9913195** 🕐 **Daily 8 am–evening**

Café Hafa £
Hafa means "cliff", and this large café built on the cliff is worth visiting for its panoramic sea views. With tables set among flowerpots and plants, and with cats strolling

around, you could linger here for hours. It's easy to understand why this was the writer Paul Bowles's (▶ 32) favourite spot; somehow the mint tea here tastes better than anywhere else in town.

➕ **183 E5** ✉ **Behind the sports stadium in Quartier Marshan, Tangier** 🕐 **Daily morning–late evening; closed in the day during Ramadan**

Comme Chez Soi ££
You'll always get a warm welcome from Nassira and Kourou, the friendly owners of this delightful restaurant offering fine Moroccan and European cuisine in beautiful and cosy surroundings.

➕ **186 C4** ✉ **rue Sjilmassa, Oujda** ☎ **(05) 5686079** 🕐 **Daily lunch and dinner**

Las Conchas ££
The best French restaurant in Tangier features a very good and inventive menu that varies according to what's available in the local market. It is popular, with a friendly,

lively atmosphere, which makes booking in advance advisable.

➕ **183 E5** ✉ **30 rue Ahmed Chaouki, Tangier** ☎ **(03) 9931643** 🕐 **Daily lunch and dinner**

Le Dauphin ££
Less friendly than Comme Chez Soi (see above) but with similarly good food, Le Dauphin offers excellent Moroccan dishes and delicious grilled fresh fish.

➕ **186 C4** ✉ **38 rue de Berkane, Oujda** ☎ **(05) 5686145** 🕐 **Daily lunch and dinner**

Estrella del Mar ££
Opposite Bab el-Khemis you'll find Larache's best restaurant. The interior is decorated with ceramics, and small windows look out over the ocean. The food of choice here is the excellent Spanish paella, which needs to be ordered in advance. The fish tagine is also worth trying.

➕ **183 E5** ✉ **68 calle Mohammed Zerktouni, Larache** ☎ **(03) 9912243** 🕐 **Daily lunch and dinner**

114 The North

Guitta's ££

Guitta's was once the most exclusive hang-out in town, but unfortunately it has now fallen on hard times. It's quite difficult to find but is definitely well worth the search, as it's a place for nostalgics – a reminder of the glory days when Tangier was an International City. It now has a little less flair and serves up European cuisine, including a passable Sunday roast.

✚ 183 E5 ☒ 110 Sidi Bouabid, near Hassan II mosque on place de Kuwait, Tangier ☎ (03) 9937333
🕐 Tue–Sun lunch and dinner

Laachiri £–££

This roadside restaurant, boasting a large terrace overlooking the river, the sea and the old fortress, is popular with Moroccan families. They come to enjoy large portions of fresh fish and seafood at very reasonable prices.

✚ 183 E5 ☒ Ksar es Seghir, 33km from Tangier on the road to Ceuta and Tetouan

El-Oceano (Casa Pepe) £–££

The outdoor terrace just outside the ramparts is an excellent place for a lunch of Spanish-style fried fish. The place is suffering a little from its own popularity, and the staff are not as attentive as they used to be, but it is one of the best of several similar restaurants in the area.

✚ 183 E5 ☒ place Zellaka, Asilah ☎ (03) 9917395 🕐 Daily lunch, dinner

Palais Bouhlal ££

One of the very few good restaurants in Tetouan serves well-prepared traditional Moroccan food in a lavish *riad* with painted ceilings and mosaics. If it's packed with tour groups, ask for a quieter table on the first floor.

✚ 183 E5 ☒ Next to the Grand Mosque, Tetouan 🕐 Daily morning–early evening

Patisserie la Durée £

Behind a beautiful façade and a great signpost, this good patisserie specialises in sweet honey cakes and other pastries to take away or enjoy in the tea room next door.

✚ 183 E5 ☒ avenue de la Résistance, Tangier 🕐 Daily morning–early evening

Patisserie Rahmouni £

The Tetouan branch of the famous Tangier patisserie sells excellent Moroccan and European sweets, ice-cream and fresh juices. It's also a popular meeting spot, particularly in the late afternoon when everyone in town goes for a stroll.

✚ 183 E5 ☒ 10 rue Youssef ben Tachfine, Tetouan 🕐 Daily early morning–evening

Populaire Saveur £

The dining room of this authentic little restaurant is decorated with crafts, fishing nets and herbs, so it's easy to enjoy the simple fish dishes here. There's no menu, but the friendly owner offers his suggestions and he always has a pot of delicious fish soup on the stove.

The sardines stuffed with *chermoula* (a mixture of onion, spices, chilli and lemon), and the shark marinated in saffron are heavenly.

✚ 183 E5 ☒ Behind el-Minzah hotel in Tangier (▶ 112) ☎ (03) 9336326
🕐 Daily lunch and dinner

Rainari ££

This excellent Moroccan restaurant with typically colourful décor is famous for its couscous with chicken and vegetables and *pastilla* with pigeon. Alternatively, there is also a French-Mediterranean menu.

✚ 183 E5 ☒ 10 rue Ahmed Chaouki, Tangier ☎ (03) 9934866 🕐 Daily lunch and dinner

Le Restinga £

The service is efficient and friendly at this old-fashioned restaurant, which serves excellent budget Moroccan meals, including couscous, fried fish and tagines, either inside or in the pleasant courtyard.

✚ 183 E5 ☒ 21 rue Mohammed V, Tetouan 🕐 Daily 11:30–11:30

Where to...
Shop

Although Tangier has a good range of shops, with so many expats living in the medina there are no real bargains to be had. However, check out the antique and junk shop opposite el-Minzah hotel, **Bazar Tindouf** (64 rue de la Liberté, tel: (03) 9931525), which has a seemingly endless collection of lanterns, carpets, copper and other *objets d'art*. The **Centre Artisanal Coopartim** in the kasbah and on rue de Belgique (tel: (03) 9933100) sells all the usual Moroccan crafts.

Tangier also has some interesting art galleries. **Boutique Majid** at 66 rue des Chrétiens has a good selection of international and local art,

as does **Tanjah Flandria Art Gallery** (rue Ibn Rochd). And at **Volubilis** (6 rue Sidi Boukoiya, near the kasbah) you'll find a range of fine crafts as well as some interesting Moroccan fashions.

The **Ensemble Artisanal** on avenue Hassan I in Tetouan has a good if rather dusty selection of local crafts, but for a better choice you'll need to head for the souks in the medina. Stalls in **Souk el-Hots** sell traditional *foutas* – hand-woven cloth in red, white and black stripes or in plain brown – while at the weavers' co-operative you can buy fine woollen cloth normally used for jellabas. The **Souk el-Foki** is a good place to look for woodcarvers, coppersmiths and leather-workers.

Chefchaouen has a good souk on Monday and Thursday, and the **Galerie Hassan** at the Hotel-Restaurant Tissemlal (▶ 111) has a beautiful collection of local crafts for sale, as well as works by local and Spanish painters, friends of the owner. Shops in the souks sell all

the usual Moroccan crafts, as well as the beautiful hand-woven cloth for which the town is famous.

Ouezzane is known as a good place to buy carpets, especially in the **weavers' souk**, where you'll need to bargain fiercely, or at the fixed-price **Ensemble Artisanal** on place de l'Indépendance, where the Thursday souk takes place. Colourful painted **furniture**, found in the souk, is also a local speciality.

ANTIQUES AND JEWELLERY

Tangier's **rue Touahin**, the first road off rue Siaghin from Grand Socco, has a line of jewellery stalls selling some interesting Berber jewellery, but don't expect to find any real antiques.

PERFUME

The Madini family has been making **essential oils** and **perfumes** for 14 generations and their shops are well worth checking out. At their oldest

shop, at 14 rue Sebou in Tangier's medina, they will patiently explain the processes involved in making different essences. The American millionairess Barbara Hutton was a devoted customer, as is the current emir of Kuwait; at these reasonable prices, you might become one too. Give them a little time and the Madinis can match any perfume at a fraction of the original price.

FOOD

Still in Tangier, the **Marché de Fes** on rue de Fes is a good place to go food shopping for spices and dried fruits.

BOOKS

The **Librairie des Colonnes** at 54 boulevard Pasteur in Tetouan has an excellent collection of French books, as well as a small range of English books on Morocco, and also Moroccan novels translated by Paul Bowles (▶ 32).

ARTS AND CRAFTS

116 The North

Where to...
Be Entertained

Listings for cultural and other events in and around Tangier can be found in the weekly *Les Nouvelles du Nord*, published on Friday and available free in most restaurants and hotels.

NIGHTLIFE

The nightlife of Tangier is not what it was, though in summer the **beach bars** attract quite a crowd. Tourists should stick to the bars and avoid strolling on the beach at night as it can be dangerous. Many of the city's **discos** are in the streets off place de France. The liveliest is the **Morocco Palace** (13 rue du Prince Moulay Abdallah, tel: (03) 993564), featuring Moroccan or Egyptian belly dance music. **Regine** (8 rue Mansour ed Dahabi) is a large, very fashionable disco playing more European music.

Much of Tetouan's nightlife also takes place near the beach, and the most popular nightspot is **Club Olivia Valère** at Cabo Negro on the road to Martil. The clientele is young and chic; at weekends, particularly in summer, the atmosphere hots up. Most nightclubs in hotels in Cabo Negro, Mdiq and Restinga Smir cater for young Moroccan men and tourists.

MUSIC, CINEMA AND THEATRE

The Spanish **bullring** in Tangier's Ville Nouvelle has been converted into a rock concert venue, but it rarely stages large gigs. Information on venues and dates for musical performances is available from the Tourist Office (tel: (03) 9961915). **Institut Français de Tanger** (86 rue de la Liberté, tel: (03) 9932134) and **La Légation des États-Unis** (▶ 101) have regular films, theatre, dance and exhibitions.

Tangier's best **cinemas** are **Dawliz**, in the Istiraha Tourist Complex on rue d'Hollande, and **Flandria** on rue Ibn Rochd. Many films are shown in their original version, but some are dubbed into French or Arabic. In Tetouan try the **Monumental** cinema on avenue Youssef ben Tachfine and the **Avenida** on place el-Adala, off avenue 10 May, which show mainly American or French movies.

SPORTS

The **Tangier Royal Golf Club** (tel: (03) 9944484; fax: (03) 9945450) in the suburb of Boubana has a good course, as does the **Cabo Negro Royal Golf Club** just outside Cabo Negro (tel: (03) 9978303; fax: (03) 9978305).

Horse-riders of all abilities can hire excellent mounts for trips into the surrounding countryside at the **Club Équestre de l'Étrier**, on the road to Boubana (tel: (03) 9934884).

Upmarket beach hotels and clubs in Tangier, Tetouan, Cabo Negro, Mdiq and Restinga Smir provide **watersports** such as waterskiing, jetskiing and windsurfing.

BIRDWATCHING

Birdwatchers can discover habitats in the wetlands and flatlands around Larache, and on the road from Larache to Tangier. Try the beautiful **Loukos** wetlands, southeast of Larache on the Ksar el-Kebir road. About 175km south of Tangier is the protected **Moulay Bousselham Lagoon** and the **Merdja Zerga** (Blue Lake), attracting a diversity of birds, including flamingoes. About 4km north of Asilah, the dry flatlands attract bustards, cranes and crested larks in winter.

Imperial Cities and Middle Atlas

Getting Your Bearings 118 – 119
In Five Days 120 – 121
Don't Miss 122 – 130
At Your Leisure 131 – 133
Where to... 134 – 138

Imperial Cities and Middle Atlas

Getting Your Bearings

The plain of Saïss and the Imperial cities of Fes (Fez) and Meknes are Morocco's heartland, and their history was for a long time also the country's history. Protected from the Mediterranean by the Rif Mountains and from the Sahara Desert by the Middle Atlas range, the fertile plain amply provided for the cities. Outside the grand urban centres the region's gentle natural attractions include the cedar woods near Azrou, picturesque landscapes, romantic lakes and the splendid Cascades d'Ouzoud.

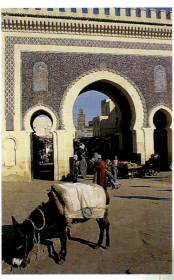

The highlight of the Middle Atlas is undoubtedly Fes, the country's ancient political and administrative capital, and still its religious and intellectual centre. The city's medina – a Unesco World Heritage Site – has a wealth of medieval monuments, some of them outstanding jewels of Islamic architecture. Its people, the Fassi – a mixture of Andalucian, Tunisian and Berber – have always had an independent identity and are often intellectuals and political leaders.

In the 17th century Moulay Ismail turned his back on Fes and moved the capital to Meknes, but over the years his megalomaniac building projects have fallen into spectacular ruin.

Even the Romans appreciated the area, and built Volubilis, the most important Roman ruins in Morocco. Not far from Volubilis is the shrine of the kingdom's most venerated Muslim saint, Moulay Idriss, the founder of Fes.

Previous page: Bab Mansour in Meknes.
Above: The 15km-long tour of the walls of Fes is a perfect introduction to the city. Right: Fes is the most complete medieval city in the Muslim world

Getting Your Bearings 119

★ Don't Miss

1 Fes (Fez) ➤ 122
2 Volubilis ➤ 126
3 Meknes ➤ 128

0 ———————— 80 km
0 ———————— 50 miles

Karia-Ba-Mohamed
Âin-Âicha
Dar-Caïd-Medboh
Sidi-Kacem
P28
Sebou
P3
Guercif
2 **5** Moulay-Idriss
Fez
1
P1
4 Taza
Volubilis
P1
3
El-Menzel
Jebel Bou Iblane
Meknès
P24 **7** Sefrou
El-Hajeb **6**
3340m
Imouzzèr-du-Kandar
P21
Ifrane
Boulemane
Outat-Oulad-El-Haj
mes **8** Azrou
Âin-Leuh
Moulouya
Atlas
P20
Enjil
Mrirt
P24
Moyen
Missour
enifra
Itzèr
Midelt
9
iba
Boumia
Jebel Ayachi
Talsinnt
Arhbala
P21
Amouguèr
Gourrama
Ziz
Rich
12
milchil

At Your Leisure

4 Taza ➤ 131
5 Moulay-Idriss ➤ 131
6 Imouzzèr-du-Kandar ➤ 131
7 Sefrou ➤ 132
8 Azrou ➤ 132
9 Midelt ➤ 132
10 Beni-Mellal ➤ 132
11 Cascades d'Ouzoud ➤ 133
12 Imilchil ➤ 133

Imperial Cities and Middle Atlas

A tour filled with urban pleasures, from marvellous Islamic architecture and gastronomic delights to busy medinas. Rural attractions include the country's most evocative Roman ruins.

Imperial Cities in Five Days

Day One

Morning
Hop in a taxi and start a tour of **Fes** (➤ 122–125) by viewing the city from a height, such as the terrace near the **Merenid tombs** (right). Drive to **Bab Boujeloud** at the entrance to the medina, then walk to the **Dar Batha Museum**. Follow rue Talaa Kebira to the **Medersa Bou Inania** and on to the **Medersa Mesbahiya** and the **Medersa Attarine**. Have lunch at the Dar Saada in Souk Attarine (➤ 136).

Afternoon
Walk to the **Kairaouine Mosque** and the **Nejjarine complex**, then stop for tea in the lovely café of the **Nejjarine Museum**. Stroll around the **souks** and return to Bab Boujeloud.

Evening
Have a romantic dinner in the Fassia restaurant of the Palais Jamaï (➤ 135), on the terrace overlooking the medina (book in advance).

Day Two

Morning
From **Bab Jamaï** walk to **Bab Guissa**, then follow rue Hormis to place Sagha for refreshments before continuing through the **jewellers' souk** to the Medersa Attarin. South of the Seffarine Medersa is the **dyers' souk**, and near by the **tanneries** (below). Continue to the **Andalous quarter**, then take a taxi to Bab Boujeloud for lunch at the Noria café in the Boujeloud Gardens.

Afternoon
Stroll through **Fes el-Jedid** and the *mellah*, then tour the city walls by taxi before dinner in one of the medina's *riad* restaurants.

In Five Days

Day Three

Morning
Take a *grand taxi* to **Moulay-Idriss** 65km away, then walk the 4km to the fascinating archaeological site of ❷ **Volubilis** (left; ➤ 126–127). Have lunch at Hotel Volubilis (➤ 135).

Afternoon
Return to the sacred village of ❺ **Moulay-Idriss** (➤ 131) for a look around and a drink at a café on the square before returning to the hotel for the night.

Day Four

Morning
Starting again from Moulay-Idriss, take a *grand taxi* 30km to ❸ **Meknes** (➤ 128–130) for a stroll around sights such as the **Tomb of Moulay Ismail**, **Bab Mansour** and **Heri es Souani**.

Afternoon
Have lunch at the *riad* restaurant signposted from Bab er Rih before visiting the **Dar Jamaï Museum**, the **Bou Inania Medersa** and the **souks**. Stroll around the lively Ville Nouvelle before dinner at Le Dauphin or Annexe de Metropolis (➤ 136).

Day Five

Morning
Buy a picnic in Meknes market and drive 55km south to the important market town of ❽ **Azrou** (➤ 132). Continue south on the Midelt road and after 8km take the gorgeous forest **Route Touristique des Cèdres**. At Ain Leuh turn left on the S303 to the waterfalls of **Oum er Rbia**, the source of Morocco's largest river, and a popular picnic spot.

Afternoon
After lunch and a careful swim drive north to the beautiful Berber village of ❻ **Imouzzèr-du-Kandar** (➤ 131), then continue to the ancient walled town of ❼ **Sefrou** (➤ 132) before heading back to Fes.

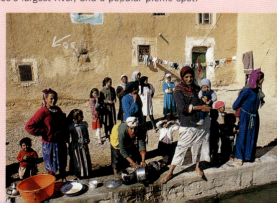

122 Imperial Cities

Fes

The oldest of Morocco's imperial capitals is also the most complete Islamic city in the Arab world, and site of the ultimate medina. Built in a valley surrounded by hills, this huge and vibrant area is home to 800,000 people – a quarter of the city's population. The medina's streets and alleys may be confusing at first, but it's a great place to get lost as there are grand buildings and magnificent sights around every corner.

Moulay Idriss I founded Madinat Fas in the 790s, but it was his son Idriss II who developed it into a grand Arab city, with Muslims from Cordoba in the Andalucian quarter, Tunisian Arabs in the Kairouanese and a Jewish community. Without these foreigners' sophisticated urban culture and artistic traditions, Fes may never have developed such grandeur.

At the end of the 11th century, the Almoravid prince Youssef ben Tachfine united the two parts of the city within walls. The city flourished further under the Almohades and enjoyed its golden age in the 13th and 14th centuries under the Merenids.

Top: Bird's eye view over Fes.
Above: Stucco Koranic calligraphy is part of the decoration of Attarine Medersa

Fes el-Bali

To understand the city's complicated layout it's best to start with a panoramic overview, especially from the terrace near the crumbling **Merenid Tombs** or from the **Borj Nord** fortress, both on a hill just outside the medina. The fortress also houses a small armoury museum. The main entrance to the old medina of Fes el-Bali is **Bab Boujeloud**, a gate built in 1913. Near by is **Dar Batha**, a beautiful Moorish building with a tranquil courtyard, where you can see one of Morocco's most interesting collections of popular arts, including carpets, *zellij* work, outstanding ceramics and calligraphy. Two main lanes lead from the gate to the **Souk el-Attarine**, the **Talaa es Seghira** and the more interesting **Talâa el-Kebira**. Here you'll find one of the country's most magnificent monuments: the grand **Medersa Bou Inania**, built in the 14th century by Merenid sultan Abou Inan, who had a reputation for being more interested in sex and murder than religion. Legend says that the religious leaders of the Qairaouine Mosque (see opposite) wanted Abou Inan to build his *medersa* on a rubbish dump if he wanted to build one at all. The sultan was then determined that his *medersa* would be more beautiful

Fes

and more important than the Qairaouine Mosque. And his wish came true, at least for a short time, when his simple yet ornate construction became Fes's most important religious building. The skillful stucco, zellig and carving remain well preserved.

Opposite the *medersa* is Bou Inania's amazing **water-clock** (under restoration), which kept perfect time despite no one ever discovering exactly how. Further along the street are several *fondouks* (caravanserais), of which the city was supposed to have over 200. Along rue Cherabliyin, several stalls sell reputedly the best *babouches* (slippers) in Morocco. The **Souk el-Attarine** (spice market), the focus of the old medina, is where the most precious goods were sold, such as fine cloth, silk thread and jewellery. The grand **Qairaouine Mosque**, founded in the 9th century by Fatima el-Fihriya, the pious daughter of a wealthy Fes merchant, was the largest in Morocco until the opening of Casablanca's Hassan II Mosque in the early 1990s. It also claims to be the oldest university in the world and still plays a leading role in the country's religious life. For non-Muslims it

Fascinating tanneries and bustling souks sum up the best of Fes

Imperial Cities and Middle Atlas

is hard to see the mosque, its exterior hidden behind surrounding buildings, the fine interior off limits. Also closed to non-Muslims is one of the city's holiest shrines, the **Zaouia and Tomb of Moulay Idriss II**. Nearby **place en Nejjarine** has the most beautiful of the city's fountains. The square is dominated by the 18th-century **Nejjarine** *fondouk*, with its small **woodwork museum** that houses well-displayed, beautifully made traditional objects, carvings and tools. The 14th-century **Medersa el-Attarine** approaches the Bou Inania in beauty and refinement of decoration and also has great views from the rooftop.

Near place Seffarine is the colourful **Souk Sabbighin** (dyers' souk), and on the other side are the pungent but fascinating **tanneries**, best seen from the rooftops.

Andalous Quarter

Although the residential Andalucian Quarter has no souks or major sights, being away from the tourist area, it's somehow more authentically Fassi. Highlights here include the **Andalucian Mosque** with its elegant courtyard. It was built in the 9th century by Myriem, the sister of Fatima el-Fihriya (founder of the Qairaouine Mosque), but was largely rebuilt by the Almohads in the 13th century. The 14th-century **Medersa es Sahrij**, a crumbling jewel of the Merenid period, is still partly used to accommodate Islamic students.

Fes el-Jedid

The huge, ornate entrance gates to the King's palace in Fes el-Jedid

New Fes is not new at all, but was built by the Merenids in the 13th century. Like Djemaa el-Fna in Marrakech, **Petit Mechouar** square was the playground for assorted performers until it was closed for repairs in the 1970s. These were never really finished, so it has not reopened. It is flanked on one side by the **royal palace** (closed to the public), one of the most sumptuous in Morocco.

The **Grande Rue des Mérénides** cuts through the *mellah* (Jewish quarter) of synagogues, cemeteries, abandoned 18th- and 19th-century houses, and a few less touristy souks. Most of Morocco's Jewish population left for Israel after its creation in 1948, and particularly after the Suez Crisis in 1956 when there were strong

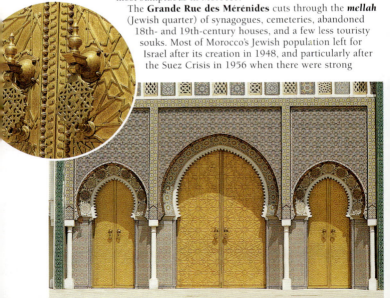

The Zaouia of Moulay Idriss II is a pilgrimage site, particularly for pregnant women and boys who are about to be circumcised

anti-Jewish feelings throughout the Arab world. The French-built **Ville Nouvelle** has hotels and restaurants but otherwise little of interest.

TAKING A BREAK

Enjoy the superb views from the beautiful garden of the hilltop **Palais Jamaï** hotel (➤ 135). The café-terrace of the **Musée Nejjarine** is another great place, as is the **Fes Hadara** (22 Sidi Ahmed Chaouki; tel: (05) 5740292) with its large garden.

183 F4

Borj Nord Armoury Museum
✉ Off avenue des Mérénides, near the Hotel des Mérénides
☎ (05) 5645241
🕐 Wed–Mon 8:30–noon, 2:30–6
💲 Inexpensive

Medersa Bou Inania and other medersas
✉ Talaa Kebira, Fes el-Bali
🕐 Daily 8:30–5:30 (in Ramadan 9–4); closed sometimes during prayer time and on religious holidays
💲 Inexpensive

Musée Nejjarine
✉ Place en Nejjarine
☎ (05) 5740580

🕐 Daily 10–5
💲 Inexpensive

Dar Batha,
✉ place de l'Istiqlal
☎ (05) 5634116
🕐 Wed–Thu 8:30–noon, 2:30–6, Fri 8:30–11:30 am, 3–6 pm, Sat–Mon 8:30–noon, 2:30–6
💲 Inexpensive (guided tours only)

FES: INSIDE INFO

Top tips If the medina looks overwhelming, **walk around it first with an official guide** from the tourist office and then return alone to stumble upon its secrets.
• See the medina from Borj Sud in the early hours or from Borj Nord or Palais Jamaï at night, when it is lit by **thousands of small lights**.
• Sample some famous **Fassi gastronomy**, such as *choua* (steamed mutton with cumin), mutton stuffed with almonds, semolina and raisins, or tagine with wild artichoke hearts. These dishes usually need hours of preparation, so you need to order them when you book.

126 Imperial Cities and Middle Atlas

2 Volubilis

The well-preserved Roman town of Volubilis, surrounded by lush countryside at the foot of Jebel Zerhoun, is one of the finest and most romantic archaeological sites in the country. The Berbers call it "Oualili" after the oleander flowers covering the nearby, and usually dry, riverbed. A guided tour of the highlights usually takes about an hour, but it's certainly worth spending a few hours strolling among the monuments.

Through the Ages

The original Berber settlement was taken by Caligula in AD 45. As the Roman Empire's most remote outpost, the city flourished during the 2nd and 3rd centuries. But the Berbers returned at the end of the 3rd century and by the time the Arabs arrived in the 7th century there was a mixed population of Latin-speaking Berbers, Jews and Syrians. Volubilis declined after 786 when Moulay Idriss (► 122) founded his capital in nearby Fes, but it remained in good repair until Moulay Ismail (► 128) plundered the city's marble for his new settlement at Meknes. The ruins suffered more damage as a result of the 1755 Lisbon earthquake.

The complex straddles the Fertassa River, with the entrance on one side and most of the sights on the other. There are several Roman villas to explore, all divided into public and private rooms and now named after the mosaics found in them. The largest is the **House of Orpheus**, with fine mosaics of Orpheus with his lyre, of dolphins and of Amphitrite, wife of Neptune and goddess of the sea. Next door are the **Gallienus Baths**, which extended over 1,000sq m.

The **Forum** is dominated by the impressive arcaded wall of the 3rd-century courthouse and the raised **Capitoline temple**, with elegant Corinthian columns, dedicated to Jupiter, his wife Juno and the goddess Minerva. North of the Forum is the **House of the Athlete** and the city's largest **public baths**, probably built by the Emperor Hadrian, covering over 1,500sq m. The **Triumphal Arch** was built in AD 217 in honour of the Emperor Caracalla and his Syrian mother Julia Domna. It was once topped with a six-horse chariot and water would cascade from carved nymphs into marble basins below. More villas line the **Decumanus Maximus** road, at the end of which is the **Gordian Palace** and the **House of Venus** with splendid mosaics, where the beautiful busts of the Berber king Juba II and Cato were found (► 77).

TAKING A BREAK

Grand mosaic floors are still in situ

Corbeille Fleurie, a small cafeteria-restaurant, offers cool drinks and good tagines. Out of summer the site and surrounding countryside are perfect for a **picnic**.

Volubilis 127

Right: View of the residential area of Volubilis, still set in the countryside

Below: The impressive Triumphal Arch is built in local Zerhoun stone

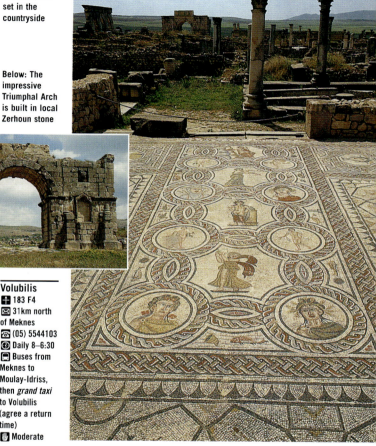

Volubilis
- 183 F4
- 31km north of Meknes
- (05) 5544103
- Daily 8–6:30
- Buses from Meknes to Moulay-Idriss, then *grand taxi* to Volubilis (agree a return time)
- Moderate

VOLUBILIS: INSIDE INFO

Top tips The site measures just under 800m by 600m and offers almost **no shade**, so wear sun protection and bring enough water.
- Visit early morning, late afternoon or dusk to **avoid the midday sun** and tour groups, and to get a warmer light on the stones.
- The most important sights are well labelled and arrows point out a **circuit**.

In more depth The site's most important finds, including bronze statues, are now in the **Archaeological Museum in Rabat** (➤ 77).

Imperial Cities and Middle Atlas

3 Meknes

Once the pride of the Morocco's most fearsome ruler, Meknes is now a thriving provincial town surrounded by farmland and vineyards. It boasts a fascinating medina and the remains of Moulay Ismail's grand plans to rival the capital cities of Europe, his legacy of marble and blood.

Above: The walled medina of Meknes.
Right and inset: The lavish tomb of Moulay Ismail

Meknes was founded in the 10th century by the nomadic Meknassa tribe, who were drawn to this fertile area of abundant water.

The Almohades and Merenids embellished the city with mosques and *medersas*, but it remained a small provincial town until 1672, when the new king Moulay Ismail made it his capital. Moulay Ismail greatly admired the French sun King Louis XIV and was keen to encourage cooperation between Morocco and France. Architecture was his passion and in Meknes he built huge palaces, mosques and walls, sometimes with marble plundered from Volubilis (► 126–127) and Marrakech's el-Badi Palace (► 62). Soon after his death in 1727 his dream city fell into ruins, looted by his successors and damaged by the effects of the 1755 Lisbon earthquake.

Place el-Hedim is where the imperial city and the medina meet. Monumental **Bab Mansour**, with fine *zellig* decoration and ancient columns from Volubilis, is often used as a promotional symbol for the city, and even the whole country. Just past the gate the large, central square of **Lalla Aouda** is a popular meeting place for families. This was the processional square of **Dar el-Kebira**, Moulay Ismail's palace with 24 separate compounds, secluded gardens and mosques, most of which were destroyed by his son. A gate in the southwest corner of the square leads to the pavilion of **Koubbet el-Khiyatin**, which was used by Ismail to receive foreign dignitories.

Through the left-hand arch is the sumptuous **Tomb of Moulay Ismail**, which attracts pilgrims from all over the country. Only the courtyard can be visited, however, but the decoration, restored by King Mohammed V, is rich and exquisite. On the opposite side is

A Cruel Sultan

Morocco's most brutal ruler was Moulay Ismail, who reigned from 1672 to 1727. He reputedly had a harem of over 500 women, with whom he fathered 700 sons and countless daughters, all ruled by the heavy hand and heavier whip of his legitimate wife, Sultana Zidana. His plans for the new capital required the labour of some 50,000 captives. It's said that if the sultan was not happy with the work, he would crush the worker's head with a brick, decapitate him or slit his throat. Their blood was mixed with the cement.

Imperial Cities and Middle Atlas

The vast old granaries of the Heri es Souani are the most impressive sight of the Imperial City

Dar el-Makhzen, a "small" royal palace. Another impressive sight is **Heri es Souani** (or Dar el-Ma), the vast imperial granary. Next to it the **Aguedal Tank**, a huge basin that once supplied water to the palaces and gardens, is now a popular picnic spot.

On the other side of place el-Hedim is the **Dar Jamaï Museum**, a 19th-century palace, which has fine Moroccan arts and a tranquil Andalucian garden. The main street of the souk is **Souk es Sebat**, leading to the 14th-century **Bou Inania Medersa**, one of the country's finest. Outside Bab el-Berdain, the *marabout* of Sidi ben Aissa (closed to non-Muslims) is the centre of one of Morocco's largest *moussems* on the eve of Mouloud – the Prophet Mohammed's birthday.

TAKING A BREAK

The rooftop café of the **Heri es Souani** has great views. Try the **Restaurant Riad** in Dar el-Kebira for lunch and **el-Hedim's market** for snacks. In the late afternoon and evening head for the **Ville Nouvelle**. Stop at **Patisserie Moosberger** (avenue Hassan II, near the Marché Central), which has excellent Moroccan sweets and French gâteaux.

🕂 183 E3

🚌 Buses from Fes, Tangier, Rabat, Ouezzane and Chefchaouen
🚆 Trains from Fes, Tangier, Rabat, Oujda and Taza

Dar el-Ma
✉ Imperial City
🕐 Daily 9–noon, 3–6; closed Aid el-Kebir (a moveable Islamic festival depending on the lunar calendar, but about 10 weeks after Ramadan)
💰 Inexpensive

Koubbet el Khiyatin
✉ Bab Fillala, off place Lalla Aouda
🕐 Daily 9–noon, 3–6
💰 Inexpensive

Tomb of Moulay Ismail
✉ Imperial City
🕐 Daily 9–noon, 3–6; closed Fri morning
💰 Inexpensive

Dar Jamaï Museum
✉ place el-Hedime
☎ (05) 5530863
🕐 Wed–Mon 9–noon, 3–6; closed national and religious holidays
💰 Inexpensive

Medersa Bou Inania
✉ rue Sebat, medina
🕐 Daily 9–noon, 3–6
💰 Inexpensive

Haras Stud Farm
✉ Outside Meknes, on the road to Azrou
☎ (05) 5539753
🕐 Mon–Fri 9–12, 3–5
🚌 Buses 14, 15 and 16 from the Ville Nouvelle

MEKNES: INSIDE INFO

Top tips Official guides wait near Bab Mansour, but both the city and medina are fairly **easy to get around**.

Hidden gems Check out the *kissarias* in the souks, with shops selling textiles, as they are better preserved than those of Marrakech.
• Just outside town you'll find the amazing **Haras stud farm**, home to some of the world's most valuable Arab horses and mules (▶ 138).

At Your Leisure

4 Taza

Perched impressively on the edge of a plateau, the medina of Taza overlooks the strategic pass between the Rif and the Middle Atlas, the origin of numerous invasions. It was said that whoever ruled Taza would eventually conquer Fes. A tour of the Almohad walls offers great views, while a walk in the charming medina leads through partially covered souks and past grand houses with beautiful, heavy, wooden doors and ornate window grilles.

✠ 186 A4 ✉ 120km east of Fes
🚌 Buses from Fes, Oujda and Nador
🚆 Trains from Fes, Oujda and Meknes

The picturesque village of Moulay-Idriss takes its name from the "Father of Morocco"

5 Moulay-Idriss

Morocco's most sacred village, hugging Jebel Zerhoun, is arguably also one of the most picturesque. Although its main attraction – the tomb of its eponymous founder – is closed to non-Muslims (who are also not allowed to stay overnight in the village), its beautiful alleys and narrow streets are well worth a visit, particularly combined with nearby Volubilis (➤ 126–127). Moulay Idriss I, a *sherif* (descendant of the Prophet Mohammed), founded the first Muslim kingdom in Morocco in the 8th century when he came from Mecca and converted the Berbers in Oualili to Islam.

A year later he founded Fes, and is considered the "Father of Morocco". Every August, the country's largest *moussem* attracts pilgrims from all over Morocco for several weeks.

✠ 183 E4 ✉ 30km north of Meknes 🚌 Bus from Fes; *grand taxi* from Meknes

6 Imouzzèr-du-Kandar

In summer, Fassis come to this Berber village and mountain resort to enjoy the cooler air, the parks, the tree-shaded avenues and a swimming pool filled with spring water. A souk is held every Monday in the ruined kasbah of the Aït Seghrouchen, which features the Seghrouchen tribe's unusual underground habitations. These offer increased security and protection from heat and cold. A track east out of town leads to the watchtower on Jebel Abad, from

Imperial Cities and Middle Atlas

where it's a short walk to the summit for spectacular views.
🞤 183 F3 ✉ 40km south of Fes
🚌 Bus from Fes

7 Sefrou
This ancient walled city, nestled in the foothills of the Middle Atlas, features a small, picturesque and charming medina that's ideal for a leisurely wander. Sefrou was strongly influenced by its once-thriving Jewish community, though Moulay Idriss I (► 122) passed through on his way from Mecca and converted many of its Berber and Jewish inhabitants to Islam. In the hills, within easy walking distance of the medina, are several springs and waterfalls.
🞤 183 F3 ✉ 28km south of Fes
🚌 Bus from Fes

8 Azrou
The charm of this small town of pretty, whitewashed houses with green-tiled roofs perhaps lies in its tranquillity. Built on the crossroads of two important routes (Meknes to Tafilalt and Fes to Marrakech) it's the main market for the semi-nomadic Beni Mguild Berber tribe, who cultivate lands in the mountains. In winter they descend to the plains with their herds and in summer they climb to the higher forests. Azrou is famous for its Berber carpets and cedarwood carving, on sale at the **Ensemble Artisanal** or the Tuesday souk. It also makes a perfect base for hiking the vast and beautiful cedar forests near by.
🞤 183 E3 ✉ 80km south of Fes
🚌 Buses from Meknes, Fes, Midelt, Ifrane and Casablanca

Ensemble Artisanal
✉ Town centre, near the Grand Mosque ☎ (05) 5562430 🕒 Sat–Thu 8:30–noon, 2:30–6:30

9 Midelt
Midelt, a friendly and relaxed town of red-tiled, French colonial chalets at the foot of Jebel Ayachi, makes a pleasant stop on the road between the Middle and the High Atlas. It's also an excellent base for hiking in summer or skiing in winter. Berbers in the surrounding villages make beautiful carpets and embroideries, which are sold in the kasbah at the **Atelier de Tissage**, run by Franciscan nuns. About 25km out of town on Road 3419 you'll find a

Berbers at the carpet shops enter negotiations with a fortifying cup of mint tea

beautiful gorge along the Oued Moulouya.
🞤 183 F2 ✉ 125km southeast of Azrou

Atelier de Tissage
✉ Kasbah Miriem, on the road to Tataouine ☎ (05) 5582443 🕒 Daily, but weavers do not work Fri, Sun and Aug

10 Beni-Mellal
On the road from Fes to Marrakech, Beni-Mellal is a green

At Your Leisure

> **5 Great Picnic Spots**
> - **Cascades d'Ouzoud** (➤ below)
> - **Volubilis** (➤ 126–127)
> - The pools near **Immouzèr-du-Kandar** (➤ 131)
> - **Heri es Souani** and **Aguedal Tank**, Meknes (➤ 130)
> - The hills outside **Sefrou** (➤ 132)

and pleasant town whose lushness is due to its many springs and its location near the Bin el-Ouidane dam. The town is surrounded by olive groves and citrus plantations, its oranges claimed to be the best in Morocco. The oldest and most pleasant part of town lies within the Kasbah Bel Kush, built by Moulay Ismail in the 17th century, but almost entirely rebuilt in the 19th. The **Aïn Asserdoun** ("Source of the Mule") is a powerful spring 3.5km south of town that feeds the orchards and the adjacent modern public garden. The restored stone fortress of **Borj Ras el-Ain** (about 1km further on) commands wonderful views over the town.

🟥 183 D2
✉ 190km south of Fes
🚌 Buses from Fes, Marrakech and Azilal

⓫ Cascades d'Ouzoud

A popular excursion from Beni-Mellal, these 110m waterfalls are one of Morocco's most beautiful natural sights. Don't be tempted to dive into the shallow pools at their base; instead admire the falls from the promontory near Café Immouzzer, where you can see the water cascade through a permanent rainbow. The striking surroundings include red cliffs, oleanders and wildlife such as turtles, crabs and monkeys. Stunning the falls may be, but the site can get overcrowded, particularly at weekends or during the summer when Moroccan students camp in the area.

🟥 183 D2
✉ 120km southwest of Beni-Mellal
🚌 *Grands taxis* from Beni-Mellal

The Cascades d'Ouzoud are a popular day trip for local Moroccans

⓬ Imilchil

Nestled remotely amid spectacular scenery in the heart of the High Atlas is this pleasant and authentic town. Although it's only accessible by 4X4, it's definitely worth the effort for the famous wedding festival. However, a new highway was due to open near by in 2002. The Berber Aït Haddidou tribe meets here every September to celebrate the feast of the local saint. But this festival is now better known as an occasion for young Berber men and beautifully dressed girls to meet the partner of their dreams, to get married (or sometimes divorced). It is a spectacular event with dancing, singing and romance. The event has been so overrun by tour groups that the tribe now holds one event for tourists, and one for themselves, only announcing the date of the latter at the last minute.

🟥 183 E2 ✉ 45km northwest of Agoudal 🚌 Four-wheel-drive from Fes, Meknes and Marrakech (expensive)

134 Imperial Cities and Middle Atlas

Where to... Stay

Prices

Expect to pay for a double room, including breakfast and taxes
£ under 640dh **££** 640–1,600dh **£££** over 1,600dh

When in Fes, the place to stay is in or near the medina, close to most of the sights and monuments. However, many budget options in the medina are either dirty or have water problems. There is a better range of inexpensive or mid-priced hotels in the Ville Nouvelle, although some recent *riad* conversions are a welcome change.

Amros ££

A pleasant mountain hotel, surrounded by superb scenery, which is a great base for hikers who want to explore the Middle Atlas. The rooms are cosy and comfortable,

but the food isn't great. The roof and chimneys are covered in storks' nests and, when in residence, the birds provide a wonderful spectacle.

✚ 183 E3 ◻ 6km south of Azrou, on the road to Meknes ☎ (05) 5563663; fax: (05) 5563680

Bab Mansour ££

This modern hotel is very popular with tour groups and businessmen and offers spacious *en suite* rooms, each with TV, telephone and excellent beds. There's no swimming pool, but you can dance the night away at the popular nightclub.

✚ 183 F3 ◻ 38 rue Emir Abdelkader, Meknes ☎ (05) 5525239; fax: (05) 5510741

Hotel Batha £

Situated right outside the medina, this modern building is in traditional *riad* style. It has 62 spotless rooms with bathroom, TV, air-conditioning and telephone, surrounding a courtyard. There's also a swimming pool. Book well in advance.

✚ 183 F4 ◻ place Batha, Fes ☎ (05) 5634860; fax: (05) 5741078

Grand Hotel £

One of the first to be built in Fes, this old colonial hotel boasts a very central location, overlooking the gardens on place Mohammed V. Behind an impressive art deco façade, its 80 spacious rooms have high ceilings and *en suite* bathrooms, although only some have air-conditioning.

✚ 183 F4 ◻ Southern end of boulevard Chefchaouni, Ville Nouvelle, Fes ☎ (05) 5932026; fax: (05) 5653847

Hotel-Restaurant Islane £

One of the few places to stay in Imilchil, this tiny hotel has some

clean but spartan bedrooms. The owner is very friendly and knowledgeable about the area and can recommend Berber friends who work as guides in the mountains.

✚ 183 E2 ◻ Imilchil, near the main village square ☎ (02) 3442806

Kasbah Asmaa ££

This converted *pisé* kasbah offers 30 comfortable *en suite* rooms, some with a fireplace and superb views over the mountains. Meals are served in salons around the courtyard or, in summer, in Berber tents in the beautiful garden. For those on a budget the hotel also rents out sleeping bags for use in a dormitory or on a terrace. The owner organises hikes and mule excursions.

✚ 183 F2 ◻ 3km outside Midelt, on the road to Er Rachidia ☎ (05) 5583945; fax: (05) 5580405

La Maison Bleue £££

The entrance to this early 20th-century *riad* is through a gateway from a busy square, but once inside all is calm and peaceful. Its six individual suites, all stylishly furnished with local antiques, overlook a blue-and-white tiled courtyard or the medina. The restaurant, in a beautiful salon, serves pastillas, tagines and couscous on the owner's family silver. The house is also known for its elegant Fassi evenings, when a set menu of delicious salads, tagines, dessert and wine is accompanied by live classical *oud* or Gnaoua music. The owners also run a less expensive and livelier bed and breakfast with a pool near by.

➕ 183 F4 ☒ 2 place de l'Istiqlal Batha, Fes ☎ (05) 5636052; fax: (05) 5741843; maisonbleue@festnet. net.ma

Majestic £

This old-style, appealing hotel in the Ville Nouvelle has particularly friendly staff. All rooms have a bathroom or shower, heating and balcony, but those facing the street can be noisy despite being larger and more airy. Breakfast is served in a lovely courtyard.

➕ 183 E3 ☒ 19 avenue Mohammed V, Meknes ☎ (05) 5522035; fax: (05) 5527427; majestic-hotel@excite.fr

Menzeh Zalagh ££

This beautiful S-shaped hotel in 1960s style is set in a lovely garden with an olive grove and swimming pool. The tiled rooms, some overlooking the medina, are spacious and have gorgeous bathrooms, but rooms on the first floor above the nightclub can be noisy.

➕ 183 F4 ☒ 10 rue Mohammed Diouri, Ville Nouvelle, Fes ☎ (05) 5932234; fax: (05) 5651995; menzeh.zalagh@fesnet.net.ma

Palais Jamaï £££

Set in an 18th-century pleasure pavillion built by a major Fassi family, this is the place to stay if you can afford it. Some rooms overlook the ramparts, but opt for the rooms on the other side that offer magnificent views over the medina and the mature Andalucian garden with *zellig* decoration and fountains. The views are particularly spectacular at night, with the lights of the medina and the floodlit mosque at its centre. Non-residents can have dinner at al-Fassia restaurant (▲ 136) or a drink on the terrace.

➕ 183 F4 ☒ Bab Jamaï, medina, Fes ☎ (05) 5634331; fax: (05) 5635096; cresa@palais.jamai.co.uk

Riad al-Bartel ££

A French couple run this small hotel of five amazing suites in a 1930s trader's house. The ordinary facade hides a splendid interior – the rooms have high ceilings, blue-and-white tiled walls and are heavily stuccoed in traditional Fes style. The rest of the decor is more eclectic, a mixture of beautiful local finds and old French furniture, and the marvellous bathrooms are decorated in mosaics. Children are welcome, too.

➕ 183 F4 ☒ 21 rue Sournas, Ziat, Fes ☎ and fax: (05) 5637053

Transatlantique ££–£££

With rooms spread over two wings, this is the most luxurious hotel in town, although there's not really much competition. The old Moroccan wing has charming rooms with painted doors and *zellig* tiles, while the modern wing has cosier, European-style rooms. Whichever section you choose, ask for a room overlooking one of the well-kept garden's two swimming pools and the medina.

➕ 183 E3 ☒ rue el-Miryine, Meknes ☎ (05) 5525050; fax: (05) 5520057

Hotel Volubilis ££

Set in a well-maintained garden, with superb views over the valley and the site of Volubilis, this is a delightful and very peaceful upmarket hotel. There's a lovely, refreshing swimming pool, and good food is on offer in the panoramic restaurant.

➕ 183 E4 ☒ 1km north of Volubilis on the main road ☎ (05) 5544405; fax: (05) 5636393

136 Imperial Cities and Middle Atlas

Where to...
Eat and Drink

Prices
Expect to pay for a three-course meal, excluding drinks but including taxes and service
£ under 160dh ££ 160–350dh £££ over 350dh

Annexe de Metropolis ££

This Moroccan restaurant is set in splendid stucco and mosaic surroundings. It uses fresh produce from the market next door to prepare simple dishes, such as salads, couscous and tagines.

➕ 183 E3 ✉ 11 rue Sherif Idrissi, Ville Nouvelle, Meknes ☎ (05) 5525668 🕐 Daily 10 am–10 pm

Hotel Atlas £

Everyone sits at one long table in this tiny but popular family-run restaurant. Mother cooks simple but delicious Moroccan specialities, including a quince and chicken tagine, and *bissarha* – a hearty peasant soup made of fava beans.

➕ 183 F2 ✉ rue Mohammed Amraoui, Midelt ☎ (05) 582938 🕐 Daily lunch and dinner

El-Baraka de Zerhoun ££

This excellent and popular restaurant in a small white building offers high-quality local dishes, including the renowned Zerhoun olives, a spicy salad and chicken tagine with preserved lemons. No alcohol is served.

➕ 183 E4 ✉ 22 Ain Smen Khiber, on the road to Moulay-Idriss ☎ (05) 5544184 🕐 Daily lunch and dinner

Dar Saada ££

Four Moroccan menus, including a selection of salads, *harira* and various tagines or couscous, are served in the courtyard of a palace in the medina. Despite its location near the Grand Mosque, alcoholic drinks are served. Booking is advisable.

➕ 183 F4 ✉ Souk Attarin, Fes el-Bali, Fes ☎ (05) 5637370 🕐 Daily lunch only

Le Dauphin ££

Le Dauphin offers a varied menu with French brasserie and Moroccan dishes, and is one of the only restaurants in town that specialises in fresh fish and shellfish. The décor is plush and comfortable, and the waiters swift. There's even a separate room for noisy tour groups.

➕ 183 E3 ✉ 5 avenue Mohammed V, Ville Nouvelle, Meknes ☎ (05) 5523423 🕐 Daily noon–3, 7–11

Al-Fassia £££

The grand Palais Jamaï hotel's restaurant offers an interesting Moroccan menu, slick service and a romantic setting in a tiled hall. The food comes with an excellent show of belly dancers and musicians. If you want to try some of the labour-intensive Fassi specialities, such as one of the best *pastillas* in the country, roast lamb shoulder or sea bass with *chermoula*, order them the night or morning before.

➕ 183 F4 ✉ Palais Jamaï hotel, Bab Jamaï, medina, Fes 🕐 Daily 7.30–11 pm

Zagora ££

This trendy restaurant serves more sophisticated Moroccan and international cuisine than most, in colourful, contemporary surroundings. The set menu, which includes *harira* soup, *pastilla*, tagine and a Moroccan dessert, is good value, while the à la carte menu offers a range of well-prepared dishes. The service is efficient and friendly.

➕ 183 F4 ✉ 5 boulevard Mohammed V, Ville Nouvelle, Fes ☎ (05) 5940686 🕐 Daily lunch and dinner

Where to...
Shop

ARTS AND CRAFTS

The **souks** in the medina in **Fes** are open Mon–Sat 9–8. Some also open on Sunday, while others close for Friday prayers around lunchtime. You'll find a large concentration of shops selling leather, ceramics, carpets, metalwork and musical instruments. Another good place in the city is the **Ensemble Artisanal** on avenue Allal ben Abdallah (tel: (05) 5625654), which has workshops and a large shop selling very reasonably priced local crafts.

Fes reputedly produces the best *babouches* (leather slippers) in the country. The best and most expensive are made from *ziouani* goatskin with no visible stitching. You'll find the main **leather souk** on rue ech

Cherabliyin, the continuation of rue Talla Kebira leading from the Medersa Bou Inania to the Medersa el-Attarin (▶ 124). Fes is also famous for its blue-and-white **pottery**, found in the Potters' Quarter at the edge of the city on the road to Taza, and particularly in the shop of **Fakhkhari Hamida.**

Souk Joutiya ez Zerabi (closed Sun), in an arcade off the textile souk in **Meknes** medina, sells good-quality carpets at a price, but it's worth bargaining. Near Bab el-Jedid is a small **flea market** (closed Sun) and a **souk** where you can buy handmade traditional musical instruments such as *ouds* (classical Arab lutes), *lotars* (Berber lutes), *rababs* (fiddles) and *tabls* (drums). The **Souk es Sebbat** (behind Dar Jamai) and the *kissarias* sell more tourist-orientated items such as jewellery, kaftans, *kelims* and carpets. For pottery head for the **Village des Potiers** in the Oued Boufekrane, between Hotel Transatlantique and Bab Berdain.

Azrou has a long tradition of producing carpets and blankets, and some good examples are sold in the Tuesday souk on the Khenifra road near the Grand Mosque. Alternatively, the **Ensemble Artisanal** sells work from the local weaving school, which was founded to preserve traditional patterns and to experiment with new designs inspired by them.

The Saturday market in **Souk Sebt des Oulad Nemaa**, 35km southwest of **Beni-Mellal**, is the largest in the Middle Atlas, where Berbers from all over the region sell their excellent carpets at reasonable prices. A good selection of Berber blankets, carpets and gorgeous embroideries are also available from the shop at **Kasbah Miriem** run by Franciscan nuns, 500m from central **Midelt** on the 3418 road (tel: (05) 5582443; ▶ 132). The prices may be slightly higher than elsewhere, but the quality is superior. Carpets are also sold in the small daily souk in the centre of

Midelt and at the Thursday souk in **Sefrou's** small medina.

JEWELLERY AND ANTIQUES

Berrada, at 40 boulevard Mohammed V in Fes, runs the most famous silver shop in Morocco, producing jewellery and other objects for the king. **Mohammed ben Abdeljali** (35 rue Talaa Seghira) sells a good selection of antiques and *objets d'art*. The jewellery souk in the medina at **Sefrou** has silver items inspired by the town's Jewish heritage.

GIFTS

Spices, essential oils and traditional herbal potions and remedies are on sale in the **Souk el-Henna**, just off place en Nejjarine in Fes. To the left of place el-Hedim in Meknes is a beautiful covered market (Mon–Sat 9 am–7 pm, but some stalls close 2–5 pm) selling fresh produce, spices and dried fruits.

138 Imperial Cities and Middle Atlas

Where to...
Be Entertained

SPORT AND LEISURE

The mountains of the Middle Atlas are gorgeous and less visited than many other parts of the country. The region is perfect for **hiking**, particularly around Sefrou, Taza, Midelt and south of Azrou. From December to March there's often enough snow for **skiing**, but don't count on it. **Mischliffen**, the crater of an old volcano 12km from Ifrane (50km south of Fes), has some antiquated but functional ski-lifts and equally old-fashioned rental equipment. About 35km southeast of Fes is also **Jebel Bou Iblane** (3,190m) with just one ski-lift.

Anglers will find the region's lakes and rivers well stocked with a variety of fish, including trout, bass and pike. You'll need your own

equipment and a permit from the Water and Forest Department (11 rue du Devoir in Rabat). The same organisation can also provide **hunting** permits, while the **Royal Moroccan Hunting Federation** (rue Akhlil, Rabat; tel and fax: (03) 7707835) has further information.

Horse-riders can visit the largest stud farm in Morocco at the **Haras of Meknes** (tel: (05) 5539753), on the road to Azrou (bus 14 or 16 from the Ville Nouvelle). You can also take out temporary membership to exercise or ride the horses. Riding is also possible at the **Club Equestre** in Moulay Idriss at the racecourse (tel: (05) 5623438).

If your hotel in Fes lacks a **swimming** pool the best in town is at the **Hotel Zalagh** on rue Mohammed Diouri in the Ville

Nouvelle, where non-residents can swim for a fee. In summer swimming is also possible at two campsites: **International**, 3km out of town on the road to Sefrou (tel: (05) 5731439) and **Diamant Vert** in Ain Chkeff, 6km south of the city (tel: (05) 5608367). The two public swimming pools in Meknes are rather unhygienic, but most hotel pools there are open to non-residents.

Near Fes are two important **spa** villages, where Moroccans go in search of a cure for their ailments. **Sidi Harazem** (15km southeast) is the source of one of Morocco's most popular bottled waters and has age-old thermal baths and a swimming pool, but it does tend to be crowded. **Moulay Yaqoub** (20km northwest) also has thermal baths used for medical treatments.

MUSIC, THEATRE AND CINEMA

At the end of June each year, the prestigious Festival of Sacred Music

takes place in Fes, when international artistes perform at Dar Batha (► 122) and other venues around town (tel: (05) 5740535; www.fezfestival.com).

In Meknes, as elsewhere in Morocco, the **Institut Franeflais in Zenkat Farhat Hached** (avenue Hassan II; tel: (05) 5524071) organises concerts, films and exhibitions (call for details). The Fes branch can be found at 33 rue Loukili, Ville Nouvelle; tel: (05) 5623921. Meknes also holds an international theatre festival during the first ten days of July in the Jardins Haboul. The tourist office has details.

NIGHTLIFE

While in Meknes, the bars can be seedy, but you can try the lively **nightclub** (daily 9 pm–3 am) at the **Hotel Volubilis** (45 avenue des FAR; tel: (05) 5525082) and the **Cabaret Oriental** on avenue Hassan II, which sometimes features live local bands.

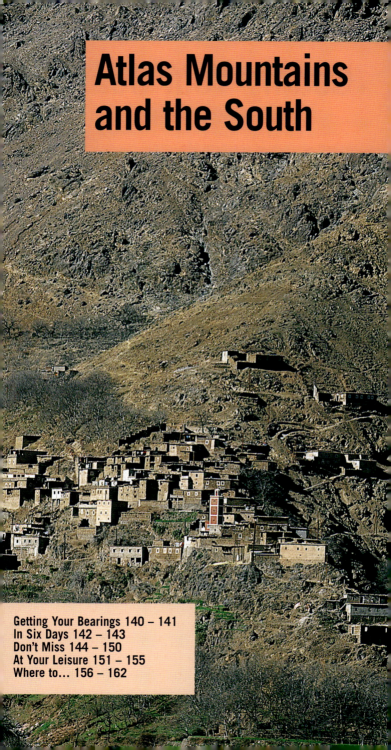

Atlas Mountains and the South

Getting Your Bearings 140 – 141
In Six Days 142 – 143
Don't Miss 144 – 150
At Your Leisure 151 – 155
Where to... 156 – 162

Atlas Mountains and the South

Getting Your Bearings

Tourism has arrived since Edith Wharton wrote of southern Morocco's feudal chiefs and heat and savagery in her book *In Morocco* (1929). But the south is still exotic, and the chance of adventure remains. The tourist images of Morocco are often of the south: endless ripples of immaculate sand dunes, grand kasbahs, oases with thousands of palm trees, Berber villages hugging the mountains, and the "blue men" – nomadic Tuaregs who epitomise adventure and harsh desert life. But perhaps most evocative of the region are the majestic peaks of the High Atlas, where Africa really begins.

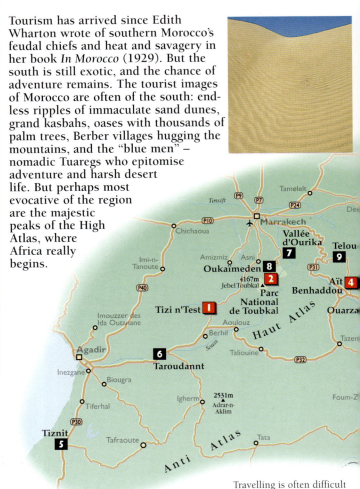

Travelling is often difficult here, but almost every road offers spectacular vistas. Tourist facilities may be less luxurious than elsewhere, but there are plenty of other delights. The region has kept its authenticity and many of its traditions – the isolation of its villages gave rise to many reformist movements, including Ibn Toumert's Almohads. Life is hard in these extreme landscapes, but it's also simple and often joyous, and the people, mostly Berbers, are friendly and welcoming.

Getting Your Bearings 141

★ Don't Miss

1. Tizi n'Test ➤ 144
2. Toubkal National Park (Parc National de Toubkal) ➤ 146
3. The Dadès Valley: La Route des Kasbahs ➤ 148
4. Aït Benhaddou ➤ 150

At Your Leisure

5. Tiznit ➤ 151
6. Taroudannt ➤ 151
7. Ourika Valley ➤ 152
8. Oukaïmeden ➤ 152
9. Telouet ➤ 152
10. Ouarzazate ➤ 153
11. Zagora ➤ 153
12. Tamegroute ➤ 154
13. Mhamid ➤ 154
14. Tinerhir ➤ 154
15. Erfoud ➤ 155
16. Merzouga ➤ 155

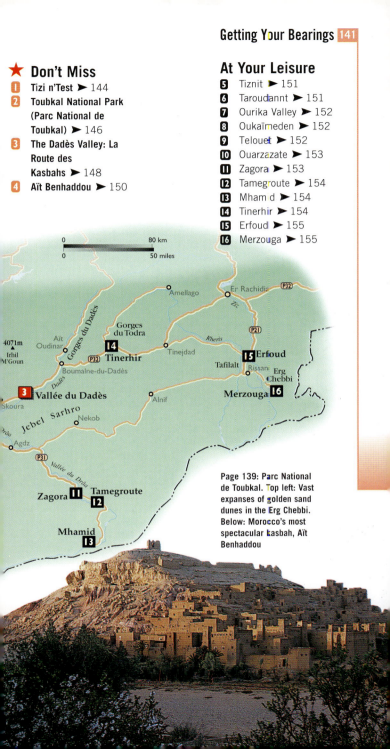

Page 139: Parc National de Toubkal. Top left: Vast expanses of golden sand dunes in the Erg Chebbi. Below: Morocco's most spectacular Kasbah, Aït Benhaddou

Atlas Mountains and the South

Morocco's most exotic region includes its highest mountains, its hottest desert and its most picturesque kasbahs.

The South in Six Days

Day One

Morning
Start from the market town of **6 Taroudannt** (➤ 151) and take the P32 to Oualed Behril (39km) for refreshments at Riad Heda, a former palace (tel: (04) 8531226). Beyond the village, take the S201 to the panoramic **1 Tizi n'Test pass** (➤ 144–145), and the **Mosque of Tin Mal** (pictured above). Have lunch in **Ouirgane** at La Bergerie (➤ 156).

Afternoon
Go for a walk or a horse ride in **2 Toubkal National Park** (Parc National de Toubkal, ➤ 146–147) around Ouirgane, especially the **Gorges Nfiss**, a popular picnic spot. Stay overnight in Ouirgane or continue 16km to Asni (➤ 144).

Day Two

Morning
Drive to Marrakech, then follow signs for Ouarzazate via the **Tizi n'Tichka** mountain road (➤ 170–172). Turn left after the highest point for the kasbah of **9 Telouet** (➤ 152–153). Have lunch opposite Glaoui kasbah (➤ 152, 171).

Afternoon
Return to the main road and turn left before Ouarzazate to explore the ksar of **4 Aït Benhaddou** (left; ➤ 150), then continue to Ouarzazate.

Day Three

Morning
Spend time exploring **10 Ouarzazate** (➤ 153), then continue to the **Atlas film studios** and have lunch at the **Kasbah Tiffoultoute** (tel: (04) 4885899), 8km west of town on the P31E to Zagora.

Afternoon
Take the **3 Dadès Valley: La Route des Kasbahs** (Vallée du Dadès, ➤ 148–149) to Skoura for a stroll through the palms and a visit to the kasbahs of **Dar Aït Sidi el-Mati** and **Amerdihil**. Drive on to **Kelaa M'Gouna** and its rose gardens, before heading for **Boulmane du Dadès** and a night in the Kasbah Tizzarouine.

Day Four

Morning
Take the 6901 towards **Msemrir**, following the Dadès Valley (above). After Aït Oudinar cross the bridge to reach the **Dadès** and **Todra gorges**, after which the road becomes a piste. Lunch at Auberge Chez Pierre (➤ 158).

Afternoon
The auberge and other places in the area offer 4X4 excursions to isolated Berber villages, along difficult pistes with spectacular mountain views, but you need to book in advance (tel: (04) 4830267). Alternatively, walk in the gorges before returning to the Chez Pierre for the night.

Day Five

Morning
Start early for the 75km drive to **14 Tinerhir** (➤ 154) and enjoy views over the palmeraie from the Hotel Saghro, north of town. Or rent a bike from the Hotel Tomboctoo (➤ 157), explore the oasis then return for lunch.

Afternoon
Drive north following the Todra River to the Hotel Yasmina at the entrance to the **Todra Gorges**. Admire the gorges on foot, then return for the night.

Day Six

Morning
Return to Tinerhir early and take the P32 to Tinejdad and then the 3451 – lined with kasbahs, palmeraies and oases – east towards Erfoud. About 2km from town stop for lunch at the Kasbah Tizimi (tel: (05) 5576179).

Afternoon
Continue to **15 Erfoud** (➤ 155), a good base for exploring the region. Book a four-wheel-drive with guide in advance from the Salam hotel (➤ 157), about 200m from town on the road to Rissani to visit the sand dunes in **16 Merzouga** (➤ 155). Return to the Salam for the night.

Atlas Mountains and the South

Tizi n'Test

The Tizi n'Test pass lies on a road that cuts through the High Atlas between Asni and Taroudannt. As well as being an amazing feat of engineering, the road is also one of the most spectacular in Morocco.

Ibn Toumert
After studying in the Orient, the 12th-century Berber Mohammed ibn Toumert returned to Morocco convinced that the country's Islamic faith needed purifying. When he forced the king's sister off her horse because she was not veiled, he was banished from Marrakech and set up a base in Tin Mal, where he declared himself the Mahdi or "Chosen One". In exile he and his lieutenant Abd el-Moumen preached to the Berbers, formed a religious and military force – the Almohad or "Unitarian" movement – and went on to conquer Morocco and southern Spain.

As a main access to the south of the country, the highway has played a significant role in Morocco's history. Before the road was built, the mountain Berbers could easily close the pass and block the passage to the south. But since the French opened the Tizi n'Test in November 1928, the south and the mountains have become much more accessible.

The Tizi n'Test starts at **Asni**, a pleasant little town in a fruit-growing area and with an interesting Saturday souk. This is the turn-off point for Imlil and hikes in the High Atlas. After Asni the landscape gets increasingly dramatic – the mountains become wilder and more barren as you climb, and there is often snow on the peaks. **Ouirgane**, a peaceful village 16km away with a few comfortable hotels serving good food, makes an excellent hiking base. The road follows the Nfiss River, which is full of trout in spring.

Tizi n'Test

At the beginning of the 20th century the Tizi n'Test was controlled by the powerful Goundafa family, who built several kasbahs along the way. These include the privately owned one at **Agadir n'Gouj**, just before the Almohad **Great Mosque of Tin Mal** that rises high up above the Tizi n'Test on a mountain slope. Looking more like a fortress than a mosque, it was built by Abd el-Moumen in around 1153 as a cult centre for his leader Ibn Toumert (see box).

About 8km further south is the 19th-century kasbah of **Tagoundaft** perched on a steep rock. Another 22km from here is the actual *col* (pass) of the Tizi n'Test which, at 2,092m, offers panoramic views over Toubkal (➤ 146–147) and the Sous Valley. Once past the *col* the road descends steeply, dropping about 1,600m in less than 30km. Along the road, picturesque hamlets overlook cultivated terraces.

Left: A different view is around every bend of this spectacular highway. **Below:** The valleys are dotted with small Berber villages

TAKING A BREAK

Café La Belle Vue (1km past the *col*) really does have a great view and serves delicious tea and snacks. For something more elaborate try **Chez Momo** in Ouirgane, but book in advance (tel: (04) 4485704; ➤ 158).

🔳 184 C3
✉ Between Asni and Taroudannt
🚌 Buses from Marrakech

Great Mosque of Tin Mal
✉ 40km from Ouirgane
🕐 Sat–Thu; caretaker will open on demand
💰 Inexpensive (plus tip)

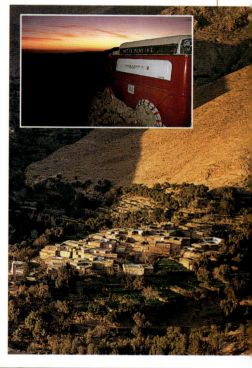

TIZI N'TEST: INSIDE INFO

Top tips From November to April the road can be blocked by snow. Signs in Asni, Marrakech and Tahanoute usually announce **road closures**, but check with tourist offices in Marrakech or Taroudannt beforehand.
• The best way to see it is by **driving yourself**, but experience of handling mountain roads is essential.
• **Avoid driving around midday** in summer as cars can overheat.
• Fill up before you leave as there are **no petrol stations** between Asni and Ouled Berrhill.

Atlas Mountains and the South

2 Toubkal National Park

On a clear day, the snow-capped peaks of Jebel Toubkal, the highest mountain in North Africa, are visible from both Taroudannt and Marrakech. Hiking in the mountains is becoming increasingly popular, which isn't surprising given the majestic landscapes, where lush garden terraces and little rivers contrast with the harsh, rocky wilderness. The reserved but friendly Berbers still maintain a fascinating and relatively traditional lifestyle in their picturesque villages.

The snow-covered peak of Jebel Toubkal

Jebel Toubkal rises to 4,167m, but even the surrounding mountains are all above 3,000m. The main paths are well trodden, particularly from Imlil to Jebel Toubkal, and are suitable for walkers of all levels (▶ 167–169). The full hike can be completed in about 16 hours, though going too fast may cause altitude sickness. Despite its popularity, the area is so vast that it is easy to escape the

Useful Addresses
For information on hiking in the Jebel Toubkal area, contact:
- **Tourist Office**
  ✉ avenue Mohammed V, Marrakech
  ☎ (04) 4436131; fax: (04) 4436057
- **Délégation de la Jeunesse et des Sports**
  ✉ stade du Hartsi, Marrakech
  ☎ (04) 4447448
- **Club Alpin Français (CAF)**
  ✉ PO Box 6178, Casablanca
  ☎ (02) 2270090

Toubkal National Park

"crowds" which, in reality and away from Toubkal itself, seldom comprise more than a few other walkers. The paths are generally well kept and there is a good network of refuges and *gîtes*; some villagers also rent out basic rooms in their houses for the night.

The small town of **Imlil**, at 1,740m, is the most obvious starting point for walks and hikes up Jebel Toubkal and around the area. It has shops selling or hiring out equipment and provisions, and numerous mountain guides and muleteers on hand; mules can be rented by the day to carry luggage and food.

An hour's walk away is **Aremd**, a gorgeous Berber village perched on a rock overlooking the surrounding plain. Most people sleep at the Neltner hut (3,207m) of the Club Alpin Français, four hours from Imlil, before climbing to Toubkal's summit, from where there are fantastic views. From Imlil, other paths lead to the main ski resort of **Oukaïmeden** (➤ 162) in about seven hours, the Berber village of Tachedirt (8km east of Imlil, about three to four hours) or to **Ouirgane**, a day away on the Tizi n'Test road.

The mountains are home to a variety of wildlife including several species of butterfly, squirrels, vultures, larks and golden eagles, and the local Berbers raise large herds of Barbary sheep and goats.

Several rivers and streams cut through these mountains and flash floods occur in the spring

Jebel Toubkal
🟥 184 C3
✉ 65km south of Marrakech
🚌 Buses from Marrakech and Taroudannt to Asni, then regular trucks to Imlil

TAKING A BREAK

Berber-run kiosks at popular stops sell tea, cold drinks and, occasionally, simple food. There are also **small restaurants** in Aremd and Imlil.

TOUBKAL NATIONAL PARK: INSIDE INFO

Top tips The **best time to visit the mountains** is in September and October or May and June; in summer visibility may be poor and thunderstorms or flash floods can occur. Between April and November, reasonably fit and determined walkers can also tackle the route. From December to March, snow, ice and short days make climbing to the top dangerous, even for experienced hikers.
• There are also other beautiful, **less demanding walks** on the lower slopes starting from Imlil, Aremd or Ouirgane (➤ 167–169).
• **Take** decent walking boots, hat, sun cream, sunglasses and plenty of water.
• The Toubkal Massif is popular in winter with **ski-mountaineering groups** and some of the descents, including Toubkal to Sidi Chamarouch, are spectacular.

In more depth For **more detailed information** on the great trails across the Atlas read Richard Knight's *Trekking in the Moroccan Atlas* and Michael Peyron's *Great Atlas Traverse* or other guidebooks available in Imlil.

Atlas Mountains and the South

3 The Dadès Valley: La Route des Kasbahs

The Dadès River drains off the peaks of the High Atlas and cuts a deep and dramatic gorge before it flows, more gently, into the Draa River. Most visitors follow the river upstream, from Ouarzazate to Tinerhir, taking in Berber settlements, surprising oases and, best of all, the spectacular gorges of Dadès and Todra.

The Dadès Valley (Vallée du Dadès) is often exaggeratedly described as the "road of a thousand kasbahs"; however, several kasbahs along the route are both beautiful and intriguing. Along most of the route the river is hardly visible above the ground and the P32 road follows the plain, which is flanked dramatically by the High Atlas and Jebel Sarhro on either side. Oases appear like mirages in this harsh and desolate landscape. This is certainly true for **Skoura** (30km east of Ouarzazate), one of the most beautiful oases, with lush vegetation and kasbahs appearing through the trees. At the entrance to this 17th-century oasis is the Kasbah de Ben Moro, now a fine hotel. Behind this you'll find **Amerdihil** – this is the most extravagant and impressive of all the Glaoui kasbahs. Directly across the river is the grand kasbah of **Dar Aït Sidi el-Mati**.

Another 50km on is the town of **el-Kelaa M'Gouna**, famous for its fields of pink *Rosa damascina*. About 4,000 tonnes are collected annually and distilled into rose water for cooking or essential oils for perfume. A rose festival is held each year in May or June. The town has a Wednesday souk, but rose water is always on sale in local shops and at the kasbah-like factory.

About 15km further along the main road is the hilltop

The long line of kasbahs along the Dadès River reveals an amazing variety of features, shapes and decorations

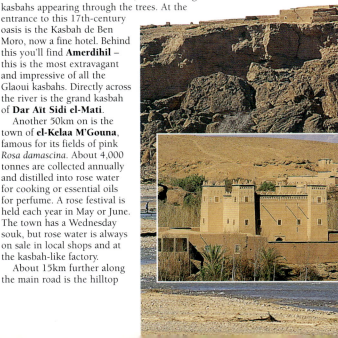

The Dadès Valley: La Route des Kasbahs

town of **Boulmane de Dadès**. This makes a perfect base for exploring the **Jebel Sarhro** region of volcanic peaks, gorges and picturesque Berber villages, and the **Vallée des Oiseaux** – a birdwatchers' paradise offering a wealth of species that include desert larks, eagle owls and sand grouse. The town is also the gateway to the **Gorge du Dadès**.

The route to the gorge, which veers off the main road, is spectacular in itself, lined with kasbahs and *ksour* amid luxuriant gardens. But the gorge, with its high limestone cliffs and strange rock formations, is definitely worth a detour. The kasbahs, many of which are still inhabited, come in all colours from chalk-white and earthy-reds to dark green.

The area of **Tamnalt**, 3km from Boulmane en route to the gorges, is also called the "Hill of Human Bodies" because of its bizarre rock formations. Further on, the river forms deep canyons past the bridge of **Aït Oudinar**. From here it's only possible to cross over to the Todra Gorge by four-wheel-drive. Otherwise you have to return to Boulmane de Dadès and continue to **Tinerhir** (➤ 154) to visit the extensive palmeraies and the **Todra Gorge**.

The setting sun turns the rocks of the Dadès Gorge a deep golden orange

TAKING A BREAK

The **Chems Hotel** in Boulmane serves good simple food on a terrace. The **Auberge Chez Pierre** in a *pisé* building near pont d'Aït Oudinar (tel: (04) 4830267) offers exceptional food.

The Dadès River meanders slowly past kasbahs in the broad valley at the foot of the High Atlas

THE DADÈS VALLEY: INSIDE INFO

Top tips You'll need a **rented car** (preferably four-wheel-drive) if you want to try out a few pistes. An ordinary car will do for the main sights. You can rent vehicles from the local hotels, which also organise guides for the more difficult treks in the area.

• In **palmeraies** such as Skoura you need to walk and the gardens are vast: to save time and effort it may be useful to hire a local guide.

• The best way to visit the valley around the Dadès Gorge is by **walking along the river**.

4 Aït Benhaddou

One of the best-preserved and most photogenic *ksour* in the Moroccan south features a cluster of deep-red houses and intricately decorated kasbahs on a steep rock towering over a shallow river.

185 D3
30km north-west of Ouarzazate
Daily 8–5
Grands taxis from Ouarzazate
Moderate

Aït Benhaddou was an important caravan stop between Ouarzazate and Marrakech, and the fortress commanded views over the entire area. It lost its importance when the French built the Tizi n'Tichka road in 1928 (▶ 170–172). However, a few families still live in the old village, some of whose buildings are said to be over 500 years old. As the *pisé* (mud-clay) from the riverbed used in the buildings threatens the *ksar*, Unesco has declared it a World Heritage Site and is slowly repairing the erosion to the amazing buildings.

The kasbah was so well protected that the way in is not always obvious, especially after the main entrance was apparently boarded up during a film shoot. Strangely, entry is now through a kitchen, which gives way to a small square from where you can easily explore the narrow streets, the Berber houses and the fortress at the top of a steep hill. Film buffs may recognise certain areas, as the *ksar* is a popular film location, seen in David Lean's epic *Lawrence of Arabia* (1962) and the Hollywood blockbuster *Gladiator* (2000).

TAKING A BREAK

Hollywood can't top this spectacular setting

Visit **La Kasbah** (▶ 156), a short walk across the river from the kasbah, for a cooling mint tea, a delicious set lunch and perhaps a dip in the pool. Stay overnight at the auberge or in one of several simple little hotels and see the changing colours of the *ksar* at sunset or by moonlight.

At Your Leisure

5 Tiznit

Standing on the arid Sous plains, the salmon-pink houses of Tiznit are enclosed by 6km of red mud ramparts. The town was founded at the end of the 19th century by Sultan Moulay Hassan, who brought in the Jewish craftsmen who made Tiznit famous for its fine silver jewellery, often regarded as the best in Morocco. Both traditional and contemporary styles can be found in the **jewellers' souk**. The minaret of the **Grand Mosque** is strewn with little perches, jutting out of the brickwork to provide resting places for the souls of the dead as they ascend to paradise. The style is unusual for Morocco, but is fairly common south of the Sahara. Near the mosque is the **tomb of Lalla Tiznit**, a prostitute who reformed and became extremely pious. Legend has it that when she was martyred, God created the pool across the street, which is rather optimistically known as the Source Bleue.

➕ 184 A2 ✉ 90km south of Agadir
🚌 Buses from Tata, Ifni, Agadir, Guelmim, Casablanca and Tafraoute

6 Taroudannt

At the heart of the fertile Sous Valley, this is the main market town in the area, renowned for its crafts – Berber jewellery, marble animal carvings and other sculpture, and heavy woollen cloaks and jellabas. Taroudannt's two souks, the **Souk Arabe Artisanal** and the **Marché Berbère**, are among the most relaxed in Morocco (Thursday and Sunday), with fewer touts and less pressure to buy. The town flourished during the 16th century when the Saadian kings made it their first capital before moving to Marrakech. They built the well-preserved, ochre city ramparts around the kasbah, but the rest of the walls and bastions date from the 18th century. The most pleasant way to admire them is by caleche, particularly at dusk or in moonlight. The **kasbah**, a village within the town, contains the winter palace of the Saadians, the ruins of a fortress built by Moulay Ismail and the wonderful Palais Salam hotel (▶ 157).

➕ 184 B3 ✉ 80km east of Agadir
🚌 Buses from Agadir, Ouarzazate, Marrakech and Essaouira

Taroudannt has a more African feel than the other cities in Morocco

Atlas Mountains and the South

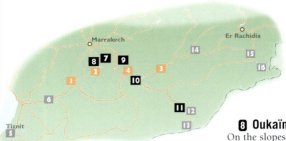

8 Oukaïmeden

On the slopes of Jebel Oukaïmeden, at 2,650m Morocco's premier ski resort is also the highest in Africa. The snow varies annually, but there can be good piste and off-piste skiing from mid-December to April. A ski-lift runs to the top of the mountain (3,273m) and guides are available for cross-country trips and skiing on other slopes. "Ouka" is also a summer resort, providing respite from the heat in Marrakech, or as a base for trekking in the surrounding area and Toubkal National Park (► 146–147).

🚩 184 C4 ✉ 74km south of Marrakech 🚌 Private car or taxi

Riding, walking or driving along the Ourika Valley are great ways to explore the nature of this region

7 Ourika Valley (Vallée d'Ourika)

Do as the Marrakchis when temperatures soar in the city, and escape to the gorgeous and lush Ourika Valley. You'll find country houses, small hotels, and numerous café-terraces, from where you can admire the views and enjoy the cooler climate. At km34 on the S513 road from Marrakech is **Tnine l'Ourika village**, which has an excellent Monday souk. The Ourika River curves through a deep-cut valley dotted with small mud-brick *douar* (villages). The road has superb viewpoints and follows the river up to Setti Fatma, ideal for a walk, a picnic and a dip in one of its waterfalls.

🚩 184 C4 ✉ Tourist office: valley entrance, route S513, km32 (Ourika) ☎ and fax (04) 4484858 🚌 Buses, minibuses, *grands taxis* from Marrakech

9 Telouet

The sleepy village of Telouet is overlooked by its magnificent crumbling **Glaoui kasbah**, built in the early 20th century. This remote spot now seems an unlikely place to built a fortress, but before the construction of the Tizi n'Tichka in 1928 (► 170–172) it

On Location at Atlas Studios

The Last Temptation of Christ (1988): controversial, but earning an Oscar for director Martin Scorsese and starring Willem Dafoe.
Kundun (1997): Martin Scorsese's biopic of the Dalai Lama.
Gladiator (2000): Ridley Scott, starring Russell Crowe and some great effects.

At Your Leisure

was an important caravan stop between Ouarzazate and Marrakech. For three years, 300 workers sculpted the walls and the ceilings of the headquarters of the powerful Glaoui brothers, but they were abandoned in 1956. The labyrinthine buildings are now fast melting back into the red earth, and today only a few of the sumptuous apartments are open to visitors.

🚩 185 D4 ✉ 21km east off the Tizi n'Tichka 🕐 Glaoui kasbah: no opening hours, but the caretaker is usually around during the day 🚌 Bus from Marrakech 💰 Free (tip the caretaker)

⑩ Ouarzazate

At the foot of the High Atlas, this is a good base for exploring the Sahara, the kasbahs and river valleys. This modern town, developed in the 1920s as a French garrison and administrative centre, is less picturesque than other Moroccan cities, which might explain why the anticipated tourism boom has not quite happened, in spite of its luxury facilities. However, the town's only sight – the **Taourirt kasbah** – is one of the most beautiful in Morocco. This sumptuous residence of the Glaoui family, built entirely in *pisé*, has remarkable decoration, but neglect means that only the courtyard and some very ornate rooms in the harem can be visited. There are great views over the kasbah from the terrace, and the **Centre Artisanal** opposite sells good-quality crafts. The **Atlas Studios** on the other side of town have earned Ouarzazate a reputation as the Hollywood of the desert. A rather surreal sight because of the grand film sets in a wilderness, the studios can usually be visited via the Oscar Salam Hotel inside the compound.

🚩 185 D3 ✉ 204km southeast of Marrakech

Tourist Office
✉ avenue Mohammed V, near the post office ☎ (04) 4882458

Taourirt Kasbah
✉ avenue Mohammed V, 1.5km from the centre 🕐 Daily 8–6:30 💰 Free

Centre Artisanal
✉ Opposite Taourirt kasbah
🕐 Mon–Fri 8:30–noon, 3–6:30, Sat 8:30–noon, Sun 10–noon

Atlas Studios
✉ 6.5km out of town on the Marrakech road ☎ (04) 4882212
🕐 Daily 8:30–6:30

⑪ Zagora

The town has become famous for a signpost that reads "Tombouctou 52 jours" or 52 days by camel to Timbuctoo in Mali. It was from here

Ouarzazate has more hotels and modern buildings than most southern towns, but traditional life continues in some corners

Atlas Mountains and the South

that the Saadians from Arabia began their conquest of Morocco in the 16th century. And it was from here that they later began the adventure that led them to conquer Timbuctoo and control the Saharan gold trade. The large administrative town has little charm, but it does have a good souk on Wednesday and Sunday. It also makes an excellent base for venturing into the sand dunes near M'Hamid, about 30km south, and Jebel Zagora commands superb views over the DraaValley, the Amazrou palmeraies and the dunes.

➕ 185 E3 ✉ 168km southeast of Ouarzazate 🚌 Buses from Ouarzazate and Mhamid

12 Tamegroute

This intriguing village is an old religious centre famous for its **Zaouia Naciri**, a Koranic school founded by Mohammed ben Nassir in the 17th century. Its important library of Islamic manuscripts includes Korans written on gazelle skin. The school and library are open to visitors, but the sanctuary containing ben Nassir's tomb is closed to non-Muslims. Pilgrims suffering from mental problems and hypertension stay at the *zauoia* hoping for a miraculous cure. The village is interesting in itself, and its kasbahs and *ksour* connected by dark passages are well worth exploring. The **potters' co-operative** has some archaic kilns and produces some wonderfully simple green and brown pottery, colours obtained from local manganese and copper.

➕ 185 E3 ✉ 22km south of Zagora 🚌 Bus from Zagora

Zaouia Naciri
✉ Off the main road 🕐 Daily 8–noon, 2–6 💷 Donations welcome

Potters' Co-operative
✉ Off the main road 🕐 Mon–Fri 7–6:30

13 Mhamid

That Mhamid was once an important stop on trans-Saharan caravan routes is best illustrated by its population of Berbers, Saharan Arabs and people thought to originate from Sudan. The modern town is small, with a colourful Monday souk. The real interest lies in the surrounding sand dunes, which should only be visited by four-wheel-drive and with a guide, or by camel. The Tuareg owner of the Hotel Sahara (tel: (04) 4848009) organises excursions for one or more days.

➕ 185 E2 ✉ 40km from the Algerian border 🚌 Daily bus from Tinfou and Zagora (94km)

14 Tinerhir

Charming Tinerhir overlooks magnificent palm groves, some of the largest and most beautiful in Morocco, alongside the Todra River. The palmeraies belong to the Aït Atta tribe, many of whom live in small kasbahs scattered around the palm groves and orchards. The centre is dominated by a ruined but still impressive Glaoui kasbah (officially closed). The town is noted for its ironwork and has a lively souk on Tuesday. The dramatic **Todra Gorge** is only 15km away and can be reached by walking, cycling or driving.

➕ 185 E4 ✉ 70km northeast of Ouarzazate 🚌 Buses from Ouarzazate and er Rachidia

Tourist Office
✉ Avenue Mohammed V

At Your Leisure

Marathon des Sables
Every year a long-distance run is held in the desert around Merzouga and Foum Zguid, when hundreds of runners try to cover 229km in six days. Not surprisingly, the race is considered to be the toughest of its kind.

"Blue Men" have an almost mythical status as the nomads who inhabit the desert.
Right: Merzouga sand dunes at sunrise

🄵 Erfoud
This small settlement on the edge of the Ziz Valley was built in the 1930s by the French Foreign Legion. The town itself has little to offer besides a Saturday souk, but is the departure point for excursions to the **Tafilalt** region of vast palmeraies, remote Berber *ksar* and the sand dunes of Merzouga. Every October many visitors and several Berber tribes gather in Erfoud for the **Date Festival**, which features a large souk, camel races, folk dancing and the election of the Date Queen. Nearby **Rissani** is the birthplace of **Moulay Ali Cherif**, founder of the Alaouite dynasty, whose tomb remains an important pilgrimage site (closed to non-Muslims).

✚ 186 A1 🚌 Buses from er Rachidia and Rissani

🄶 Merzouga
The road from Erfoud to Merzouga requires a four-wheel-drive and should not be attempted during a sandstorm, which can happen all year round. This village has a few hotels and restaurants, but its attraction is the surrounding desert, and the nearby **Erg Chebbi** dunes are truly spectacular and stretch for several kilometres. At 150m high, the dune outside the Hotel Merzouga (1km before the village) is the tallest in Morocco. It's an interesting place: Berbers swear by a sand bath for longevity, being buried up to the neck in sand in midsummer (▶ 162). Local hotels will organise activities from sunset camel rides to several days of trekking.

✚ 186 A1 ✉ 50km from Erfoud, 20km from Algeria

156 Atlas Mountains and the South

Where to... Stay

Prices
Expect to pay for a double room, including breakfast and taxes
£ under 640dh **££** 640–1,600dh **£££** over 1,600dh

Amnougour ££

This is a modern hotel with simple but spotless rooms overlooking the Ourika River and surrounding mountains. There's a good Moroccan restaurant, an international restaurant and also a terrace that's great for a drink or for lunch. A small pool is open in summer.

➕ **184 C4** ✉ **Route d'Ourika, km49, Aghbalou Region** ☎ **(04) 4484545; fax: (04) 4432913**

Auberge Kasbah Derkaoua (Chez Michel) ££–£££

The best place to stay in the region is undoubtedly this French-run auberge in the middle of the desert, with a few simple but very tasteful

rooms and bungalows. Half board is obligatory but the food, served in the olive grove garden or in the grand salon at night, is excellent. The owner Michel, a desert buff, can advise on local excursions, and the hotel has its own camels, horses and mules for exploring the desert. Guests can also swim in the small irrigation tank that's used as a pool.

➕ **186 A1** ✉ **km23, between Erfoud and Merzouga** ☎ **and fax: (05) 5577140** ⊘ **Closed Jan, Jul and Aug**

La Bergerie ££

All the cosy *en suite* rooms have a fireplace and a little garden in this small but charming French-run auberge in a mud-brick building

arranged around a traditional courtyard. Excellent Moroccan-European food is served in the pleasant dining room.

➕ **184 C4** ✉ **Marigha, km59 on the road from Marrakech** ☎ **(04) 4485716; fax: (04) 4485718**

La Fibule du Draa £–££

This long-established hotel
(▲ 159) offers a range of simple and comfortable rooms with air-conditioning; alternatively, you can sleep under the stars in tents on the terrace. Moroccan specialities are served in a large dining room. The swimming pool is set in a beautiful garden, and the very friendly staff can advise on desert excursions. The same management also runs the more upmarket and splendid Ksar Tinsouline in central Zagora (tel: (04) 4847252; fax: (04) 4847042; tinsouli@iam.net.ma), which has a great pool and its own oasis.

➕ **185 E3** ✉ **2km from Zagora** ☎ **(04) 4847318; fax: (04) 4847271 email: fibule@atlas-net.net.ma**

La Kasbah £–££

This wonderfully located little hotel has great views over one of Morocco's most impressive kasbahs. The rooms vary from basic but very clean to air-conditioned suites, and there's a swimming pool and a good restaurant serving set menus of fresh salad, Berber omelette and chicken tagine.

➕ **185 D3** ✉ **Across the river from the kasbah, Aït Benhaddou** ☎ **4890302; fax: (04) 4883787**

Kasbah Asmaa ££

Within the impressive pisé walls is a kasbah with rooms surrounding a courtyard. Rooms in the new building are more comfortable, but those in the towers have splendid views. The lush garden has a belvedere overlooking the large palmeraie and a gorgeous shaded pool. Candlelit dinners are served in the garden in summer, or in the beautiful Moroccan salons.

➕ **185 E3** ✉ **2km from Zagora** ☎ **(04) 4847241; fax: (04) 4847527**

Where to... 157

Ksar Sania £

This small *ksar* at the foot of the sand dunes is set in its own oasis and isn't easy to find. Many *faux guides* in Merzouga will be quick to point out that there is no road, or that it is closed or lost under the sand, so call the hotel for directions. Rooms come with *en suite* or communal bathrooms, and there's also a Bedouin tent on the terrace where you can sleep out in summer. The friendly and helpful French host couple organise trips in the area.

⊞ 186 A1 ⊠ 1.5km outside Merzouga, on the piste to Taouz
☎ (05) 5577414; fax: (05) 5577230

Palais Salam ££

The sultan's old pleasure palace, this hotel's abundant charm stems from its beautiful décor and the fabulous fountain-filled gardens surrounding it. There are more than 100 comfortable, Moorish-style rooms set around terraced courtyards containing banana trees. There are also two pools and a

---

couple of restaurants: try the Moroccan one for high-quality traditional food (though you need to order elaborate dishes several hours in advance).

⊞ 184 B3 ⊠ Kasbah, Taroudannt
☎ (04) 8852312; fax: (04) 8852854;
palsalam@agairnet.net.ma

Riad Salam ££-£££

Built as two adjoining *pisé kasbahs*, and with a large and pleasant pool featuring a waterfall, this quiet hotel near the Taourirt kasbah attracts fewer tour groups than the other luxury hotels in town. Its sister hotel, the Oscar Salam, is rather surreal, set within the Atlas Film Studios and decorated with large parts of old film sets.

⊞ 185 D1 ⊠ avenue Mohammed V, Ouarzazate ☎ (04) 4883335; fax: (04) 4882766

Salam ££

Built in the regional style of a kasbah with *pisé* walls, this large, upmarket hotel has airy and

---

spacious rooms, some overlooking the splendid swimming pool in the central, lush courtyard. As the best hotel in town, it's popular with tour groups, but the friendly staff will do their utmost to welcome everyone.

⊞ 186 A1 ⊠ Erfoud, on the road to Rissani ☎ (05) 5576665; fax: (05) 5576426

Le Soleil £

A rarity in town is this small hotel set in a lovely garden, with only nine quiet, simple and spotless rooms (some *en suite*). The restaurant serves very good Moroccan meals and the garden is a good spot for a drink.

⊞ 184 A3 ⊠ Dar m'Bark, near Bab Targhount on the road to Agadir
☎ (04) 8551707

Taroudannt £

Situated next door to the train station, this French colonial hotel is as old-fashioned as it gets. The basic rooms, with either washbasin or shower, are fairly clean, but

---

those located on the street side are much noisier.

⊞ 184 B3 ⊠ place al Alaouyine (Assarag), Taroudannt ☎ (04) 8852416

Tomboctoo £-££

An old kasbah has been restored by the friendly Catalan Roger Mimo, who fell in love with the region. The charming *en suite* rooms, decorated in Moroccan style with *pisé* details and locally made furniture, have phone, fan and winter heating. It doesn't have an alcohol licence but you can bring your own bottles.

⊞ 185 E4 ⊠ avenue Anzarane, Tinerhir ☎ (04) 4834604; fax: (04) 4833505

Ziz £

This family-run hotel has clean, air-conditioned, *en suite* rooms, some with a balcony overlooking the courtyard. The Moroccan restaurant is especially recommended.

⊞ 186 A1 ⊠ 3 avenue Mohammed V, Erfoud ☎ (05) 5576154; fax: (05) 5576811

158 Atlas Mountains and the South

Where to...
Eat and Drink

Prices
Expect to pay for a three-course meal, excluding drinks but including taxes and service
£ under 160dh **££** 160–350dh **£££** over 350dh

Most eating places in the south of Morocco are housed either in the hotels or in smaller *gîtes*. You may find that some of the nicest restaurants are often booked by tour groups, particularly at lunchtime, which sometimes means that individual travellers are set aside and easily overlooked. Take care if you want to buy food from street stalls in this region, as hygiene is often poorer than in the rest of the country and the higher temperatures make the food perish more quickly.

Auberge Chez Pierre ££

Besides the eight tastefully decorated rooms is an excellent restaurant where the Belgian owner Pierre is also the chef. The surprisingly good food, based on local produce, has the inventiveness of *nouvelle cuisine*, but without its small portions. Specialities include quiches with seasonal vegetables and spices, roast chicken with herbs and home-made goats' cheese with local honey. In fact, everything from bread and cheese to delicious ice-cream is home-made. This is a charming place, where advance booking is essential.

➕ 185 E4 ✉ 22km from Boulmane, 3km past the Aït Oudinar bridge ☎ (04) 4830267 🕐 Daily lunch and dinner

Chez Dimitri ££

This typical French-Moroccan restaurant has lots of old-fashioned charm and character. Founded in 1928 – at the same time as Ouarzazate – it served as a post and telephone office, bar and ballroom for the legionnaires stationed here. Now the high-ceilinged room is decorated with signed black-and-white pictures of visiting movie stars and other celebrities. The menu includes traditional French and Moroccan dishes, good pastas and salads, and there's an extensive wine list.

➕ 185 D3 ✉ 22 avenue Mohammed V, Ouarzazate ☎ (04) 4887346 🕐 Daily lunch and dinner

Chez Momo £

Housed in a basic mountain refuge with great views of the Atlas range

you'll find this amazing little place serving really delicious tagines with salads and grills.

➕ 184 C3 ✉ Ouirgane village ☎ (04) 4485704 🕐 Daily lunch and dinner

Chez Nada £

Taroudannt's reputation for good food is well maintained by this simple but very popular Moroccan restaurant. Delicious couscous, tagines and salads are served in a pleasant dining room on the first floor, or else under the stars on the terrace. Remember that specialities such as the excellent *pastilla* with pigeon need to be ordered several hours in advance.

➕ 184 B3 ✉ rue Ferk Lahbab, near Hotel Les Saadiens, Taroudannt ☎ (04) 8851726 🕐 Daily early morning–late evening

Dar Tioute (Restaurant du Sheikh) £

In this small restaurant with a beautiful courtyard you can enjoy a

Where to... 159

fantastic couscous made, like everything else here, by the women of the house. The surrounding palmeraie, with more than 20,000 trees, is perfect for strolling. If you wish, you can also rent a simple room for the night.

🕀 184 B3 ⊠ Douar Azour, in Tioute palmeraie, 29km southeast of Taroudannt ☎ (04) 8550555; fax: (04) 8850293 🕲 Daily lunch and dinner

La Fibule du Draa ££

The hotel's restaurant is set in an enormous Berber-style dining room. You can choose between good-value set menus, à la carte or local specialities, such as a delectable *pastilla* stuffed with dates and nuts, which need to be ordered in advance. Service is slow but the atmosphere makes up for it. There's also a popular, palm-shaded garden bar offering a wide selection of (mainly French) aperitifs (▶ 156).

🕀 185 E3 ⊠ 2km from Zagora ☎ (04) 8847318; fax: (04) 8847271; email: fibule@atlas-net.net.ma

Gazelle d'Or £££

The exclusive hotel is one of the most beautiful spots in Morocco, but the atmosphere can be somewhat frosty. The lunch buffet by the pool is more than pleasant, but the five-course dinner can be disappointing, as the food is not really up to its ambitious standards. It's popular, though, so ensure that you book in advance.

🕀 184 B3 ⊠ 1km outside Taroudannt ☎ (04) 8852039; fax: 8852737; gazelle@marocnet.net.ma 🕲 Daily lunch and dinner

Jnane Dar (Chez Abdessadek Naciri) ££

Freshly prepared Moroccan food is served under tents in a pleasant garden or in the cosy dining room. There's always a friendly welcome and the restaurant often hosts sessions with local musicians in the evening.

🕀 185 E3 ⊠ Opposite the Naciri Medersa, Tamegroute ☎ (04) 4848622

La Kasbah £–££

A pleasant restaurant with several terraces overlooking the kasbah, and more intimate dining rooms inside, this serves good Moroccan food, particularly the copious couscous, but no alcohol.

🕀 185 D3 ⊠ Opposite the Taourirt kasbah, Ouarzazate ☎ (04) 4882033 🕲 Daily lunch and dinner

Kasbah Asmaa ££

Excellent Moroccan meals are served in the poolside garden or in sumptuous Moroccan salons. The house speciality of *mechoui* (roast lamb) needs to be ordered a day in advance, and alcohol is only available at meal times.

🕀 185 E3 ⊠ kasbah Asmaa hotel, 2km from Zagora ☎ (04) 4847241; fax: (04) 4847527 🕲 Daily lunch and dinner

Ksar Sania £

Ksar Sania is well worth the short walk from Merzouga for its splendid location and well-prepared

Moroccan-French food. It's served outside in the garden overlooking the sand dunes and oasis in summer or in the large dining room in winter. The mainly Moroccan menu includes an excellent couscous with lamb, Moroccan salads and tagines, but the French owners always offer a few traditional French dishes as well.

🕀 186 A1 ⊠ Ksar Sania Hotel, 1.5km outside Merzouga, on the piste to Taouz 🕲 Daily breakfast, lunch and dinner

Al-Mechouar £

This is an excellent patisserie offering delicious Moroccan and European pastries, as well as fresh fruit juices, including sweet almond milk. It's particularly recommended for breakfast.

🕀 184 A2 ⊠ 66 place du Mechouar, Tiznit 🕲 Daily 7 am–11 pm

Ouarzazate Complex £££

With splendid Moorish-style salons and large Berber tents around a

Atlas Mountains and the South

lovely pool, the setting is spectacular, but the Moroccan food, while good, is not very inventive. However, it's worth it because dinner comes with a fine and colourful folkloric show, including local Berber musicians and a belly dancer. It's mainly for tourists, but is also popular with Moroccan families, especially at weekends.

✚ 185 D3 ⊠ Edge of Ouarzazate, on the road to Tinerhir ☎ (04) 4883110 ⏱ Daily lunch and dinner

Palais Riad Hida ££–£££

Another 19th-century kasbah is now a beautiful hotel-restaurant set in a large, well-maintained garden. There is only a choice of several set menus that include salads, tagines or grilled meats and dessert, and the restaurant prefers to take orders in advance by phone; otherwise hang out by the pool while your meal is being prepared. At lunchtime it may be crowded with tour groups, but at dinner it's usually a lot quieter.

✚ 184 B3 ⊠ Ouled Berhil, 40km from Taroudannt ☎ (04) 8531044; fax: (04) 8531026 ⏱ Daily lunch and dinner

Le Petit Prince de l'Aviation ££

Another nostalgic, French-themed restaurant, this features a beautiful dining room fitted with slow-moving fans and adorned with old photographs, including some of the French aviator and writer Antoine de Saint-Exupéry (1900–44), whose popular and touching novel *Le Petit Prince* was published the year before he was declared missing during a flight. The excellent food includes French and Moroccan specialities, or a mixture of both, such as pigeons stuffed with almonds and served with fine crêpes or Atlas trout.

✚ 185 D3 ⊠ 13 avenue Moulay Abdallah, Algods, Ouarzazate ⏱ Daily lunch and dinner

Restaurant Gastronomique ££

Although this upmarket restaurant in a large Moorish dining room in the smartest hotel in town serves fine Moroccan food, it's not as good as the name suggests. However, the bar near the pool is livelier, popular with locals and serves good international and Moroccan snacks.

✚ 184 A2 ⊠ Hotel Tiznit, rue nin Anzarane, Tiznit ☎ (04) 8862411 ⏱ Daily 5 am–1 am

Les Roches £–££

This hotel-restaurant superbly located right in the Todra Gorge is a popular stop for tour buses at lunchtime, when you can eat outdoors in the shade of Berber tents. At night the place calms down a bit, offering romantic candlelit dinners with good Moroccan food. There's no alcohol, but you can bring your own.

✚ 185 E4 ⊠ Todra Gorge ☎ (04) 4834814 ⏱ Daily lunch and dinner

Taroudannt Hotel-Restaurant £–££

Good old-fashioned French and Moroccan dishes are served in a colonial-style restaurant with high ceilings. Service can be erratic, but that's part of the charm in this, Taroudannt's oldest hotel (▶ 157), and the four-course menu is excellent value for money. It's on the busiest square in the town, and there's also a bar to enjoy a drink in the evening.

✚ 184 B3 ⊠ place al Alaouyine (Assarag), Taroudannt ☎ (04) 8852416; fax: (04) 8851553 ⏱ Daily breakfast, lunch and dinner

Tombouctoo Hotel-Restaurant ££

Like the hotel (▶ 157), this excellent restaurant shows much charm and inventiveness, offering some great Spanish dishes as well as delicious Moroccan food. Specialities such as couscous or *mechoui* (roast lamb) need to be ordered in advance. There's no alcohol, but you are welcome to bring your own if you'd like it.

✚ 185 E4 ⊠ avenue Anzarane, Tinerhir ☎ (04) 4834604; fax: (04) 4833505 ⏱ Daily lunch and dinner

Where to...
Shop

SOUKS AND MARKETS

Erfoud has a daily market near place des FAR, and a larger weekly souk in the same place on Saturday. There's a large souk on Sunday at the entrance to **Ouarzazate** coming from Marrakech, and smaller souks are held in **Sidi Daoud** on Tuesday and in **Tabounte** on Saturday.

Taroudannt is known for its craftsmen, and the town's two souks are less touristy than in Marrakech, but the *faux guides* can be pretty fierce. The Arab souk has a great spice market, and there's an excellent jewellery souk with lots of Berber jewellery and local sculpture. The Marché Berbère is aimed more at locals and sells good, inexpensive pottery, clothes and food.

Tiznit is famous for its silver Berber jewellery, both in traditional and contemporary designs, on sale in the little alleys of the jewellery souk. The town's new souk on place du Mechouar offers a wider choice, but the old souk is more authentic. There is a Thursday souk on the road to **Tafraoute**.

The covered souk in **Zagora** is open daily, but gets busier on Wednesday and Saturday when Berbers from the region come to sell their produce.

JEWELLERY AND ANTIQUES

Aït Benhaddou has several shops within its lower kasbah that sell local "antiques", carpets and Tuareg jewellery, but you won't find many bargains. Tuareg jewellery is also on sale opposite the Tinsouline hotel in Zagora, at **Maison Berbère**, which also sells the best crafts in town. The **Centre Artisanal** on avenue Mohammed V in Tiznit also has jewellery on sale, as well as

other crafts. For a selection of good antiques and carpets try **Lichir el-Houssaine** in souk Smata, Taroudannt (tel: (04) 8851680).

ARTS AND CRAFTS

The **Ensemble Artisanal** opposite the kasbah in **Ouarzazate** is the place for Berber pottery, wood and alabaster, carpets and silver jewellery with big orange copal beads. The town's **carpet weavers' co-operative** (Mohammed V, opposite the police station) has a good selection of local carpets, particularly the loosely woven, brightly coloured wool examples made by the Ouzquita tribe. The **Centre Horizon Artisanat** on avenue de la Victoire (tel: (04) 488698; as.hor.hand@cybernet.net.ma) sells excellent crafts, produced in their workshops with the help of local youngsters with disabilities.

At the top of the kasbah in Aït Benhaddou, artists sell *aquarelles* (transparent watercolours) and

other **paintings**. And in the village across the river you'll find many craft shops catering to passing tour buses.

Erfoud is famous for its dark **marble**, which is exported all over the world. But here it's used for smaller objects such ashtrays or fake fossils on sale in craft shops and tourist bazaars along avenues Mohammed V and Moulay Ismail, or direct from the marble factory near Tizimi hotel on the road to Tinerhir. A more unusual souvenir from Erfoud would be a **water-colour** by Madeleine Laurent, whose studio is at 68 rue el-Wahda, near the Salam hotel.

DATES

Dates make excellent gifts, and those from **Zagora** are considered the best in Morocco. Traders will no doubt let you sample the varieties before you buy. **Erfoud** is also a major exporter of dates, which can be bought at the market.

Atlas Mountains and the South

Where to...
Be Entertained

DESERT EXCURSIONS

The entertainment in **Merzouga** focuses on the desert, and anything from guided sunset walks or camel trips to fully equipped expeditions by motorbike or four-wheel-drive are on offer at most hotels. **Camel trips** are also big in Zagora, where three operators offer similar trips at the same prices – for an hour, half a day or full day, including meals. They can be booked through the hotel **La Fibule du Draa** (▶ 156) or **Caravane du Sud** (tel: 04) 484797).

Near the Atlas Film Studios on avenue Moulay Rachid in Ouarzazate is **Kart Adventure** (tel: (04) 486374) which organises **karting** and **quad-bike** excursions. **Mountain bikes** (and ordinary

models) can be rented from **Ksour Voyages** at 11 place du 3 Mars.

SAND BATHS

Merzouga is the place where Berbers come for a sand bath, which is believed to aid longevity, invigorate the body and cure rheumatism. However, it's not for the faint-hearted because it involves being buried up to the neck in the sand under the hot sun. You can stay there for a maximum of 20 minutes, after which you are wrapped in blankets and served hot drinks. The local hotels can put you in touch with people who specialise in sand baths in particular areas. Prices vary according to different cures and lengths, but are relatively inexpensive.

SPORT AND LEISURE

Oukaïmeden has an impressive ski-lift at 3,273m, and offers the best **skiing** in Morocco, including off-piste, between December and March. **Hiking** is possible on the lower slopes for most of the year. For information contact the **Club Alpin Chalet** (tel: (04) 4319036). **Golfers** should head for the **Golf Royal** course in Ouarzazate (tel: (04) 4882653). Most of Ouarzazate's upmarket hotels allow non-residents to use their **pools** if they pay or eat there. Non-residents can use the splendid pool at the **Palais Salam** in Taroudannt (▶ 157), the heated indoor pool of the **Kenzi** hotel in Oukaïmeden or the pool at the **Tinsouline** (avenue Hassan II, Zagora) for a fee.

The municipal gardens near the Palais Salam in Taroudannt have six **tennis** courts, with ball and racket hire. A **cycle** ride around the town walls is also recommended; bikes can be hired from a small nameless

stall on avenue Mohammed V, just off place al-Alaouyine.

For **horse-riders** the **Gazelle d'Or hotel** (▶ 159), 1km outside Taroudannt, has good stables, or try **Chez Habib** (368 rue Mansour ed Dahabi) near Bab Zorgane in town.

Cinema Atlas on rue de la Poste in Ouarzazate shows mostly French, Indian and Arab films.

BIRDWATCHING

The **Oued Souss** between Taroudannt and Taliaouine is a rich bird habitat in winter and spring. Keen birdwatchers can check out **Aoulouz Gorge**, 90km from Taroudannt along the same road.

DATE FESTIVAL

Every October, Erfoud holds a **Date Festival** – a mixture of religious celebrations and more worldly entertainment such as a fashion show, music and dance, and athletics competitions.

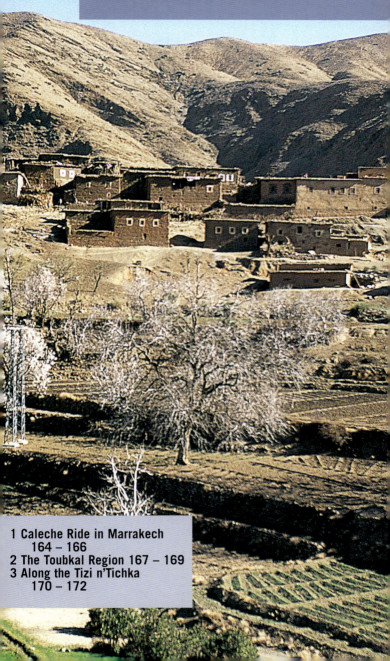

Walks & Tours

1 Caleche Ride in Marrakech
 164 – 166
2 The Toubkal Region 167 – 169
3 Along the Tizi n'Tichka
 170 – 172

164 Walks and Tours

1 CALECHE RIDE IN MARRAKECH

Tour

This relaxed horse-drawn cab ride takes you through the southern quarters of the medina, where you can see some of the city's greatest sights as well as people going about their daily business regardless of passing tourists.

The fixed rates per person are advertised on the seats of the caleche, but it is worth negotiating a fee for the whole tour in advance, including stops to visit sights *en route*. Either start the tour at 9 am or, if it's not too hot, at 2 pm, as many of the attractions close at lunchtime.

DISTANCE 4–5km **TIME** 3–4 hours, including visits
START POINT Caleche stand behind the Koutoubia Mosque on avenue Houmman el-Fetouaki (bus No 1 from the main squares in Guéliz) 182 C1 **END POINT** Djemaa el-Fna 182 C1

Caleches are one of the best ways to explore the medina

1–2

Take a good look at the minaret of the **Koutoubia Mosque** (Mosquée de la Koutoubia), one of Marrakech's main landmarks. Turn right on to rue Sidi Mimoun, with the Koubba de Youssef ben Tachfine on the right-hand side. This leads to two gates, **Bab Agnaou** and **Bab er Rob** (▶ 57). Bab Agnaou, a contemporary of the Koutoubia and a beautiful example of an elegant Almohad gateway, led from the medina to the imperial city. Enter the city walls via the passage next to Bab Agnaou. Straight ahead is the **Kasbah**

1 Caleche Ride in Marrakech

The Mellah

In 1558, considerably later than in other Moroccan cities, the Saadians moved the Jewish community into a district known as the mellah. Located near the sultan's palace, this was a safe quarter with only two entrance gates. Most sultans valued the Jewish community, recognising its skills as bankers, traders and craftsmen. A council of rabbis controlled the community, which had its own cemeteries, gardens and markets. Until the 1950s, the population was over 16,000 but after 1948 most emigrated to the new State of Israel, leaving only a few today.

Mosque (Mosquée de la Kasbah), also known as the Mosque of el-Mansour as it was built in 1190 by the sultan Yaqoub el-Mansour. An explosion destroyed part of it in 1569, but it was restored by successive kings, including Hassan II (1929–99). A narrow corridor to the right of the mosque leads to the entrance to the splendid **Saadian Tombs** (Tombeaux Saadiens, ▲ 63), one of the city's highlights.

2–3

Continue on rue de la Kasbah and, at the end, turn left into rue du Méchouar. At the end of this, to the right, is a gateway in the ramparts leading to a large square. Take the left route through the Porte de l'Aguedal leading to the **Méchouar** where, in the 18th and 19th centuries, the sultan gave audiences and received European ambassadors. Go across the Méchouar (the Royal Palace, on the left, is closed to the public) and through the gate. Take the next gate immediately

to the left, leading into rue Berrima with the **Mellah** (Jewish quarter) beyond on the right. At the end of the street, at Bab Berrima, a corridor between two walls leads to the 16th-century **el-Badi Palace** (Palais el-Badi,

Ahmed el-Mansour is buried in the Saadian cemetery with his son and successor Zaidan, and his grandson Mohammed esh Sheikh II

166 Walks and Tours

The el-Badi Palace has been robbed of all its former splendour

▶ 62). Go back through Bab Berrima to place des Ferblantiers, a large, rectangular *fondouk* (caravanserai) of metal workshops, where many of the lanterns on sale in the souks are made. Turn right on to avenue

Houmman el-Fetouaki, with the cemetery on your left and the *mellah* on the right. At the corner with rue Riad ez Zitoun el-Jdid is the entrance to the late-19th century **el-Bahia Palace and Museum** (Palais el-Bahia, ▶ 63).

3–4

After visiting el-Bahia, continue north along rue Riad ez Zitoun el-Jdid until you reach a square with a public garden. Walk through a narrow passage called rue de la Bahia to the right, then take the first alley to the left to visit the **Dar Si Said Museum** of Moroccan arts (▶ 63). Return to rue de la Bahia where, on the left at No 8, you'll find **Maison Tiskiwin** (▶ 63), a beautiful Moorish mansion named after a Berber dance from the High Atlas.

4–5

Return to rue Riad ez Zitoun el-Jdid and turn right. Where the road forks, turn left, towards Café de France on **Djemaa el-Fna** (▶ 50–51).

Taking a Break

Several of the splendid late 19th- and early 20th-century mansions along rue Riad ez Zitoun el-Jdid have been converted into upmarket restaurants, including **Palais Gharnata** (5–6 derb el Arsa; tel: (04) 4440615) and **Douirya** (14 derb Jdid; tel: (04) 4403030). Alternatively, if you wait, there are plenty of refreshments available at **Djemaa el-Fna** (▶ 50–51).

2 THE TOUBKAL REGION

Walk

DISTANCE 12km **TIME** 1 day
START/END POINT Le Soleil Hotel, Imlil (minibus, truck or taxi from Asni) 184 C3
INFORMATION or qualified guides from the mountain refuge of Club Alpin Franéflais: PO Box 6178, Casablanca (tel: (02) 2270090); or from Le Soleil (tel: (04) 4485622)

Hikers rest beside the blessed waters of Sidi Chamarouch

This hike takes you through spectacular mountains and beautiful Berber villages. It's the first and easiest part of the most popular ascent of Jebel Toubkal, but for Berbers it is also a pilgrimage route to the shrine of Sidi Chamarouch.

Although long, this is an easy walk for most fit people, but if you're in any doubt, consider going by mule, which can be rented by the day or half day from Imlil or Aremd (ask in the cafés or restaurants). Rates are about 100dh a day, plus a tip for the muleteer. You shouldn't need a guide on this well-trodden path, especially if you have a muleteer, but if you do decide to take one, expect to pay him about 200dh a day. Imlil and Aremd have several simple hotels where you can spend the night. The hotel Kasbah du Toubkal also offers rooms to hikers, through Hotel de Foucauld in Marrakech (▶ 65) or the British company Discover: to book through its Marrakech office, tel: (04) 4485611.

1-2
Start at around 8 or 9 am from the Hotel du Soleil, following the mule track past the Hotel de l'Etoile and several small shops. Take the first track to the right at Laiterie Toubkal and follow the well-defined path, zigzagging up to the right of the **Mizane**

168 Walks and Tours

The rivers in the High Atlas are dry for most of the year, except in spring

River. The path goes past several houses and the **Hotel Kasbah du Toubkal**, an old Glaoui kasbah with great views. Soon the path climbs above the walnut trees and the landscape opens out. After about 45 minutes (2km) turn left along a trail wide enough for cars. Across the river is the picturesque village of Aremd, built on a large spur.

2–3

Aremd is the largest village in the Mizane Valley and has benefited from tourists climbing Jebel Toubkal. It's an authentic place where you can meet Berbers and see how they live and work. Cross the river (there is a bridge but the river is usually pretty dry) and climb through the winding streets to the top of the village. Retrace your steps back across the river and walk 100m to the left, towards a cluster of houses opposite the village, for refreshments at the **Hotel Aremd**.

3–4

Take the path opposite the hotel, through the flood plain and orchards towards the

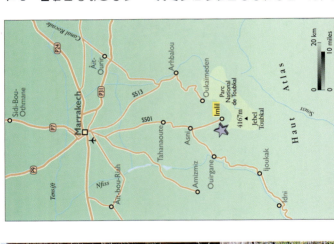

2 The Toubkal Region

mountains on the other side of the valley. After about 15 minutes, at the foot of the slopes a well-worn path to the right climbs into the mountains, through the hard grey rocks overlooking the river. After another 15 minutes you reach a spring, but continue along the path, which now looks down over apple orchards. After another hour's walk the boulders become larger, the river forming pools and small waterfalls around them. Suddenly you can see a white *koubba*, the **shrine of Sidi Chamarouche**, a Muslim saint associated with the traditional Berber spirits of the mountains. His tomb is closed to non-Muslims, who are requested not even to cross the bridge to the shrine. He is known as the "King of Jinns" and many pilgrims possessed by a *jinn* (that is, those with psychological problems) come to the shrine so that Sidi Chamarouche can take control of their *jinn* and thus cure them. Some serious cases stay for several years in the cells near the shrine, but most come for a few days and bathe in the sacred pool near the *koubba*.

below the shrine are not sacred and can be seriously inviting on a hot day. It's usually possible for visitors to take a dip, but be careful not to offend the locals – women should wear bathing suits at least, and go a little further upstream.

5–6

The walk goes back along the same path, past the fossil and mineral shops of Sidi Chamarouche hamlet, whose owners sometimes adopt quite aggressive sales tactics at this stage. You will almost certainly not be alone here, especially at weekends when entire families from Marrakech take to the trail, often barefoot or wearing slippers. Continue back to Aremd or Imlil for the night.

Taking a Break

Drinks and snacks are available all along the route. You can get a good, simple lunch at the **Hotel Aremd** just below Aremd itself, or in the hamlet of Sidi Chamarouche. Alternatively, **bring a picnic** to enjoy at the top, followed by a dip in the pools of the little river.

Practical Advice

- You'll need **sturdy shoes**, preferably walking boots, and sun protection.
- This area is under snow from November until spring, but it's usually possible to complete the walk **all year round**. The best time to go is late spring to early autumn. Afternoons are often cloudy.
- Although well trodden, the path is not signed so a **map would be handy**. You can sometimes buy a map in Imlil or Marrakech, but it's better to get one before you go to Morocco. If you get lost, just ask a local.

4–5

The trail continues the steep climb from here to Jebel Toubkal, but this is a perfect place to stop for a picnic or a meal in the small hamlet of **Sidi Chamarouche**, which surrounds the tomb and is mostly inhabited by the saint's descendants. The pools behind and

3 ALONG THE TIZI N'TICHKA

Tour

Together with the Tizi n'Test (▶ 144–145), at over 2,000m the Tizi n'Tichka is one of the highest and most spectacular roads in the High Atlas. It also offers the chance to visit some of Morocco's most impressive kasbahs.

This tour is possible by public transport – there are frequent buses across the mountains from Marrakech to Ouarzazate – but it would be difficult to include everything in one day, as the kasbahs of Telouet (▶ 152) and Aït Benhaddou (▶ 150) are off the road. It's therefore easier either to hire a car or a *grand taxi* for the day. The road is good and relatively fast, but if you have a four-wheel-drive you can take the more adventurous piste from Telouet to Aït Benhaddou. A tarmac road from Telouet leads east to Anemiter, 11km away. From there a rough, unsurfaced track (piste) leads for 30km through barren landscape to Tamdaght, just north of Aït Benhaddou.

DISTANCE 273km **TIME** 1 day
START POINT Bab Doukkala, Marrakech ✚ 184 C4
END POINT Ouarzazate (daily buses and *grands taxis* from Marrakech via Telouet) ✚ 185 D3

The vendors of rocks and minerals are also skilled in faking, some in almost fluorescent colours

1–2

From Bab Doukkala follow the signs out of town for Fes-Ouarzazate. After about 7.5km when the road forks, take the P31 to the right towards Ouarzazate, through a eucalyptus plantation dotted with the occasional large villa. After 36km

3 Along the Tizi n'Tichka

you'll see the first big village along the road, **Aït-Ourir**, with the attractive Hotel le Coq Hardi and the ruins of a crenellated kasbah. Beyond this, the road becomes more beautiful as it follows the River Oued Zate, and all along the route are clusters of villages dramatically set into the mountains. Amid deliciously scented pine forests is the picturesque little Berber village of **Toufliat**.

2–3

After 17km you'll reach the small alpine town of **Taddert**, surrounded by walnut trees and invaded by sellers of minerals and fossils, who also display their wares all along the road.

About 12km further on is a **viewpoint** with excellent views back over the valley, and a small café for refreshments. The Col du Tichka, 5km after this, is the highest road in Morocco, at 2,260m. There is always a strong wind blowing at this altitude, but the view of the mountains is now obscured by the stalls and shops selling pottery and fossils.

3–4

Another 5km further on, take a small road to the left signposted to the village of **Telouet**, which you'll reach after 20km (▶ 152–153). Continue along the road and through the village to the Auberge de Telouet, which is on your left. Turn right here on a narrow track signposted to the kasbah, and after about 500m you will arrive on the small square in front of it. Look out for the caretaker outside the **Glaoui kasbah** to let you in for a look around, then return to the Auberge de Telouet for lunch or drinks.

Children in the village around Telouet kasbah

172 Walks and Tours

4–5
Return through a windswept landscape with an occasional terraced village to the main Marrakech–Ouarzazate road and turn left. After 10km you'll reach Irherm n'Ougdal, a typical High Atlas village at 1,970m, with low houses and a beautiful *irherm* or *agadir* (fortified communal granary). The next village of Tiurdjal (20km), which seems to be sliding downhill, features a pretty marble minaret permanently topped with a stork's nest. The road now follows the Asif Imini River and becomes straighter and considerably faster, with a panoramic view over some of the highest peaks in the Atlas. After about 8km, just before **Agouim**, there are panoramas over some of the highest peaks in the Atlas; the village has a weaving cooperative set up by Franciscan friars, on road 6849, a dirt track on the right that leads to Sour.

Back on the main road, after about 20km look out for the splendid kasbah of **Tiseldei** on the left and, 2km further on, the *ksar* of Iflilt, a village set among olive groves. Some 8km to the south is el-Mdint, and another 2km outside the village, to the right, is a fine kasbah with ornate towers and the pretty *ksar* of Taddoula, both set in palm groves.

5–6
At a crossroads 10km further on, turn left on to the 6803 leading to the magnificent *ksar* of **Aït Benhaddou** in another 10km (▶ 150). The best view of this remarkable site is from a viewpoint 2km before the village. From the village return to the main road and turn left to continue to **Ouarzazate** about 25km away (▶ 153).

Lords of the High Atlas
The powerful Glaoui family ruled over the Atlas from 1875 to 1956. They began as simple tribal leaders but came to control the important mountain road of Tizi n'Test (▶ 144–145). Unlike other mountain tribes, who fought against the French colonisers, the Glaouis made a pact with them. The French Marshal Lyautey appreciated their support and did nothing to stop their rise to power. The two brothers Madani and T'hami appointed themselves pashas of Marrakech and established other family members as *caïds* (tribal chiefs), who ruled as despots over all the main Atlas and desert cities. The brothers built many kasbahs in the region, and were notorious for their lavish parties.

If you only see one kasbah, let it be well-maintained Aït Benhaddou

Taking a Break
The **Auberge de Telouet** (tel: (04) 4890717, open 7–7) serves a set lunch (fresh salad and excellent tagine) under a Berber tent overlooking the crumbling kasbah. The terrace of **La Kasbah** (▶ 156) commands great views over Aït Benhaddou and serves delicious Moroccan food or cool drinks near the pool.

Practicalities

GETTING ADVANCE INFORMATION
Websites
- Moroccan Tourist Office www.tourism-in-morocco.com
- Accommodation: www.hotelstravel.com/morocco

- General information www.al-bab.com/maroc
- Culture and politics www.multimania.com/aza/ugzil.htm

- Moroccan contemporary music www.maroc.net/baraka

BEFORE YOU GO

WHAT YOU NEED

	UK	Germany	USA	Canada	Australia	Ireland	Netherlands	Spain
● Required ○ Suggested ▲ Not required △ Not applicable								
Passport/National Identity Card	●	●	●	●	●	●	●	●
Visa (check with your Moroccan consulate)								
Onward or Return Ticket	○	○	○	○	○	○	○	○
Health Inoculations (tetanus, polio and malaria)	○	○	○	○	○	○	○	○
Health Documentation	○	○	○	○	○	○	○	○
Travel Insurance	●	●	●	●	●	●	●	●
Driving Licence (national, International for US nationals)	●	●	●	●	●	●	●	●
Car Insurance Certificate (included if car is hired)	●	●	●	●	●	●	●	●
Car Registration Document	●	●	●	●	●	●	●	●

WHEN TO GO

Rabat/Casablanca

High season　　　　Low season

JAN	FEB	MAR	APR	MAY	JUN	JUL	AUG	SEP	OCT	NOV	DEC
17°C	18°C	19°C	21°C	23°C	25°C	28°C	28°C	27°C	25°C	20°C	18°C

☀ Sun

🌦 Sunshine and showers

Morocco is not called a cold country with a hot sun for nothing – **temperatures can vary dramatically** between night and day, depending on the season and the region. In summer the beaches will be hot but crowded, and on the Atlantic side the sky is very often overcast. The **coast is temperate** all year round, but the resorts will feel cool out of season. The summer months are excellent for visiting the High and Middle Atlas Mountains, but cities like Fes and Marrakech can be unbearably hot. The **best time to visit** the south and the Sahara region is in winter, from October to February, as the summer temperature here can easily soar to over 45°C. For a general tour of Morocco **the best periods** are March to May and September to October, when it's cooler and there's less chance of rain.

174 **Practicalities**

In the UK	In the USA	In Canada
205 Regent Street	Suite 1201, 20 East 46th	2001 University Street,
London W1R 44B	Street, New York,	Suite 1460, Montréal,
☎ 020 7437 0073	NY 10017	Québec H3A 2A6
Fax: 020 7734 8172	☎ 212/557-2520	☎ 514/842-8111
	Fax: 212/949-8148	Fax: 514/842-5316

GETTING THERE

By Air Royal Air Maroc (tel: 020 7439 4361; web: www.royalairmaroc.com) operates **direct, scheduled flights** from London Heathrow, Paris and other cities in France. New York and Montréal also have **direct flights** to Morocco. British Airways (tel: 0345 222111; web: www.britishairways.com) operates flights from London to Casablanca, Tangier and Marrakech. Air France (tel: 0845 0845 111; web: www.airfrance.co.uk) has **daily flights** to several Moroccan cities via Paris, as does KLM (tel: 08705 074 074; web: www.klm.com) via Amsterdam to Casablanca.
Travel times Direct flights from London to Casablanca take just over three hours, and to Marrakech 3 hours and 40 minutes.

By Sea Several ferry companies operate between France or Spain and Morocco. The **keenest prices** are available from Transmediterranea in Algeciras, Spain (tel: 956 583 444, in Algeciras or c/o Southern Ferries in London, tel: 020 7491 4968). There are **several crossings a day** between Algeciras in Spain and Ceuta **by vehicle ferry** (1hr 30 min), **by fast ferry** (40 min) or **by catamaran** (30 min). Passengers need to take a bus to the Moroccan border and then another one to their final destination.

By Car You can cross **by ferry from Spain or France**, but, as cars can face slow land border crossings from Ceuta into Morocco due to custom controls, it's better to arrive in Tangier.

TIME

Morocco stays at Greenwich Mean Time all year, with no Daylight Saving Time in summer. However, Ceuta and Melilla keep Spanish time, which is GMT +1 in winter and GMT +2 in summer.

CURRENCY AND FOREIGN EXCHANGE

Currency The monetary unit of Morocco is the dirham (dh), divided into 100 centimes. **Notes** are issued in 20, 50, 100 and 200 dirhams. There are **coins** for 10, 20 and 50 centimes and for 1 and 5 dirhams. Notes are issued in 20, 50, 100 and 200 dirhams. Currency is labelled in Arabic and French.

Exchange Keep all exchange receipts and budget carefully at the end of your stay, as on departure you will only be allowed to reconvert half of what you can prove to have changed. **Eurocheques** are accepted in at least one bank in each major city, and both hotels and banks will change cash and traveller's cheques. Hotels usually offer slightly lower exchange rates than banks.

Traveller's cheques (sterling and US$) are easily exchanged in most banks, but there is usually a surcharge on each cheque. There are numerous cash machines in tourist areas and even in smaller towns. Hotels usually offer slightly lower exchange rates than banks.

Credit cards are widely accepted at banks, top hotels, restaurants and shops, but it is wise to check first.

Practicalities 175

TIME DIFFERENCES

GMT
12 noon

Morocco
12 noon

USA (East)
7 am

USA (West)
4 am

Germany
1 pm

Australia
(Sydney) 10 pm

WHEN YOU ARE THERE

CLOTHING SIZES

UK	Morocco	USA	
36	46	36	**Suits**
38	48	38	
40	50	40	
42	52	42	
44	54	44	
46	56	46	
7	41	8	**Shoes**
7.5	42	8.5	
8.5	43	9.5	
9.5	44	10.5	
10.5	45	11.5	
11	46	12	
14.5	37	14.5	**Shirts**
15	38	15	
15.5	39/40	15.5	
16	41	16	
16.5	42	16.5	
17	43	17	
8	36	6	**Dresses**
10	38	8	
12	40	10	
14	42	12	
16	44	14	
18	46	16	
4.5	37.5	6	**Shoes**
5	38	6.5	
5.5	38.5	7	
6	39	7.5	
6.5	40	8	
7	41	8.5	

NATIONAL HOLIDAYS

1 Jan	New Year's Day
11 Jan	Independence Manifesto
1 May	Labour Day
23 May	National Day
30 Jul	Feast of the Throne
14 Aug	Allegiance Day
20 Aug	King's Birthday
6 Nov	Day of Green March
18 Nov	Independence Day

Morocco observes the traditional feast days of the Muslim year, together with Ramadan, the month of fasting. The dates of these change to follow the lunar calendar and move backwards by 11 days each year.

OPENING HOURS

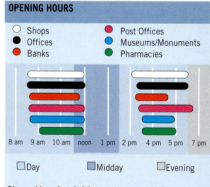

Shops Mon–Sat 8:30 am–noon and 2–6 pm. Souks in the medinas are open 8 am–7 or 8 pm, sometimes longer in summer/high season. Some shops in the souks close for the Friday prayers.
Banks Mon–Thu 8:30–11:30 am and 2:15–4:30 pm; on Fridays they open slightly earlier and close slightly later.
Post offices Mon–Fri 8:30–noon and 2:30–6:30.
Museums Generally closed on Tuesday and between noon and 3 pm on other days.
Pharmacies 9 am–noon and 3–5 pm.
All times may vary.

Practicalities

POLICE 19

FIRE 15

AMBULANCE 15

HIGHWAY EMERGENCY SERVICE 177

PERSONAL SAFETY

- Watch out for *faux guides* posing as "students" or "friends"; extreme caution should be taken in accepting help from them. Use official tourist office guides or manage without. The grey-uniformed Sûreté police are tourist friendly.
- Do not accept offers of hashish cannabis (*kif*) – penalties for possessing drugs are high.
- Beware of pickpockets in crowded places.
- Keep money and passports out of sight.
- Do not walk alone at night in medinas.
- Women should dress modestly when away from the beach and hotel.

Police assistance:
 19 from any phone

ELECTRICITY

Moroccan power supply is 220 volts, but some areas are still on 110 volts. Sockets accept two-round-pin plugs, so an adaptor is advisable, as is a transformer for appliances operating on 100–120 volts.

TELEPHONES

Téléboutiques, clearly marked in blue, are plentiful in towns. They give information and change, and are easy to operate. Card phones are increasingly available and are also easy to use. The cards can be bought at post offices, newsagents and tobacconists. Calls can be made from phone offices with operator assistance. The number is given to a telephonist who will dial the call number required and direct the caller to a cabin where the call is waiting. Although it is simpler to call from hotels, the charges can be double that paid elsewhere.

POST

All cities and most towns have post offices (PTT). The postal service is reliable, but international post can be slow. Post to and from Europe can take up to a week; post to the USA, Canada and Australia takes two weeks. Letters are collected more frequently from post offices, so it's worth posting your letters in the box inside or just outside the buildings.

TIPS/GRATUITIES

Tips are often expected by caretakers who open up attractions on demand. As a general guide:

Restaurants (service incl.)	7–10%
Cafés/bars	10%
Taxis (agree price first)	Change
Museum and site guides	5–10dh
Porters, hotel workers	5–10dh
Hairdressers	5–10dh
Petrol pump attendants	2–4dh
Toilets (in bars etc)	2–5dh

Practicalities 177

EMBASSIES and HIGH COMMISSIONS

UK/Ireland
☎ (03) 7729696

USA
☎ (03) 7762265

France
☎ (03) 9932039
(Tangier)

Germany
☎ (03) 7709662

Canada/Australia
☎ (03) 7672880

HEALTH

 Insurance Morocco has well-qualified doctors in the larger towns and cities. State hospitals provide free or minimal charge emergency treatment, but full health insurance is essential.

 Dental Services Have a thorough check-up before leaving home. In case of emergency, ask a consulate in a major city to recommend a local dentist, who will be French-speaking. Medical insurance is essential.

 Weather The sun is very hot, so cover up with light cotton clothes, wear a hat, use high-factor sunscreen and drink plenty of bottled water. Avoid too much alcohol and caffeine as these contribute to dehydration.

 Drugs Although pharmacies are well supplied, check expiry dates as drugs deteriorate quickly in the heat. Drugs can be expensive, so bring a supply of painkillers, anti-diarrhoea pills and a sunburn remedy. Do not buy illegal drugs.

 Safe Water Drinking unboiled water can cause stomach problems. Use bottled water and do not eat raw food, especially salads washed in local water. Bilharzia, caused by blood flukes, can be caught by swimming in oases or slow-flowing rivers.

WILDLIFE SOUVENIRS

Importing wildlife souvenirs sourced from rare or endangered species may be illegal or require a special permit. Check your country's customs rules.

CONCESSIONS

Students and Youths Student cards are redundant in Morocco, but Royal Air Maroc gives a 25 per cent discount to under-26s on internal flights. InterRail passes for under-26s also extend to the Moroccan rail system.
Senior Citizens There are no general concessions for senior citizens, but beach-front hotels south of Agadir offer good rates for long-stay guests. However, many do not have lifts or ramps for wheelchairs.

TRAVELLING WITH A DISABILITY

Facilities for visitors with disabilities are rare in Morocco, and medinas are tricky places to get around. Although Moroccans are usually helpful, it is still difficult to get around hotels, public transport and most of the monuments. Check with a specialist organisation for travellers with disabilities before travelling: Tripscope in London (tel: 020 8994 9294; www.justmobility.co.uk/tripscope), and AccessAbility in the USA (tel: 800/610-5640). The AA *Disabled Travellers' Guide* gives details of accessible transport in Britain and abroad.

CHILDREN

Moroccans love children and will welcome and entertain them wherever you go. While Western-style amusement parks are rare, most kids will be happy to stroll through the souks, or to enjoy the country's fabulous nature, mountains and beaches. The food is usually pretty child friendly, as well.

TOILETS

Most hotels have Western-style toilets, but almost everywhere else you will find squat toilets, which are usually cleaner and more hygienic. Toilet paper is not always provided in restaurants or public loos so always travel with some tissues.

SURVIVAL PHRASES

The official language in Morocco is Arabic, but it is quite different from classical Arabic. The country also has three different Berber dialects. French is widely taught in schools, and some Moroccans speak several languages fluently, including English and Spanish. The following is a phonetic transliteration from the Arabic script. Words or letters in brackets indicate the different form that is required when addressing, or speaking as, a woman.

GREETINGS AND COMMON WORDS

Yes **Eeyeh, naam**
No **La**
Please **Min fadlak (fadlik) / Afek**
Thank you **Shukran / Baraka allah Oofeek**
You're welcome **Al Afow**
Hello *to Muslims* **As Salaam walaykum (formal)**
Response **Wa alaykum salaam**
Hello (informal) **La bes**
Response **Bikheer**
Welcome **Ahlan wa sahlan**
Response **Ahlan bik(i)**
Goodbye **Bislemah**
Good morning **Sbah 'khir**
Good evening **Msa l'khir**
Good night **Leela saieeda**
How are you? **La bes?**
Fine, thank you **Bikheer hamdulillaah**
God Willing **Inshallah**
Sorry **Smeh lee**
My name is… **Smeete…**
Do you speak English? **Ana macken Hdersh ngliziya**
I don't understand **Mafhemsh**
I understand **Fhamt**
I don't speak Arabic **Ana macken Hdersh Arbiya**

NUMBERS

0	**sifr**	5	**khamsa**
1	**wahid**	6	**sitta**
2	**tnayn (formal)**	7	**sebaa**
	joof (common)	8	**tmanya**
3	**tlaata**	9	**tseud**
4	**arbah**	10	**ashra**

DAYS

Monday	**youm al-itnayn**
Tuesday	**youm at-talaat**
Wednesday	**youm al-arbah**
Thursday	**youm al-khamees**
Friday	**youm al-gumah**
Saturday	**youm is sabt**
Sunday	**youm al-hadd**

EMERGENCY! Taari!

Help! **Atkooni!**
Thief! **Serrak / cheffar**
Police **Booleess**
Fire **Afia / nar**
Hospital **S'beetar**
Go away **Seer Fhalek!**
Where is the toilet? **Feyn atoilet?**
I'm sick **Ana m'reed**
We want a doctor **B'gheet T'beeb**

SHOPPING

Shop **Hanoot**
I would like… **B'gheet**
How much…? **Bech Hal?**
That's my last offer **Aakhir kelma**
That's too expensive **Had she b'zzaf**
Cheap **Rakhees**
Big / small **S'gheer**
Open / closed **Maftooh / mooglak**

DIRECTIONS AND TRAVELLING

I'm lost **Ana T'left**
Where is…? **Feyn…?**
Airport **Mataar**
Boat **Babor / bato**
Bus **Kar**
Bus station **Mahattat delkeeran**
Embassy **Sifaara**
Market **Souk**
Mosque **Gaama; masjid**
Museum **Mathaf**
Square **Saaha**
Street **Zenka**
Taxi rank **Mahattat at taxiyat**
Train station **La gare**
Near / far? **near / kreeb?**
How many kilometres? **Sh hal min kilomet?**
Left / right **Leeser / leemin**
Straight on **Toul / neeshan**
When does the bus/train leave **Waktash tren / kar yamshi?**
I want a taxi **B'gheet taxi**
Ticket **warka / tickita**
Car **tonobeel**
Train **Tren**

Useful words and phrases 179

RESTAURANT: Mattaam / restauran

I would like to eat... **B'gheet nakul...**
Alcohol / beer **Alcohol / shrab**
Bread **Khobz**
Coffee / tea **Tea / atay**
Meat **L'ham**
Mineral water **Mae maadini**
Milk **Halib**
Salt and pepper **el-melha / lebzak**
Wine red / white **Nabit rouge / blanc**
Breakfast **Ftoor**
Waiter **Garsson / serbaay**
Menu **La carte / menu**
Bill **L'hssab**

MONEY: Flooss

Where is the bank? **Feyn el-banka?**
Small change **Ssarf**
Post office **Bosta / beriol**
Mail **Barid**
Cheque **Cheque**
Traveller's cheque **Traveller's cheque**
Credit card **Cart visa**
How much is that? **Bsh hal hadeek**

GLOSSARY TO THE TEXT

Aim spring
Aït tribe
Arabesque geometrical and floral decoration, including caligraphy
Bab gate in city walls
Babouche traditional leather slipper
Baraka blessing of a saint, sought at his *marabout*
Berbers the first inhabitants of Morocco and North Africa
Borj fort/tower
Caid district administrator
Caleche horse-drawn carriage
Caravanserai lodgings for travellers and animals, around a courtyard
Cherif (or shrif) descendant of the Prophet Mohammed
Djellaba (or Jellaba) hooded outer dress worn by men and women
Djemaa/jamaa mosque
Drar house
Ensemble artisanal fixed-price government shop
Eye sand dune
Fantasia spectacular party traditionally held at Berber festivals
Fassi inhabitant of Fes
Fondouk inn, caravanserai
Gnaoua brotherhood descended from slaves from Mali and Senegal

Haik traditional veil
Hammam steam bath, usually near mosques for ablutions before prayers
Harira rich meat soup
Jinn genie, good or evil spirit
Joutia flea market
Khanqah Sufi monastery
Kasbah fortified village
Kif cannabis
Kissaria covered market where more expensive goods are sold
Koran (Qu'ran) Muslim holy book
Koubba tomb of a saint/ dome (see *marabout*)
Ksar tribal stronghold
Ksour plural of ksar
Makhzen government
Marabout holy man, as well as his tomb (see *koubba*)
Maristan (Islamic) hospital
Mechouar large square for official gatherings
Medersa Koranic school
Medina old part of the city
Mellah Jewish quarter of a Moroccan town
Midan square
Minaret slender tower of a mosque
Minzah the garden in old Moroccan houses
Moulay descendant of Mohammed, title of Moroccan sultans
Mouloud birthday of the Prophet
Moussem pilgrimage and festival for a Muslim saint
Mstani Christian
Muhayyem campsite
Oud Moroccan music
Oued river or river bed
Pisé building material of packed clay and stones from river bed
Ramadan Islamic month of fasting
Ras source/head
Sahn courtyard of a mosque
Sawiris inhabitants of Essaouira
Sharia street
Shereef descendant of Mohammed
Shouaf witchdoctor
Souk street market/bazaar
Sufi Islamic brotherhood of ascetics and mystics
Tagine traditional stew of spiced meat or fish and vegetables or fruit
Tizi mountain pass
Touaref Berber nomad from the Western Sahara known for their blue clothes
Vizier chief minister of Islamic ruler
Zaouia a place of religious gathering

180 **Useful words and phrases**

Atlas

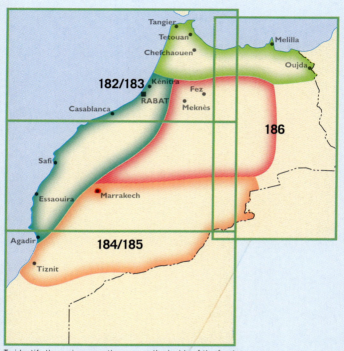

To identify the regions, see the map on the inside of the front cover

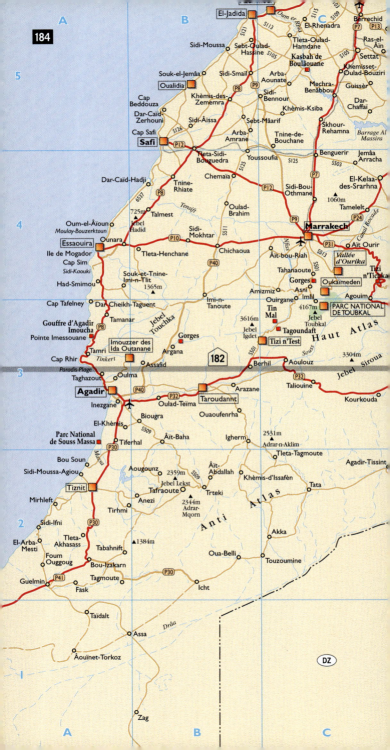

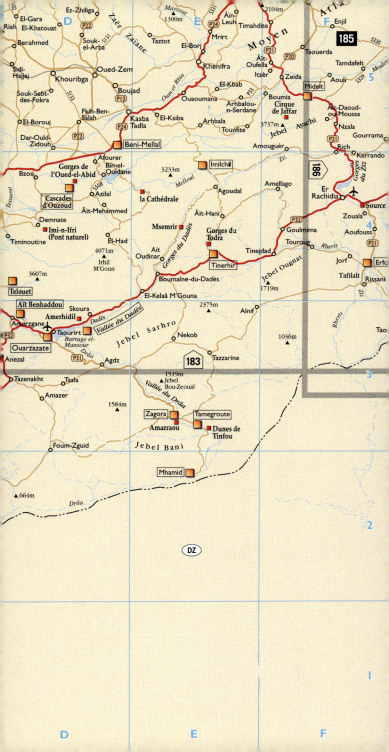

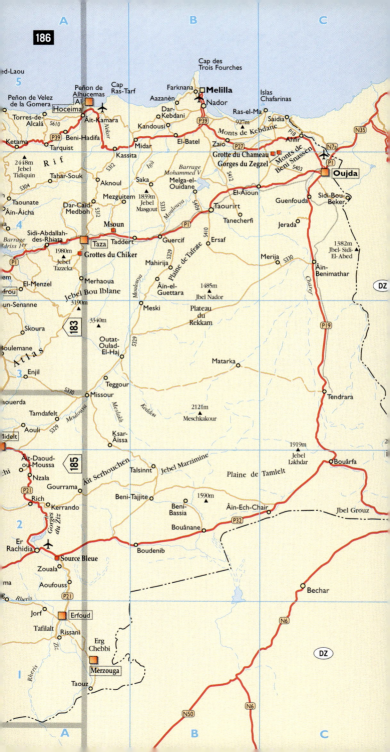

Index

Accommodation 39–40
see also individual areas
admission charges 36
Agadir 72, 87
airport 34
Musée Municipal 87
Portuguese Fortress 87
Vallée des Oiseaux 87
Agadir n'Gouj 145
agadirs 23
Agouim 172
Aïn Asserdoun 133
airports and air services 34, 37, 175
Aït Benhaddou 11, 150, 161, 172
Aït Oudinar 149
Aït-Ourir 171
Al-Hoceima 110
Amerdihil 148
amusement parks 86, 94
Aoulouz Gorge 162
architecture 23–26
Aremd 147, 168
argan oil 93
Asilah 108–109
Asni 144
athletics 22
Atlantic Coast 7, 71–94
accommodation 88–89
Agadir 72, 87
Azemmour 85
Casablanca 72, 79–80
children's entertainment 86
eating out 90–92
El-Jadida 85–86
entertainment 94
Essaouira 72, 81–83
five-day itinerary 74–75
Imouzzer des Ida
Outanane 87
map 72–73
Mehdiya 84
Mohammedia 84–85
Oualidia 86
Rabat 72, 76–78
Safi 86
Salé 72, 78
shopping 93
Atlas Mountains 8–9
see also Atlas Mountains and the South; Middle Atlas
Atlas Mountains and the South 139–162
accommodation 156–157
Aït Benhaddou 11, 150, 161, 172

Dadès Valley 148–149
desert excursions 162
eating out 158–160
entertainment 162
Erfoud 155
map 140–141
Merzouga 155
Mhamid 10, 154
Ouarzazate 153
Oukaïmeden 9, 147, 152
Ourika Valley 152
shopping 161
six-day itinerary 142–143
Tamegroute 154
Taroudannt 151
Telouet 152–153
Tinerhir 10, 154
Tizi n'Test 144–145
Tizi n'Tichka 170–172
Tiznit 151, 161
Toubkal National Park 146–147
Zagora 10, 153–154, 161
Atlas Studios 152, 153
Azemmour 85
Azrou 9, 132

Bab Mansour 128
babouches 43, 137
banks 176
Ben Jelloun, Tahar 20–21, 100
Ben Youssef Medersa 54–55
Beni Snassen Mountains 110
Beni-Mellal 132–133
Berbers 27–29, 132, 133, 144
birdwatching 83, 116, 162
Blue Lake 116
Borj Ras el-Ain 133
Boulmane de Dadès 149
Bowles, Paul 32, 102

Cabo Negro 109
cafés 11
camel trips 162
camping 39
Cap Malabata 102
Cap Spartel 102
car hire 38
carpets 28, 43, 132, 161
Casablanca 72, 79–80
airport 34
Mosque of Hassan II 79–80
Cascades d'Ouzoud 133
casinos 70
Ceuta 109
Museo de la Legión 109
Chaouen *see* Chefchaouen
Chefchaouen 97, 106–107
fondouks 107

Galerie Hassan 107, 115
kasbah 106–107
kif trade 107
Musée Artisanal 107
children 86, 178
cinemas 70, 94, 116, 162
climate and seasons 6, 174
clothing sizes 176
concessions 70
corsairs 30–31
credit cards 175
crime and personal safety 177
currency 175

Dadès Valley 148–149
Dar Aït Sidi el-Mati 148
Dar Menebhi 62
Date Festival 155, 162
dental services 178
desert excursions 162
disability, travelling with 178
Djemaa el-Fna 50–51, 166
dress code 40, 177
drinking water 178
driving 37–38, 174, 175
drugs, illegal 36, 107, 177
drugs and medicines 178

Eating out 40–41
see also individual areas
El-Badi Palace 62
El-Bahia Palace and Museum 63
El-Kelaa M'Gouna 148
El-Jadida 85–86
Portuguese Cistern 85–86
Portuguese garrison 85
electricity 177
embassies and high commissions 178
emergency telephone numbers 177
entertainment 44
see also individual areas
Erfoud 10–11, 155
Erg Chebbi 155
Essaouira 72, 81–83
fishing harbour 81
Galerie Frederic Damgaard 83, 93
Îles Purpuaires 83
Musée Sidi Mohammed ben Abdallah 82
Skala de la Ville 81–82
souks 82–83

Fantasias 44, 70
ferry services 175
Fes 118, 122–125

Index 187

airport **34**
Andalucian Mosque **124**
Armoury Museum **122, 125**
Borj Nord fortress **122**
Dar Batha **122**
Fes el-Jedid **124–125**
fondouks **123, 124**
Medersa Bou Inania **25, 122–123**
Medersa el-Attarine **124**
Medersa es Sahrij **124**
Merenid Tombs **122**
Quaraouine Mosque **123–124**
souks **123, 124, 137**
water-clock **123**
Woodwork Museum **124**
Zaouia and Tomb of Moulay Idriss II **124**
Festival of Sacred Music **138**
festivals and events **11, 44**
fondouks **23, 107, 123**
food and drink **15–17, 40–41**
drinks, wine and beer **41**
mint tea **10, 16, 41**
Ras el-Hanout **17**
shopping for **69, 93**
street food **41, 158**
tagine recipe **17**
Forbes, Malcolm **102**
foreign exchange **175**

Galerie Frederic Damgaard **83, 93**
Galerie Hassan **107, 115**
gardens
Aguedal Garden **58–59**
Jardin Majorelle **10, 58, 60**
Jardin de la Mamounia **58, 59–60**
Jardins Exotiques de Sidi Bouknadel **84**
Menara Gardens **59**
Mendoubia Gardens **100**
Palmeraie **59**
Genet, Jean **108**
Glaoui family **172**
Glaoui Kasbah **152–153, 171**
Gnaoua people **82**
golf **10, 44, 70, 94, 116, 162**
Gorge du Dadès **149**
Gorges du Zegzel **10, 110**
Great Mosque of Tin Mal **145**
Grotte du Chameau **110**
Grottes d'Hercule **102**
Guéliz **63**

Hammams **23**
Haouzia **85**
Haras Stud Farm **130**

Harris, Walter **101, 103**
Hassan II, King **21, 79**
health **174, 178**
hiking **44, 138, 146–147, 162, 167–169**
history **20–21**
horse-racing **94**
horse-riding **44, 70, 94, 116, 138, 162**
hotel ratings **39**
hunting **44, 138, 177**
hustlers and *faux guides* **34, 35, 177**

Ibn Battutah **20**
Ibn Toumert, Mohammed **144**
Îles Purpuaries **83**
Imilchil **133**
Imlil **147**
Imouzzer des Ida Outanane **87**
Imouzzèr Falls **87**
Imouzzèr-du-Kandar **131–132**
insurance **174, 178**
Irherm n'Ougdal **172**
Islam **12–14**

Jardin Majorelle **10, 58, 60**
Jebel Bou Iblane **138**
Jebel Sarhro **149**
jewellery **43, 151, 161**
Jewish community **82, 105, 124, 165**
jinns **14, 169**

Kaaseras **109**
karting and quad-bike excursions **162**
kasbahs **23–24**
Aït Benhaddou **11, 150, 172**
Chefchaouen **106–107**
Dadès Valley **148–149**
Glaoui Kasbah **152–153, 171**
Rabat **77–78**
Tangier **101–102**
Taourirt Kasbah **153**
Taroudannt **151**
Tizi n'Test pass **145**
Koubba Ba'adiyin **61**
koubbas **25**
Koutoubia Mosque **61, 164**
ksour **23–24, 29, 150**

Language
Berber **27–28**
words and phrases **179–180**
Larache **108**
Château de la Cicogne **108**
Kebibat fortress **108**
Lixus **108**

Lixus **108**
Loukos wetlands **116**

Magic potions **14**
Mainwaring, Sir Henry **31**
Maison Tiskiwin **63, 166**
marabouts **13–14, 25**
Marathon des Sables **44, 155**
Marrakech **45–70, 164–166**
accommodation **64–65**
Aguedal Garden **58–59**
airport **34**
Bab Doukkala Mosque **56**
Ben Youssef Medersa **54–55**
caleche ride **164–166**
Dar Menebhi **62**
Dar Si Said Museum **63, 166**
Djemaa el-Fna **50–51, 166**
eating out **66–67**
El-Badi Palace **62, 166**
El-Bahia Palace and Museum **63, 166**
entertainment **70**
Guéliz **63**
Jardin Majorelle **10, 58, 60**
Jardin de la Mamounia **58, 59–60**
Kasbah Mosque **165**
Koubba Ba'adiyin **61**
Koutoubia Mosque **61, 164**
Maison Tiskiwin **63, 166**
map **46–47**
mellah **165**
Menara Gardens **59**
Palmeraie **59**
ramparts and gates **56–57**
Saadian Tombs **62**
shopping **68–69**
souks **52–53, 68**
three-day itinerary **48–49**
Zaouia of Sidi Bel Abbès **57**
marriage festival **11, 133**
Martil **109**
massage **10**
medersas **24–25**
Ben Youssef Medersa **54–55**
Bou Inania Medersa **130**
Medersa Bou Inania **25, 122–123**
Medersa el-Attarine **124**
Medersa es Sahrij **124**
Merenid Medersa **78**
medical treatment **178**
medinas **25–26**
Mehdiya **84**
Jardins Exotiques de Sidi Bouknadel **84**
Musée Dar Beghazi **84**
Meknes **128–130**

188 Index

Aguedal Tank **130**
Bab Mansour **128**
Bou Inania Medersa **130**
Dar el-Kebira **128**
Dar el-Makhzen **128, 130**
Dar Jamaï Museum **130**
Haras stud farm **130**
Heri es Souani **130**
Koubbet el-Khiyatin **128**
souks **137**
Tomb of Moulay Ismail
128, 129
Merdja Zerga **116**
Merzouga **155**
Mhamic **10, 154**
Middle Atlas and Imperial
cities **8, 10, 117–138**
accommmodation **134–135**
Azrou **132**
Beni-Mellal **132–133**
Cascades d'Ouzoud **133**
eating out **136**
entertainment **138**
Fes **118, 122–125**
five-day itinerary **120–121**
Imilchil **133**
Imouzzèr-du-Kandar
131–132
map **118–119**
Meknes **128–130**
Midelt **132**
Moulay-Idriss **131**
Sefrou **132**
shopping **137**
Taza **131**
Volubilis **126–127**
Midelt **132**
Mischliffen **9, 138**
Mohammedia **84–85**
Mohammed VI, King **21, 109**
money **175**
mosques
Andalucian Mosque **124**
architecture **23**
Bab Doukkala Mosque **56**
Great Mosque of Tin Mal **145**
Kasbah Mosque **165**
Koutoubia Mosque **61**
Mosque of Hassan **77–78**
Mosque of Hassan II **79–80**
Quaraouine Mosque **123–124**
Moulay Bousselham Lagoon
116
Moulay Yacoub **138**
Moulay-Idriss **131**
mountain biking **162**
moussems **11, 14, 130**
Mrabet, Mohammed **21**
museum opening hours **176**

museums
Archaeological Museum,
Rabat **77**
Archaeological Museum,
Tangier **102**
Armoury Museum **122, 125**
Ceramics Museum **86**
Dar Jamaï Museum **130**
Dar Menebhi **62**
Dar Si Said Museum **63**
El-Bahia Palace and
Museum **63**
Ethnographic Museum **102**
Musée Archéologique,
Tetouan **105**
Musée Artisanal **107**
Musée Dar Beghazi **84**
Musée d'Art Contemporain
de la Ville de Tanger **101**
Musée d'Art Marocain **105**
Musée Municipal, Agadir **87**
Musée Sidi Mohammed
ben Abdallah **82**
Museo de la Légion **109**
Museum of Moroccan Arts
63
Oudaïa Museum **77**
Woodwork Museum **124**
music
Berber **29**
Raï music **27**

National holidays **176**
The North **95–116**
accommodation **111–112**
Al-Hoceima **110**
Asilah **108–109**
Ceuta **109**
Chefchaouen **97, 106–107**
eating out **113–114**
entertainment **116**
five-day itinerary **98–99**
Larache **108**
map **96–97**
Ouezzane **110**
Oujda **110**
Rif Coast **109**
shopping **115**
Tangier **96, 100–103**
Tetouan **104–105**

Oases **10–11**
Akka **11**
Erfoud **10–11**
Figuig **11**
Skoura **148**
Tinerhir **10**
Zagora **10**
opening hours **42, 176**

Oualidia **86**
Ouarzazate **153, 172**
Atlas Studios **152, 153**
Taourirt Kasbah **153**
Oued Laou **109**
Oued Souss **162**
Ouezzane **110**
Ouirgane **144, 147**
Oujda **111**
Oukaïmeden **9, 147, 152**
Ourika Valley **152**

Palais el-Badi **62**
Palais el-Bahia **63**
palm trees **18–19, 59, 154**
Palmeraie **59**
passports and visas **174**
pharmacies **176**
picnic spots **133**
pisé **24, 26**
police **38, 177**
post offices **176, 177**
public transport **36–37**

Quaraouine Mosque
123–124

Rabat **72, 76–78**
Archaeological Museum **77**
Chellah **77**
kasbah **77–78**
Mohammed V Mausoleum
73, 78
Mosque of Hassan **77–78**
Oudaïa Museum **77**
souks **93**
Ville Nouvelle **76–77**
Ramadan **12, 19, 40**
Ras el-Ma **107**
riad hotels **26, 39**
Rif Coast **109**
Rif Mountains **9, 96**
Rissani **155**
Route des Kasbahs **24,
148–149**

Saadian Tombs **62**
Safi **86**
Ceramics Museum **86**
Dar el-Bahar **86**
Kechla **86**
Sahara Desert **9**
Saint Laurent, Yves **60**
Salé **72, 78**
Merenid Medersa **78**
Salée Rovers **30**
sand baths **162**
sand dunes **9, 10, 154, 155**
Sefrou **132**

Index 189

senior citizens **178**
shopping **42–43, 176**
  see also individual areas
Sidi Bouzid **86**
Sidi Chamarouche **10, 169**
Sidi Harazem **138**
Sidi Kaouki **83, 94**
skiing **9, 44, 138, 152, 162**
Skoura **148**
Smir-Restinga **109**
souks **10, 26, 42**
  Essaouira **82–83**
  Fes **123, 124, 137**
  Marrakech **52–53, 68**
  Meknes **137**
  Rabat **93**
  Taroudannt **151, 161**
  Tetouan **104–105**
The South *see* Atlas
  Mountains and the South
spa villages **138**
sport **44, 70, 94, 116, 138, 162**
student and young travellers
  178
Sufi brotherhood **14, 110**
sun safety **178**
swimming pools **70, 94, 138,**
  162

Taddert **171**
Tafilalt **155**
Tagoundaft **145**
Tamegroute **154**
Tamnalt **149**
Tangier **96, 100–103**
  airport **34**

Archaeological Museum **102**
Café Detroit **103**
Church of St Andrew **101**
Dar el-Makhzen **102**
Ethnographic Museum **102**
Grottes d'Hercule **102**
kasbah **101–102**
La Légation des Étas-Unis
  101
Mendoubia Gardens **100**
Musée d'Art Contemporain
  de la Ville de Tanger **101**
port **34**
Villa Harris **103**
Taourirt Kasbah **153**
Taroudannt **151**
  kasbah **151**
  souks **151, 161**
taxis **36, 37**
Taza **131**
telephones **177**
Telouet **152–153, 171**
Tetouan **104–105**
  École des Métiers **105**
  Musée Archéologique **105**
  Musée d'Art Marocain **105**
  souks **104–105**
thalassotherapy **94**
time differences **175, 176**
Tinerhir **10, 154**
tipping **177**
Tiseldei **172**
Tizi n'Test **144–145**
Tizi n'Tichka **170–172**
Tiznit **151, 161**
Tnine l'Ourika **152**

Todra Gorge **149, 154**
toilets **178**
Tomb of Lalla Tiznit **151**
Tomb of Moulay Ismail **128,**
  129
Tombeaux Saadiens **62**
Toubkal National Park
  146–147, 167–169
Toufliat **171**
tourist information **35, 174–175**
trains **36**
travel documents **174**
travellers' cheques **175**

Vallée du Dadès **148–149**
Vallée des Oiseaux **149**
Vallée des Oiseaux (park and
  zoo) **87**
Vallée d'Ourika **152**
Villa Harris **103**
Volubilis **126–127**

Water resources **7**
websites **174**
wildlife **133, 147, 178**
windsurfing **7, 44, 83, 94**

Youth hostels **39**

Zagora **10, 153–154, 161**
zaouias **14**
  Zaouia Naciri **154**
  Zaouia of Sidi Bel Abbès **57**
  Zaouia and Tomb of
    Moulay Idriss II **124**
zellij **26**

Picture Credits/Acknowledgements

The Automobile Association wishes to thank the following photographers, libraries and museums for their assistance with the preparation of this book.

Abbreviations for terms appearing above: (t) top, (b) bottom, (l) left, (r) right, (c) centre

Front and back cover: (t) AA Photo Library/Paul Kenward; (ct) AA Photo Library/Ian Burgum; (cb) AA Photo Library/Ian Burgum; (b) AA Photo Library/Paul Kenward; Spine AA Photo Library/Paul Kenward.

ACTION IMAGES 22b; EMPICS LTD 22t; HULTON ARCHIVE 21t, 31t, 31b; © THE INTERNATIONAL PAUL BOWLES SOCIETY 32t; THE KOBAL COLLECTION/WARNER BROS 32c; MARY EVANS PICTURE LIBRARY 30/31; PICTURES COLOUR LIBRARY 78; DAVID REDFERN/REDFERNS 27b; REX FEATURES 21b; ROBERT HARDING PICTURE LIBRARY 10, 11br, 11bl, 18/19, 19c; GORDON SINGER 7c; SPECTRUM COLOUR LIBRARY 11t.
The remaining photographs are held in the Association's own library (AA PHOTO LIBRARY) and were taken by IAN BURGUM with the exception of 6t, 7t, 8/9, 23c, 28c, 29crt, 48t, 48b, 49t, 61l, 72, 73t, 74, 84/5, 85, 98t, 118, 121b, 122t, 131, 143, 148, 148/9, 149, 153 which were taken by PAUL KENWARD; 2ii, 2iii, 3i, 3iii, 3iv, 6cb, 8tr, 13t, 13, 14 inset, 15b, 15d, 15e, 15f, 15g, 15 bottom, 16ct, 17bl, 18/19, 18. 19, 19t, 23t, 23bl, 24, 25, 33, 45, 49b, 50t, 50b, 51t, 51c, 52t, 52c, 55, 57, 58b, 59c, 59cr, 60b, 61b, 81t, 81b, 95, 96/7, 97, 98b, 99t, 100, 100/1, 102/3, 102, 104, 105, 106c, 106b, 107, 119, 128, 129 inset, 130, 139, 141, 142t, 142b, 144, 145, 145 inset, 146, 146 inset, 147, 150, 163, 168, 170, 172, 176t, 176cr which were taken by SIMON McBRIDE and 8tl which was taken by Tom D Timms.

The author would like to thank the Moroccan National Tourist Office for its help in the preparation of this guide.

SPIRAL GUIDES

Questionnaire

Dear Traveler

Your comments, opinions and recommendations are very important to us. So please help us to improve our travel guides by taking a few minutes to complete this simple questionnaire.

Send to: Spiral Guides, MailStop 66, 1000 AAA Drive, Heathrow, FL 32746–5063

Your recommendations...
We always encourage readers' recommendations for restaurants, nightlife or shopping – if your recommendation is added to the next edition of the guide, we will send you a FREE AAA Spiral Guide of your choice. Please state below the establishment name, location and your reasons for recommending it.

_____

_____

_____

_____

_____

Please send me AAA Spiral_____
(see list of titles inside the back cover)

About this guide...
Which title did you buy?

_____ **AAA Spiral**

Where did you buy it?_____

When? m m / y y

Why did you choose a AAA Spiral Guide? _____

_____

_____

_____

Did this guide meet your expectations?

Exceeded ☐   Met all ☐   Met most ☐   Fell below ☐

Please give your reasons _____

_____

_____

_____

continued on next page...

Were there any aspects of this guide that you particularly liked?

_____
_____
_____
_____
_____

Is there anything we could have done better?

_____
_____
_____
_____
_____

About you...

Name (Mr/Mrs/Ms) _____

Address _____

_____ Zip ____

Daytime tel nos. _____

Which age group are you in?

Under 25 ☐   25–34 ☐   35–44 ☐   45–54 ☐   55–64 ☐   65+ ☐

How many trips do you make a year?

Less than one ☐   One ☐   Two ☐   Three or more ☐

Are you a AAA member? Yes ☐   No ☐

Name of AAA club _____

About your trip...

When did you book? m m / y y .   When did you travel? m m / y y

How long did you stay? _____

Was it for business or leisure? _____

Did you buy any other travel guides for your trip? ☐ Yes ☐ No

If yes, which ones? _____

Thank you for taking the time to complete this questionnaire.

All information is for AAA internal use only and will NOT be distributed outside the organization to any third parties.